Constructing Others, Constructing Ourselves

A Reader

Edited by
Sibylle Gruber, Ellen Riek, Desiree Butterfield, Justin Lerberg,
Rick Mangum, Alysia Rasmussen, Katie Sheridan
Northern Arizona University

KENDALL/HUNT PUBLISHING COMPANY
4050 Westmark Drive   Dubuque, Iowa 52002

Cover illustration by Rubén Vásquez

ISBN 0-7872-9359-8

Printed in the United States of America
10 9 8 7 6 5 4 3 2 1

CONTENTS

Introduction
Acknowledgements

Section 1
Construction of Community 1

Soul Searching *Pythia Peay* 3

Reclaiming Culture and the Land: Motherhood and the Politics of Sustaining Community *Winona LaDuke* 9

In Groups We Shrink From Loner's Heroics *Carol Tavris* 17

Countering the Culture of Sex *Ellen Goodman* 21

Let Gays Marry *Andrew Sullivan* 25

Leave Marriage Alone *William Bennett* 29

Section 2
Construction of Language 33

Mother Tongue *Amy Tan* 35

Coming into Language *Jimmy Santiago Baca* 41

How to Tame a Wild Tongue *Gloria Anzaldúa* 49

Language Use in Family and in Society *Lee Thomas and Linh Cao* 61

A Kind of Love *Andrei Codrescu* 73

The Debate Has Been Miscast From the Start *Henry Louis Gates* 79

Discrimination Is a Virtue *Robert Keith Miller* 85

Learning the Language *Richard Rodriguez* 89

Bilingual Education: The Key to Basic Skills *Angelo Gonzalez* 99

Section 3
Construction of Social Reality   103

A Revolution of Values: The Promise of Multicultural Change *bell hooks*   105

The Visigoths in Tweed *Dinesh D'Souza*   113

The Border Patrol State *Leslie Marmon Silko*   123

Body Ritual Among the Nacirema *Horace M. Miner*   129

Shakespeare in the Bush *Laura Bohannon*   135

Prologue from *The Invisible Man Ralph Ellison*   145

Section 4
Construction of Identity   155

Declaration of Sentiments and Resolutions *Elizabeth Cady Stanton*   157

Split at the Root: An Essay on Jewish Identity *Adrienne Rich*   163

From a Native Daughter *Haunani-Kay Trask*   175

Men as Success Objects *Warren Farrell*   185

Stranger in a Strange Land *Pico Iver*   191

Wanderers by Choice *Eva Hoffman*   197

She Had Some Horses *Joy Harjo*   203

Child of the Americas *Aurora Levins Morales*   207

Index   211

INTRODUCTION

Every day, magazines, newspapers, and television bombard us with information about products to buy, movies to watch, people to know, accidents that happened, world events, political controversies, or cultural events. When we read about the newest incident of racial discrimination, or when we hear about the new car that accelerates from zero to 60 in three seconds, we use a specific lens to make sense of the information. Our previous knowledge, our educational backgrounds, our abilities to absorb information, our abilities to be critical of what goes on around us, encourage us to think about what we hear and read in specific ways. We construct our reality, and with it, we construct others and ourselves.

With this in mind, we call this reader *Constructing Others, Constructing Ourselves*. The title of the book reflects our belief that we bring our own perspectives to every reading, to every task that we undertake. We also believe that each one of us constructs others in multiple ways, and that our construction of ourselves changes with every reading and with every interaction. *Constructing Others, Constructing Ourselves* is a reader that offers you essential materials to think critically about other's writing and to also think about your own writing. You will find thematically arranged selections which include biographical information about the writers and writing prompts that encourage you to summarize the readings, synthesize them, and to critically analyze readings in isolation and in relation to other texts. The texts and the questions are intended to help you through every aspect of the writing process.

The reader is divided into four major sections:

1. Construction of Community

2. Construction of Language

3. Construction of Social Reality

4. Construction of Identity

Each section includes writers that explore, expand, question, or problematize ideas about community, language, social reality, and identity.

In Section 1, you will read about countering the culture of sex, bystander apathy, big cities and small towns, reclaiming culture and the land, and pro and cons of gay marriage. Section 2 focuses closely on how language influences our thinking about multiculturalism, how we all use different versions of English, how we "come into language," the literariness of baseball, how language is used in family and in society, what it means to tame a wild tongue, and bilingual education issues. Section 3 leads you into the construction of social reality. You'll read about men as success objects, what it means to live in a border patrol state, how we identify ourselves through rituals, and how we identify ourselves as belonging to specific cultural groups. In Section 4 we look at constructions of identity, starting with gender issues and issues of ethnic identity. You'll find readings that discuss concerns raised by American Indians, Jewish identity, what it means to live under the power of the United States, the modern nomad, and media presentations of others.

What we hope for is that the readings in *Constructing Others, Constructing Ourselves* challenge your ideas about others and about yourself. We hope that through analyzing the texts you will become a critical reader, thinker, and writer in your classes at college and in your everyday life.

Before you start reading through the four major sections of this book, think about some of the following questions: you can discuss them with your friends, class mates, and instructor, or you can write down your ideas in your writing journal, send a note via the Internet to your instructor, or type up a few paragraphs to bring to class.

- Think about the place where you grew up and think about your childhood friends. How have your ideas about your childhood community and friends changed over the years? Why do you think we see things differently?

- Look at the words "constructing others, constructing ourselves." What do these words mean to you? Can you give some examples of when you used language to construct others or when somebody else used language to construct you?

- Walk around campus or town and take note of the people that you see. What can you tell us about them after your short encounters? How does your own background influence your descriptions of who and what you saw?

- Take a close look at an ad from a magazine, newspaper, or web site. What is depicted in the ad, and how do the advertisers try to influence you as the reader/buyer? Think about how they construct a consumer's identity by using specific language, graphics, background, or layout.

Sibylle Gruber, Ellen Riek, Desiree Butterfield, Justin Lerberg, Rick Mangum, Alysia Rasmussen, Katie Sheridan.
2002

ACKNOWLEDGMENTS

Constructing Others, Constructing Ourselves, reflects the efforts of graduate assistants, instructors, and program staff to produce a unique reader for students at Northern Arizona University. Many thanks go to all of them! We owe special thanks to Suzanne Bratcher who worked closely with the reader committee to get the process started; to William Grabe and Susan Fitzmaurice whose support helped to move us along; the Composition Committee which worked closely with the graduate assistants and instructors; Karla Brewster who was always helpful and cheerful and encouraging; and the students whose feedback helped us make this new reader an excellent resource for teaching critical reading and writing skills. Many of our colleagues and friends have given us feedback and have offered their support while we were working on this reader. We thank them for their constant encouragement. And, we thank each other—Sibylle, Ellen, Desiree, Justin, Rick, Alysia, and Katie, for working hard and long to make this reader possible.

Section 1 ————————————————

Construction of Community

A "community" is usually defined as a group of people who share similar ideas, are interested in similar social or political issues, and are a relatively self-sufficient group. Communities can be based on national or ethnic characteristics, our gender, our profession, the geographical areas we are from, organizations in which we have participated, or activities that we are engaged in. One of the most important aspects of any community is its ability to communicate effectively and to work together for the common good.

The readings in this section look at a wide variety of communities, and they provide us with an opportunity to look more closely at how we construct different communities and how we are constructed by them. Pythia Peay in "Soul Searching" shows us how we can find community in the places we live, no matter whether it's a big city or a small town. Winona LaDuke addresses a similar issue in "Reclaiming Culture and the Land" when she discusses her community of White Earth. She points out that it is every individual's responsibility to make a community work and to make it into a place that you want to live in "In Groups We Shrink," by Carol Tavris, is another commentary on how individuals, when they become members of groups, or small communities, change behavioral patterns in emergency situations. Ellen Goodman, in "Countering the Culture of Sex," provides us with some thought-provoking comments on how the entertainment industry can be seen as a "cultural message maker," contributing to the cause as well as the cure for a community of sex-saturated teenage kids. The last two articles in this selection, " Let Gays Marry," by Andrew Sullivan, and "Leave Marriage Alone," by William Bennett, discuss how the larger community can exclude or include smaller communities such as gays and lesbians.

When you read these articles, think about the communities that you belong to. Also think about the communities that you do not belong to, the ones that you would like to belong to, and the ones that you discriminate against:

- How does your childhood community influence the ways you interact with your friends, family, teachers, strangers? What did your membership in your childhood community teach you?

- What are some of the communities that you belong to now? How did you become a member of these communities? What do these communities stand for? What do they oppose?

- How have your values been shaped by members of the various communities that are part of your life? How have your perspectives on social issues, environmental issues, race and ethnicity, heterosexuality, or homosexuality been influenced by the media or by people around you?

Soul Searching

PYTHIA PEAY

Pythia Peay is a writer based in Washington, D.C., where she receives regular doses of inspiration from the Georgetown Flea Market and the Potomac River. Her book on feminine spirituality, *Soul Sisters: A Sacred Way for All Women*, was published in 2001 by Tarcher/Putnam. Her essay on "Soul Searching" looks at how we participate in the life of a town and how we define the "heart of town."

I was the proverbial small-town girl, raised in Oak Grove, Missouri. While my friends looked forward to marriage and career, I yearned for big cities. It was a dream that cast my fate and, since leaving home 30 years ago, I have lived in or near five American cities. As much as any intimate tie to friend or family, each of these places has shaped my character. To Kansas City and St. Louis I owe my ability to stay grounded; to San Francisco, my impulse to seek out life's edge; to Santa Fe, my reliance on imagination.

But it is to Washington, D.C., the metropolis where I finally settled 14 years ago, that I owe a part of my soul. Transplanted from the subtle-hued desert of Santa Fe to the highly charged atmosphere of the nation's capital, I felt turmoil within myself and dreamed of going mad. With time, however, the special charm of the place—the poetry of the passing seasons and the spirit of American history that sighs invisibly through the air—opened my heart. "As soon as man has stopped wandering and stood still and looked about him," wrote the American author Eudora Welty, "he found a God in that place." And I did, too.

The idea that cities possess a soul was common among the ancients. The Romans spoke of "genius loci," meaning the special spirit of a place. Indeed, until the 18th-century Enlightenment, when the sacred was severed from the secular in Western culture, cities were often built on foundations of myth and religion, and were thought to be watched over by gods and goddesses, nature spirits, saints, and angels. Belief in a city's mysteriously personal character lives on in the colorful images that arise when we think of certain places: Los Angeles is the city of angels and dreams of stardom. New Orleans is jazz and black magic. Boulder is breathtaking mountain views and spiritual exploration. Boston, founded by austere Puritans, is symbolized by the lowly bean. Even when they're repeated ad nauseam in travel brochures, these images connect us with the underground wells of myth that water a city's soul.

But does anyone today really care about the souls of our cities? Like giant urban gods fallen from their pedestals, they lie dying of neglect, buried beneath asphalt and artless architecture, crushed by the weight of overwhelming social problems, their inhabitants often blind to the fact that their own souls are shaped, for better or worse, within the city's larger reality. We ignore the magic of a place—hidden beyond the real estate deals, the political squabbles, and numbing commutes—at our own peril.

I embarked on my own quest to uncover the soul of Washington, D.C., as a way to quell my distress after moving here. It dawned on me recently that if I can succeed in a city renowned for its hollow-hearted power-mongering and inside-the-beltway narcissism, then anyone anywhere could do the same. Here are a few methods to help unearth the soul of your hometown, based on my own exploration and conversations with thinkers around the country as well as with Washington historians, artists, mapmakers, poets, and activists. Some may sound deceptively simple, but beware: As your perceptions are transformed, you may find yourself living in a city wholly transformed.

Unearth the Original Landscape

The essence of a place is closely tied to its landscape. According to Gail Thomas, director of the Dallas Institute for Humanities and Culture, who studies the connection between soul and cities, settlers initially were attracted to a site by some remarkable natural feature—the way the wind blows, or the abundance of good underground water. Kansas City, for example, was founded on the high bluffs overlooking the Missouri River that explorers Lewis and Clark trumpeted as an ideal location for a fort. But even though a city's topography may have been obscured by development, maps and history books may offer a vivid image of how it once looked.

I was inspired to learn from a mapmaker how Washington's landscape resembled the very principle of unity out of diversity that is the city's—and the nation's—foundation. It is a geographical crossroads where the flora and fauna of the North and the South intermingle, maples growing alongside magnolias. Most surprising to me was learning that Washington, so often described as a swamp, is predominantly a city of river terraces and hills. Archetypal psychologist James Hillman, who has thought deeply about the ties between soul and city for more than two decades, sees significance in the way the swamp image has found its way into

Washington's cultural imagination. He calls it a psychologically apt metaphor that captures the way our politicians' ideals inevitably become bogged down by less noble realities.

Steep Yourself in History

Thomas Moore, author of *The Care of the Soul*, writes that reflecting on the past is an important part of retrieving your soul. Just as individuals in therapy or on a spiritual search discern new patterns of meaning by revisiting what they've experienced, so, too, does a city's history reveal something of its intrinsic nature.

To know that the poet Walt Whitman once walked the streets of Capitol Hill after tending wounded Civil War soldiers housed in the Patent Office Building, and that the banks of the Anacostia River were lined for 3,000 years with settlements of the Nacotchtank Indians, opened my heart to the ghosts of the past still haunting its modern spaces.

Stoke Your Imagination

In some way, great cities are created by the artists who render them immortal as much as by the planners, construction workers, and business leaders who build them. Think of James Joyce's Dublin, impressionist painter Camille Pissarro's Paris, or even Bruce Springsteen's Asbury Park. Washington came magically alive when I saw it through the eyes of artist Renee Butler, who showed me slides of the city's trees printed on large screens to express the way their lacy-leafed branches evoke the sacred. Delving into the works of local poets, fiction writers, columnists, memoirists, painters, photographers, folk artists, and songwriters deepens how we experience our home, imbuing commonplace reality with awareness, appreciation, and perhaps wonder.

Find the Heart of Town

Ask your friends this question: Where do you go to find the true heart of the city? In Seattle, many would say Pike's Place Market. In Chicago, Wrigley Field. In Madison, the lakeside beer garden at the University of Wisconsin student union. Most of the people I interviewed in Washington, D.C., located the city's soul not in the famous monuments and museums but in neighborhood streets, cafés, bookstores. John Johnson, founder of Process

WorkD.C.—a multicultural group that meets to discuss race and class issues—took me on a tour of his favorite spots: a tucked-away Cheers-style café near Capitol Hill that is frequented by activists, a baseball field where Hispanic families gather on Sundays for games and picnics. Others cited Kramer's Books and Afterwords, the popular Dupont Circle hangout, or ethnic restaurants with atmosphere and inexpensive menus.

Nearly everyone finds at least a slice of the city's soul in Washington's surprising wealth of parks and natural areas. I expect you'd find the same in San Francisco, where many people connect with their city's soul in Golden Gate Park or on the winding trails of Mount Tamalpais, the gentle mountain rising up out of the ocean mists north of the Golden Gate Bridge.

Discover the Civic Wound That Needs Healing

All cities have problems, though they are often unacknowledged. While it's usually difficult and politically risky to draw attention to shortcomings, especially in a place that prides itself on being a city that "works," ignoring them perpetuates a state of soullessness. In Santa Fe, for example, conflicts arise between the economic bonanza of tourism and its rich historic, Hispanic character. The influx of wealthy Anglos purchasing vacation homes has come at the expense of indigenous residents—the Native Americans and Spanish—who can no longer afford to live where their grandparents and great-grandparents lived.

Race, of course, is an issue affecting most American cities. Almost every person I've talked with in Washington mourns the racial divide between blacks and whites; some people describe it as a city of "two souls." To drive past abandoned buildings with the U.S. Capitol looming in the background, to see how dramatically the pollution-choked Anacostia River contrasts with the cleaner, suburban Potomac River, is to witness a visible tear in the city's soul.

Volunteering at a shelter for the homeless, throwing yourself into a political reform movement, getting to know down-and-out neighborhoods, speaking out about community ills all can help you find the soul of your hometown, as well as contribute to healing it.

Find Where People Come Together

The polis, wrote Hannah Arendt, arises out of people acting and speaking together in a "sharing of words and deeds." Thus the living force of a city's soul is most palpable in those large physical spaces—the commons—where the people of a city come together to celebrate, to protest, or simply to enjoy a Sunday afternoon. As a veteran of the anti-war movement, I fondly recall the boisterous rallies held in Kansas City's Volker Park and San Francisco's Golden Gate Park. The first place I ever felt the true beat of Washington, D.C., was at the

Georgetown Flea Market, an open-air bazaar where people from every corner of the city come each Sunday to barter with vendors for produce and craftwork.

Washington, of course, is the city where the rest of the country comes to make its voice heard. The open rectangle of green grass on the Mall is one of the most powerful outdoor public spaces in the modern world. It's where Martin Luther King gave his "I Have a Dream" speech and the destination for protesters about abortion, gun control, foreign policy, and countless other causes. Yet I've also enjoyed spring days strolling along the Mall while my kids clamor to pet someone's dog.

Take note of outdoor spaces where people gather to share in the ordinariness of life and, in being together, keep city life vibrant. More than the physical landscape or architectural design of a city, it is people, individually and collectively, who are the true force that enlivens and empowers a place.

Ironically, commitment to saving the souls of our cities might lead to greater protection of wilderness. As James Hillman has frequently pointed out, Americans tend to see their cities as the place where the innocent become corrupted and where soul is lost, rather than found. He has argued passionately on behalf of reversing this trend, thus protecting nature from too much human contact and reanimating our cities from within. For to seek soul only in nature, or within ourselves, is to miss the wondrous natural creation that is a city—a convergence of community, commerce, street life, history, nature, geography, politics, art, and people that offers a perpetually renewing source of life.

Thinking About the Text _____

1. What does Peay mean by the term "cultural imagination"? How does "cultural imagina-tion" contribute to the soul of a city?

2. What, in Peay's opinion, is significant about the "heart of town"? How important is her choice of words in this particular instance?

3. How useful is Peay's organization of subheadings within the text to keep the reader focused? What other organizational techniques could you use to structure your essay?

Reclaiming Culture and the Land: Motherhood and the Politics of Sustaining Community

WINONA LADUKE

Winona LaDuke, a Native American activist raised on the White Earth reservation in Minnesota, attended Harvard University where she researched the health impacts of uranium mining on the Navajo reservation. She also worked with grassroots Native organizations in South Dakota, New Mexico, and Arizona. LaDuke founded the White Earth Land Recovery Project, an organization concerned with reclaiming 800,000 acres of land taken from the reservation. LaDuke continues to be involved with social and environmental concerns. She is the founder of the Indigenous Women's Network and serves on the board of directors of Green Peace USA. She is also a program officer for a Native American controlled foundation. LaDuke has published numerous articles, testified to governmental bodies, and spoken at various universities, including Northern Arizona University. LaDuke lives on the White Earth reservation in Minnesota with her two children. "Reclaiming Culture and the Land" is an interview transcribed in essay form, in which LaDuke addresses such issues as cultural practices, community, education, parenting, and politics.

From *The Politics of Motherhood: Activist Voices From Left to Right* edited by Alexis Jetter, Annelise Orleck and Diana Taylor © 1997 by the Trustees of Dartmouth College, reprinted with permission of the author and University Press of New England.

An interview with Winona LaDuke

Conducted and edited by Annelise Orleck and Alexis Jetter

I get called a Native American activist, which I think is kind of ludicrous. I mostly consider myself a responsible parent. I think that not letting others say what you are is important. I want my children to think that it's normal to do what I do.

In the Native community, and my community at White Earth, we parent through extended families and clan relations. That's the essence of it. So parenting is not done by you. It's done by everybody, though I'm obviously the most active of the parent people in my kids' lives. My kids spend a lot of time with me, but so do a lot of other children. That practice is an essential piece of our culture.

This came up recently because I had an intern working with me at White Earth who was really conservative. He told me, "I'm really concerned about your son. He's not with you enough." Now, in reality, he's with me plenty. My kids travel with me a lot, although right now they're off hunting with their father. They had a choice and I said, "Fine. Go spend two weeks in the bus with your dad."

What I realized was that this intern was really concerned with the absence of a nuclear family. What he hadn't grasped yet, even though he's entirely immersed in our community, what he has not fathomed, is that we do not largely operate in nuclear families. We operate in extended families. And that's how we parent.

But I do think that it's real important for a politically active parent, as with any other parent, to illustrate to children the values that you're trying to instill in them. And those lessons have to be experiential. You don't tell them how to live. It's how you live your life. That's how children learn. At least that's my experience. And so I try to practice the cultural traditions and values that I want them to absorb.

In our community, our cultural practice is that your daily life is guided by ritual. The significance is in everything that you do: how you cook, what you cook, how you prepare food, how you prepare clothing for your children, how you look, how you walk outside. In our way of living there is ceremony in everything. So for instance, a couple of weeks ago someone gave me a beaver that they had shot. They knew that I like to eat beaver meat. This was a neighbor who is part of our extended system. He and his son brought me the beaver and asked if I wanted it. And I said, "Yeah, that would be great."

And so my children and I butchered the beaver. Now there are certain things you do when you butcher an animal. You talk to it. You put tobacco out. In the case of a beaver, you don't let a dog eat its bones. And when you butcher it, you undress it. That's how you talk to it. You undress it. So what my children learn from that is a whole set of things that they can't learn from just hearing about it. They only learn from experiencing it and seeing it as a common thing, not an unusual thing.

I think that the separation of political and cultural and spiritual is an artificial separation that's articulated by industrial society. But that split doesn't actually exist. Because cultural practices are political practices. And how you live your life is political. We spend our time trying to pretend it's all separate but it isn't. In our community, we view it differently. For me, whether it's opposing cultural destruction or opposing clear-cutting, it's the same. Opposing clear-cutting is opposing cultural destruction. It would be wrong for me to talk about cultural preservation to my children and not oppose clear-cutting because they won't have forests if I don't oppose clear-cutting. So a lot of my thinking is around that.

I get called a Native American activist, which I think is kind of ludicrous. I mostly consider myself a responsible parent. I think that not letting others say what you are is important. I want my children to think that it's normal to do what I do. My children do have the sense that what I do is not necessarily common. Recently my daughter started asking me if I'm famous. I don't know where she got that. She's six. I don't know how they know what is famous and what isn't. I said, "No." She said, "Then how come everybody knows who you are?" So I don't know if they consider the things I do totally normal. But, at the same time, that's the only way they've ever known me to be. So they don't balk at the things that I do.

They have had to deal with my being arrested. We've had a lot of talks about who the police are and where they are. They don't have a sense of good police. They have experiences of going through Customs and having the person they're with pulled out. And they had some terrible experiences with cops. So they don't have a sense of cops as good guys. There are a lot of people who go in and out of jail in our community. But when I got arrested I explained to them why and they thought it was okay.

At the same time, if the kids were asked, I'm sure they'd say, "I wish mommy stayed home more." As a politically active parent, you need to strike a balance. I have seen children of politically active Native people walk away for a period of time because their parents did not attend to them as a primary part of their lives. It usually was a male parent who, not unlike my father, was not present in their lives. I think they felt that there was a competition and they resented it.

And so I try to not repeat that with my children, which is hard. I travel a lot. I cannot get a foundation to fund my social change work but I can get a college to pay me to come and talk. So I take my children with me whenever I can—but I make sure that they have a lot of fun.

Like my children, I was raised in a context in which being "responsible" for others was normal. I come from a biracial family. My mother is Jewish and my father is Ojibwe. And they're both very political. They did different things. My father, ever since I was little, was active in the Native community. My mother was active in the civil rights movement. I spent a lot of time in the anti-war movement when I was a kid. And my maternal grandmother was active in the International Ladies' Garment Workers' Union.

I was raised with the belief that "bearing witness to wrong" or engaging in more active resistance was the right thing to do. My whole upbringing was based on that. My mother instilled in me a broad sense of social justice that I hear myself repeating to my children. I am thankful in many ways for my upbringing. My mother likes to travel and she took me to Europe and I saw these churches and I was so awed. And I remember my mother's refrain: "You know how they built those churches? They didn't pay union wages. They exploited everyone to build those churches."

But I think the part of my upbringing that has stuck with me the most is that I was raised as an outsider. I think I gave up trying to be cool or an insider by about the fifth grade. There were no Jews or Indian people in our town. My mom used to get letters from the John Birch Society when I was little. And because I was the darkest kid in my school, my primary experience was being socialized as a dark kid. You get centered on your own when you're not based on affirmation by others.

Being different was valued in my home. My mother was an artist so she thought it was important not to conform. She is very earth based in her cultural practice. She writes books on Third World women and art. So she always raised me with a great appreciation for a lot of cultures and very little appreciation for American culture. Consumerism was really frowned on in our house. Because it's part of cultural destruction.

A lot of the struggle we have as parents is created by the deculturalizing of people. The taking away of people's culture is a very American thing to do—to everyone. And then that culture is replaced with a monochrome American culture. That causes a lot of psychological and social problems for people. That's largely why we have the level of consumption we have. Because it's conditioned: To become "American"—whatever that is—you shop and you buy and you wear. That same thing is happening in Native communities. So our challenge as parents in those communities is to make it really cool to be Indian. Powwows are really important for that. So are ceremonies and gatherings. Of course, my kids are into rebellion, too. My son just cut his hair! That's what he did.

For me, fighting deculturalizing takes many forms. When I moved back to White Earth, for instance, I could have, as an individual, secured my own land. But the fact was that 90 percent of White Earth land was held by non-Indians. And everybody was in the same boat that I was. Now, America would teach you that you should take care of yourself. But I have always felt that that's not right.

If I want to live in a community, then I have to make that community the kind of community that I want to live in. And if the structural causes of poverty in my community don't change—insecure land tenure, Bureau of Indian Affairs-controlled institutions, Tribal Councils dominated by BIA values, economic control that is outside of the community—then my kids, my children and I are not in a healthy community.

That's why I have my children in tribal school. I was the principal of that school when I came back. The Tribal Council fired me. Fired me for insubordination. I was proud of that. But I put my children in that school because I wanted them to be in the Indian community. It's a mediocre rural school at best, with some Indian infused in it, but barely enough. Our battle and our work is to transform it into a much better school that teaches a lot more Ojibwe language. Now students have twelve years of Ojibwe instruction, but at the end of their studies they can barely speak.

So we have a problem in our school system. It comes from a couple of sources. There are a lot of white teachers who would have preferred to work in a white school but they couldn't get jobs so they come to us. That's the first problem. My daughter's kindergarten and first grade teachers are excellent teachers. But a lot aren't. The other problem is that the Tribal Council does not make education a priority. So our struggle is to try to transform that school.

We run an early childhood language immersion program that my four-year-old son is in. We also run evening programs for adults and children, weekend classes in language immersion, and in-school programming in two of the schools.

But we're battling the school system. We really are. My thinking, my political strategy is to transform the school system so that my children have peers in their own community. I can do that best in my own school system. I am going to have a lot less pull in a non-Indian school system off reservation where Indians are just a small percentage. I could probably try to pull a bunch of strings and get my kids into a private school someplace. But that's not going to address the problem. Then my kids will have an education that someone says is a good education. But they won't be in the community. So that's how I'm thinking.

In our community, both men and women have a pretty significant role. I would say that the berries are more the women's responsibility and the syruping is more the men's responsibility. As for corn, we planted a bunch of hominy corn last year and a man planted it—and you know, when those ears came up they were about 90 percent male! So we're going to do a test this year. He's going to plant one field and I'm going to plant the other. And we'll see what happens. I didn't even know that there were male and female ears until some Six Nations people showed me that. We are just relearning our corn knowledge. Anyway, at White Earth there's a lot of balance between men and women.

But nationally, a lot of the leadership for grassroots native environmental organizations comes from women. Native Action at North Cheyenne reservation is run by a woman, Gail Small. Then you go to Dine Care, and it's run by Laurie Goodman. Indians for Cultural Environmental Protection, which is fighting toxic sewage and sludge from San Diego, is run by Marina Ortega. Grace Thorpe fought her own tribal council when they wanted to accept nuclear waste. Grace and her daughter Dagmar are a really good example of women's leadership around these issues.

There's a lot of people who say that this era, this time, is led by women. There's a lot of recognition of that. I hear it from a lot of elders. Because women didn't have enough vested interest to get corrupted. My view is that when the tribal council system, and a lot of the jobs programs, came into the reservations, women were relegated to second-class status. And consequently they didn't get as much patronage or as much vested interest. They were marginalized and thus ended up knowing more who they were. That's why a lot of that resistance started with women.

On my reservation the Tribal Council is all male. Every once in a while you get a woman in there but it's totally male dominated. And I'll tell you, those guys hate me. On the other hand, they work with me because they know what we're doing is right and because they're afraid that I'm going to bring a lot of press or that I'm going to go and fight them. They want to take credit for what we're doing. And we let them take credit for it. It doesn't matter to me. Everyone knows that they didn't do it. But they hate me because I'm everything that scares them, because I'm educated and because I'm a woman. And because I don't agree with them.

On the other hand, I'm supported by a lot of men in our community. Our community is split between the council and everyone else. Between the haves and the have-nots. We're the have-nots. The chairman of the tribal council makes $250,000 a year. For everyone else at White Earth, the per capita income is $10,000 a year.

There are a lot of Native women out in their communities fighting tribal councils and fighting corporations. Many went to college and went back to work in their communities. And what we're finding is that our relationship with each other is really what sustains us, to know that there are women who are your peers, that there are more women of my vintage. We have a point of reference, a political and human view that are similar.

A bunch of us came together in 1985 to talk about these issues and to encourage women's participation at the local, national and international levels. We wanted to talk about organizing, and strategies that are working and challenges that we're facing—and despair and hope and all those pieces. So we hosted a conference in Yelm, Washington, that drew about 500 women. And out of that came the Indigenous Women's Network.

There was a mandate to try to form something to continue that work. So IWN is about encouraging women's political and other participation, whether it is by honoring them, or raising money to support their work, or just by being a network so that they know there's other women out there. Sometimes we found ourselves battling with women's organizations and environmental groups to say that we have a voice too, whether it's in the Native community or the broader community. That's our thinking.

And so we publish a magazine a couple of times a year. We've raised money for a Venezuelan women's health project, a diaper service in Moose Factory, Ontario. We went to Geneva to the United Nations conference. And in 1993 we did a tour with the Indigo Girls that raised $58,000 for native women's projects.

On our White Earth Reservation, Ojibwe women have joined together in a marketing collective, seeking a fair price for crafts and wild rice. On the reservation, 75 percent of the people hunt, 45 percent harvest wild rice, and about the same number make handicrafts. They produce more than they can use, and women are seeking to market the surplus themselves. The collective hopes to leave out generally unscrupulous middlemen or, at the very least, capture the "value added" of their resources themselves.

The ethical code of my own Anishinabeg culture keeps communities and individuals in line with natural law. *Minobimaatisiiwin*, which means both the "good life" and "continuous rebirth," is central to our value system. In *minobimaatisiiwin*, we honor one another, we honor women as the givers of our lives, and we honor our *Chi Anishinabeg*, our old people and ancestors who hold the knowledge. We honor our children as the continuity from generations, and we honor ourselves as a part of creation.

Implicit in *minobimaatisiiwin* is a continuous habitation of place, an intimate understanding of the relationship between humans and the ecosystem and of the need to maintain this balance. That value system has made it possible for many indigenous peoples to maintain their economic, political and religious institutions for generations in a way that would now be termed sustainable.

Throughout North America, Native women, joined with families and the men of their communities, both resist environmentally and culturally destructive projects, and engage in rebuilding efforts. We have a place. And many women are positive that the best security for themselves and their families isn't in the context of the modern industrial world but in a self-defined context of our own cultures and ways of living.

So, bringing the conversation back to parenting and politics—back home, a lot of our life is about simple things. Right now we're in maple syruping season. So my children spend a lot of time in the sugarbush. I try to keep our life-style simple. I'm most comfortable in a fairly rural life-style; that way of life reiterates my values. And, you know, I would probably have a much harder time parenting if I lived somewhere else. Because I think that parenting is about living how you believe.

Thinking About the Text _____

1. How does LaDuke's narrative style compare with Peay's? Would LaDuke's essay benefit from a structure similar to Peay's? Why?

2. How do LaDuke's "home politics" relate or influence her "world politics?" Discuss with a partner the tie between the two. Does the tie make sense?

3. Write a paragraph explaining Minobimaatisiiwin. Does western culture have a term(s) for such a concept? Explain your idea with support from your general understanding of western culture.

In Groups We Shrink From Loner's Heroics

Carol Tavris

Carol Tavris, born in 1944, received her Ph.D. in Social Psychology from the University of Michigan. She has published on women's and men's mental health issues and has taught courses in psychology. Some of her articles have been published in magazines such as *Science Digest, Harpers, Redbook,* and the *New York Times.* She has also published *Anger: the Misunderstood Emotion,* and *The Mismeasure of Woman.* Tavris continues to publish a wide variety of articles on aspects of psychology. "In Groups We Shrink" looks at how people in groups tend to be less involved in helping when disaster and danger strike. Tavris asks why responsibility gets diffused when we are part of a group.

The ghost of Kitty Genovese would sympathize with Rodney King. Genovese, you may remember, is the symbol of bystander apathy in America. Screaming for help, she was stabbed repeatedly and killed in front of her New York apartment, and not one of the 38 neighbors who heard her, including those who came to their windows to watch, even called for help.

One of the things we find appalling in the videotape of King's assault is the image of at least 11 police officers watching four of their colleagues administer the savage beating and doing nothing to intervene. Whatever is the matter with them, we wonder.

Something happens to individuals when they collect in a group. They think and act differently than they would on their own. Most people, if they observe some disaster or danger on their own—a woman being stabbed, a pedestrian slammed by a hit-and-run driver—will at least call for help; many will even risk their own safety to intervene. But if they are in a group observing the same danger, they hold back. The reason is not necessarily that they are lazy, *what is?*

cowardly or have 50 other personality deficiencies; it has more to do with the nature of groups than the nature of individuals.

In one experiment in behavioral psychology, students were seated in a room, either alone or in groups of three, as a staged emergency occurred: Smoke began pouring through the vents. Students who were on their own usually hesitated a minute, got up, checked the vents and then went out to report what certainly seemed like fire. But the students who were sitting in groups of three did not move. They sat there for six minutes, with smoke so thick they could barely see, rubbing their eyes and coughing.

In another experiment, psychologists staged a situation in which people overheard a loud crash, a scream and a woman in pain, moaning that her ankle was broken. Seventy percent of those who were alone when the "accident" occurred went to her aid, compared with only 40% of those who heard her in the presence another person.

For victims, obviously, there is no safety in numbers. Why? One reason is that if other people aren't doing anything, the individual assumes that nothing needs to be done. In the smoke-filled room study, the students in groups said they thought that the smoke was caused by "steam pipes," "truth gas" or "leaks in the air conditioning"; not one said what the students on their own did: "I thought it was fire." In the lady-in-distress study, some of those who failed to offer help said, "I didn't want to embarrass her."

Often, observers think nothing needs to be done because someone else has already taken care of it, and the more observers there are, the less likely any one person is to call for help. In Albuquerque, N.M., 30 people watched for an hour and a half as a building burned to the ground before they realized that no one had called the fire department. Psychologists call this process "diffusion of responsibility" or "social loafing": The more people in a group, the lazier each individual in it becomes. *Does this happen in our days?*

But there was no mistaking what those officers were doing to Rodney King. There was no way for those observers to discount the severity of the beating King was getting. What kept them silent?

One explanation, of course, is that they approved. They may have identified with the abusers, vicariously participating in a beating they rationalized as justified. The widespread racism in the Los Angeles Police Department and the unprovoked abuse of black people is now undeniable. A friend who runs a trucking company told me recently that one of her drivers, a 50-year-old black man, is routinely pulled over by Los Angeles cops for the flimsiest of reasons "and made to lie down on the street like a dog." None of her white drivers has been treated this way.

Or the observers may have hated what was happening and been caught in the oldest of human dilemmas: Do the moral thing and be disliked, humiliated, embarrassed and rejected. Our nation, for all its celebration of the Lone Ranger and the independent pioneer, does not really value the individual—at least not when the person is behaving individually and standing up to the group. (We like dissenters, but only when they are dissenting in Russia or China.) Again and again, countless studies have shown that people will go along rather than risk the embarrassment of being disobedient, rude or disloyal.

And so the banality of evil is once again confirmed. Most people do not behave badly because they are inherently bad. They behave badly because they aren't paying attention, or they leave it to Harry, or they don't want to rock the boat, or they don't want to embarrass themselves or others if they're wrong.

Every time the news reports another story of a group that has behaved mindlessly, violently and stupidly, including the inevitable members who are just "going along," many people shake their heads in shock and anger at the failings of "human nature." But the findings of behavioral research can direct us instead to appreciate the conditions under which individuals in groups will behave morally or not. Once we know the conditions, we can begin to prescribe antidotes. By understanding the impulse to diffuse responsibility, perhaps as individuals we will be more likely to act. By understanding the social pressures that reward group-think, loyalty and obedience, we can foster those that reward whistle-blowing and moral courage. And, as a society, we can reinforce the belief that they also sin who only stand and watch.

Thinking About the Text _____

1. What structure and rhetorical appeals does Tavris use in her essay? Could the essay be presented in another way to make it more powerful? Explain your reasoning for your alternative choices.

2. Tavris uses a variety of rhetorical appeals, sometimes even displaying both pathos and ethos in the same sentence. Look through the essay and find the places that use dual appeals in the same sentence. How effective is this technique?

3. Write a paragraph detailing your experience with "social loafing." To strengthen your paragraph include the rhetorical appeals relevant to that experience.

Countering the Culture of Sex

ELLEN GOODMAN

Ellen Goodman is a Pulitzer Prize-winning columnist and has published several books, including *Keep in Touch* (1985), *Making Sense* (1989) and *Value Judgments* (1993). In "Countering the Culture of Sex," Goodman looks at how the entertainment industry can be seen as a "cultural message maker." This article originally appeared in 1995 in *The Boston Globe*.

When Kathleen Sylvester began researching welfare reform for the Progressive Policy Institute, she asked a Baltimore school principal the one thing she'd do to reduce the number of teen-age pregnancies.

The principal had an immediate two-word answer for her: "Shoot Madonna."

This was not a serious attempt on this educator's part to cure sex with violence. The principal was not a character assassin.

She was probably thinking of the Madonna of the 1980s, the one who wrote the classic paean to teen-age motherhood: "Papa Don't Preach." The Madonna of the '90s has a line in "Bedtime Stories" that sounds more like paean to Joycelyn Elders: "Happiness lies in your own hand."

But the principal was speaking in a familiar vocabulary. It's a language shared by parents, teachers, policy makers—the whole range of frustrated adults whose voices of reason are drowned out by a culture that sells kids sex as successfully as it sells them sneakers. Just Do It.

These messages that kids actually listen to ought to be piped into the hearing rooms where Congress is busy concocting a new welfare policy. The plan the House Ways and Means Committee is contemplating for teen-age mothers is called euphemistically "tough love." But our culture offers something else. Sex without consequences.

"How many times do kids see sex on TV," says Sylvester, "in which no one gets pregnant, no one gets AIDS and no one has to get up in the middle of the night to feed a baby?"

In the face of the onslaught, the true counterculture in America is not the "McGovernik elite" or, for heaven's sakes, PBS. It's parents and reasonable adults who are left to literally counter the culture, to do combat with the incessant messages of mainstream films, music, television—the conglomerate known as Hollywood—as best we can.

Hollywood may not *cause* teen pregnancy. But Sylvester and others are convinced that any national campaign that goes to the heart and hard core of the problem is going to have to engage these cultural message makers.

We're going to have to do more than label them as villains. We need them as allies.

It will take all their creativity to make a successful pitch against irresponsible sex and teen pregnancy. "Just say no" won't do it. Teen-agers are the most risk-taking part of the population. They're still being seduced by cigarette ads.

It will be harder to fashion a stand against sex than against smoking. After all, smoking is always bad for you; sex isn't. And hormones are even more powerful than nicotine addiction.

It will also be harder to campaign against unwed parenthood than against drunken driving. The campaign against drunken driving was successful in curbing dangerous behavior by creating a new social role: the designated driver. But a baby is a different sort of accident than a head-on collision.

If we can't preach, however much papa (and mama) may want to, we can say unequivocally in rhythm, rap or reel what Sylvester says in plain words: "It's wrong to bring a child into the world that you can't take care of." It's not cool, it's not manly, it's not womanly. It's wrong.

This goes beyond using Madonna for target practice. It even goes beyond lowering the sexual thermostat of the culture.

Entertainment executives like to say, on the one hand, that they are just reflecting reality and, on the other hand, that they're in the business of fantasy. With both hands they wave furious charges of censorship at any critic.

But how about more reality? In an ad campaign, in soap operas, movies, music.

Not long ago an outraged producer complained to Jay Winston, the public health guru who created the designated driver campaign: "Can you imagine that people are lobbying to have Tom Cruise use a condom? Tom Cruise?" Why is that so hard to imagine?

At Harvard's Kennedy School of Government, a nervous Barbra Streisand recently offered a spirited defense of the artist as citizen. But the problem isn't that this "cultural elite" is too political, it's that it isn't political enough. As Winston says, "They ought to be powerful players in this process. They need to come to the table."

Let's begin with some sexual truth-in-advertising: one part passion to two parts diapers. Sex and consequences. Try humming a few bars.

Thinking About the Text _____

1. Goodman, like most authors, has a specific audience in mind. Who is her audience for this essay? Where in the text does her appeal to a specific audience become apparent?

2. Based on Goodman's identification of audience, what is the purpose of her essay? Is she effective in communicating her purpose?

3. Based on the identification of audience and the purpose of Goodman's essay, what can we assume about the author?

4. List the factors you believe contribute to unplanned pregnancy. How does Goodman address what is on your list? Why do issues concerning unplanned pregnancies need to be addressed?

Let Gays Marry

Andrew Sullivan is an editor of *The New Republic* and author of *Virtually Normal: An Argument about Homosexuality*. This article discusses why gays should be allowed to marry. It originally appeared in *Newsweek*, June 3, 1996, p. 26.

"A state cannot deem a class of persons a stranger to its laws," declared the Supreme Court last week. It was a monumental statement. Gay men and lesbians, the conservative Court said, are no longer strangers in America. They are citizens, entitled, like everyone else, to equal protection—no special rights, but simple equality.

For the first time in Supreme Court history, gay men and women were seen not as some powerful lobby trying to subvert America, but as the people we truly are—the sons and daughters of countless mothers and fathers, with all the weaknesses and strengths and hopes of everybody else. And what we seek is not some special place in America but merely to be a full and equal part of America, to give back to our society without being forced to lie or hide or live as second-class citizens.

That is why marriage is so central to our hopes. People ask us why we want the right to marry, but the answer is obvious. It's the same reason anyone wants the right to marry. At some point in our lives, some of us are lucky enough to meet the person we truly love. And we want to commit to that person in front of our family and country for the rest of our lives. It's the most simple, the most natural, the most human instinct in the world. How could anyone seek to oppose that?

Yes, at first blush, it seems like a radical proposal, but, when you think about it some more, it's actually the opposite. Throughout American history, to be sure, marriage has been between a man and a woman, and in many ways our society is built upon that institution. But none of that need change in the slightest. After all, no one is seeking to take away anybody's right to marry, and no one is seeking to force any church to change any doctrine in any way. Particular religious arguments against same-sex marriage are rightly debated within the churches and faiths themselves. That is not the issue here: there is a separation between church and state in this country. We are only asking that when the government gives out *civil* marriage licenses, those of us who are gay should be treated like anybody else.

Of course, some argue that marriage is *by definition* between a man and a woman. But for centuries, marriage was *by definition* a contract in which the wife was her husband's legal property. And we changed that. For centuries, marriage was *by definition* between two people of the same race. And we changed that. We changed these things because we recognized that human dignity is the same whether you are a man or a woman, black or white. And no one has any more of a choice to be gay than to be black or white or male or female.

Some say that marriage is only about raising children, but we let childless heterosexual couples be married (Bob and Elizabeth Dole, Pat and Shelley Buchanan, for instance). Why should gay couples be treated differently? Others fear that there is no logical difference between allowing same-sex marriage and sanctioning polygamy and other horrors. But the issue of whether to sanction multiple spouses (gay or straight) is completely separate from whether, in the existing institution between two unrelated adults, the government should discriminate between its citizens.

This is, in fact, if only Bill Bennett could see it, a deeply conservative cause. It seeks to change no one else's rights or marriages in any way. It seems merely to promote monogamy, fidelity and the disciplines of family life among people who have long been cast to the margins of society. And what could be a more conservative project than that? Why indeed would any conservative seek to oppose those very family values for gay people that he or she supports for everybody else? Except, of course, to make gay men and lesbians strangers in their own country, to forbid them to ever come home.

Thinking About the Text _____

1. Describe the choices made by the author in the introduction to the essay. Are his techniques effective? How might these techniques be used in writing your own introductions to essays?

2. What are the key points of Sullivan's argument? Which points anticipate opposing viewpoints, and how are these addressed?

3. What are some specific strategies in Sullivan's essay to engage his readers? Why are these strategies effective? What other strategies would work?

Leave Marriage Alone

WILLIAM BENNETT

William Bennett is the editor of *The Book of Virtues* and co-director of Empower America. His article was written as a response to Andrew Sullivan's piece, and also appeared in *Newsweek*, June 3, 1996, p. 27.

There are at least two key issues that divide proponents and opponents of same-sex marriage. The first is whether legally recognizing same-sex unions would strengthen or weaken the institution. The second has to do with the basic understanding of marriage itself.

The advocates of same-sex marriage say that they seek to strengthen and celebrate marriage. That may be what some intend. But I am certain that it will not be the reality. Consider: the legal union of same-sex couples would shatter the conventional definition of marriage, change the rules which govern behavior, endorse practices which are completely antithetical to the tenets of all of the world's major religions, send conflicting signals about marriage and sexuality, particularly to the young, and obscure marriage's enormously consequential function—procreation and child-rearing.

Broadening the definition of marriage to include same-sex unions would stretch it almost beyond recognition—and new attempts to expand the definition still further would surely follow. On what *principled* ground can Andrew Sullivan exclude others who most desperately want what he wants, legal recognition and social acceptance? Why on earth would Sullivan exclude from marriage a bisexual who wants to marry two other people? After all, exclusion would be a denial of that person's sexuality. The same holds true of a father and daughter who want to marry. Or two sisters. Or men who want (consensual) polygamous arrangements. Sullivan may think some of these arrangements are unwise. But having employed sexual relativism in his own defense, he has effectively lost the capacity to draw any lines and make moral distinctions.

Forsaking all others is an essential component of marriage. Obviously it is not always honored in practice. But it is the ideal to which we rightly aspire, and in most marriages the ideal is in fact the norm. Many advocates of same-sex marriage simply do not share this ideal; promiscuity among homosexual males is well known. Sullivan himself has written that gay male relationships are served by the "openness of the contract" and that homosexuals should resist allowing their "varied and complicated lives" to be flattened into a "single, moralistic model." But that "single, moralistic model" has served society exceedingly well. The burden of proof ought to be on those who propose untested arrangements for our most important institution.

A second key difference I have with Sullivan goes to the very heart of marriage itself. I believe that marriage is not an arbitrary construct which can be redefined simply by those who lay claim to it. It is an honorable estate, instituted of God and built on moral, religious, sexual and human realities. Marriage is based on a natural teleology, on the different, complementary nature of men and women—and how they refine, support, encourage and complete one another. It is the institution through which we propagate, nurture, educate and sustain our species.

That we have to engage in this debate at all is an indication of how steep our moral slide has been. Worse, those who defend the traditional understanding of marriage are routinely referred to (though not to my knowledge by Sullivan) as "homophobes," "gay-bashers," "intolerant" and "bigoted." Can one defend an honorable, 4,000-year-old tradition and not be called these names?

This is a large, tolerant, diverse country. In America people are free to do as they wish, within broad parameters. It is also a country in sore need of shoring up some of its most crucial institutions: marriage and the family, schools, neighborhoods, communities. But marriage and family are the greatest of these. That is why they are elevated and revered. We should keep them so.

Thinking About the Text _____

1. How does Bennett's introduction influence your reading of the rest of the essay? What techniques is he using in his introduction to convince you of his viewpoints? How well do his strategies work?

2. How do the connotations of words such as "institution" and "shattered" impact (benefit or detract from) the argument that Bennett presents? Are there other examples of words selected that have a strong connotation?

3. What do the essays by Sullivan and Bennett have in common? Where do the two authors differ? Which argument, Sullivan's or Bennett's, do you find more compelling? Why?

Section 2

Construction of Language

Language is one of the most powerful tools in our interactions with others. We use language to let people know that we agree or disagree with them; we use it to make sure that our opinions are heard; and we use it to make a coherent argument about an issue that we care about deeply. We interpret language based on who we are and what experiences we have had. Our audience influences our language use, and our purpose leads us to argue differently in different situations. The readings in this section show you how writers can influence their readers, and how they use language to construct not only who they are but also what perspectives they want their readers to take. Amy Tan, in "Mother Tongue," Jimmy Santiago Baca, in "Coming into Language," and Gloria Anzaldúa, in "How to Tame a Wild Tongue," show us how their backgrounds influence their use of language as well as their perception of themselves and of others in their various communities. Lee Thomas and Linh Cao discuss "Language Use in Family and Society" from a linguistics perspective, pointing out that even families can be separated by language use and by changes in cultural perspectives. This essay is followed by Andrei Codrescu's explorations of the language of baseball which he considers literary and poetic, using such words as caesuras, short lines, stanzas, and prosodic regularity. In "The Debate Has Been Miscast from the Start," Henry Louis Gates argues that a multicultural approach to education might not cure all the problems we face as a society, but that it can instill and encourage social tolerance. Gates' essay is complemented by Robert Keith Miller's commentary on the virtues of discrimination in which he argues that the word *discrimination* has been misused for many years. Here again we see how language can be used and misused to fit the intent of the writer, the purpose, and the audience. The last two selections in this section address the ever-popular debate on bilingual education, showing two opposing perspectives by Richard Rodriguez and Angelo Gonzalez. Rodriguez presents his argument based on personal experiences, and Gonzalez uses his experiences as an educator and director of ASPIRA, an organization that promotes awareness and advocacy of issues related to Latinos.

When you read these articles, think about how you use language to convince your readers that your perspective is valid and valuable. Also think about how others have used language to make a point, and why they were able or unable to get your support for a cause they support:

- Think about a controversial issue (social, political, economic, etc.) that you care about deeply. What strategies would you use to convince your audience that your perspective is the right one?

- Define the word "multiculturalism." What are some of the political and social connotations of this word? How does your own schooling influence your interpretation of the word?

- Many people living in the United States speak English as a second language. What are your perceptions of people who do not speak English fluently? How do you interact with them?

Mother Tongue

Amy Tan

Amy Tan, a first-generation Asian-American, was born in 1952 to parents who emigrated from China to Oakland, California. Tan is the author of several novels including *The Joy Luck Club* (1989), and *The Kitchen God's Wife* (1991). In the following essay, Tan considers the implications of her mother's "limited English" on her self-perception as well as her perception of her mother. Ultimately, Tan realizes that the language she shares with her mother is a "language of intimacy."

I am not a scholar of English or literature. I cannot give you much more than personal opinions on the English language and its variations in this country or others.

I am a writer. And by that definition, I am someone who has always loved language. I am fascinated by language in daily life. I spend a great deal of my time thinking about the power of language—the way it can evoke an emotion, a visual image, a complex idea, or a simple truth. Language is the tool of my trade. And I use them all—all the Englishes I grew up with.

Recently, I was made keenly aware of the different Englishes I do use. I was giving a talk to a large group of people, the same talk I had already given to half a dozen other groups. The nature of the talk was about my writing, my life, and my book, *The Joy Luck Club*. The talk was going along well enough, until I remembered one major difference that made the whole talk sound wrong. My mother was in the room. And it was perhaps the first time she had heard me give a lengthy speech, using the kind of English I have never used with her. I was saying things like, "The intersection of memory upon imagination" and "There is an aspect of my fiction that relates to thus-and-thus"—a speech filled with carefully wrought grammatical phrases, burdened, it suddenly seemed to me, with nominalized forms, past perfect tenses, conditional phrases, all the forms of standard English that I had learned in school and through books, the forms of English I did not use at home with my mother.

Just last week, I was walking down the street with my mother, and I again found myself conscious of the English I was using, the English I do use with her. We were talking about the price of new and used furniture and I heard myself saying this: "Not waste money that way." My husband was with us as well, and he didn't notice any switch in my English. And then I realized why. It's because over the twenty years we've been together I've often used that same kind of English with him, and sometimes he even uses it with me. It has become our language of intimacy, a different sort of English that relates to family talk, the language I grew up with.

So you'll have some idea of what this family talk I heard sounds like, I'll quote what my mother said during a recent conversation which I videotaped and then transcribed. During this conversation, my mother was talking about a political gangster in Shanghai who had the same last name as her family's, Du, and how the gangster in his early years wanted to be adopted by her family, which was rich by comparison. Later, the gangster became more powerful, far richer than my mother's family, and one day showed up at my mother's wedding to pay his respects. Here's what she said in part:

"Du Yusong having business like fruit stand. Like off the street kind. He is Du like Du Zong—but not Tsung-ming Island people. The local people call putong, the river east side, he belong to that side local people. That man want to ask Du Zong father take him in like become own family. Du Zong father wasn't look down on him, but didn't take seriously, until that man big like become a mafia. Now important person, very hard to inviting him. Chinese way, came only to show respect, don't stay for dinner. Respect for making big celebration, he shows up. Mean gives lots of respect. Chinese custom. Chinese social life that way. If too important won't have to stay too long. He come to my wedding. I didn't see, I heard it. I gone to boy's side, they have YMCA dinner. Chinese age I was nineteen."

You should know that my mother's expressive command of English belies how much she actually understands. She reads the *Forbes* report, listens to *Wall Street Week*, converses daily with her stockbroker, reads all of Shirley MacLaine's books with ease—all kinds of things I can't begin to understand. Yet some of my friends tell me they understand 50 percent of what my mother says. Some say they understand 80 to 90 percent. Some say they understand none of it, as if she were speaking pure Chinese. But to me, my mother's English is perfectly clear, perfectly natural. It's my mother tongue. Her language, as I hear it, is vivid, direct, full of observation and imagery. That was the language that helped shape the way I saw things, expressed things, made sense of the world.

Lately, I've been giving more thought to the kind of English my mother speaks. Like others, I have described it to people as "broken" or "fractured" English. But I wince when I say that. It has always bothered me that I can think of no way to describe it other than "broken," as if it were damaged and needed to be fixed, as if it lacked a certain wholeness and soundness. I've heard other terms used, "limited English," for example. But they seem just as bad, as if everything is limited, including people's perceptions of the limited English speaker.

I know this for a fact, because when I was growing up, my mother's "limited" English limited *my* perception of her. I was ashamed of her English. I believed that her English reflected the quality of what she had to say. That is, because she expressed them imperfectly her thoughts were imperfect. And I had plenty of empirical evidence to support me: the fact that people in department stores, at banks, and at restaurants did not take her seriously, did not give her good service, pretended not to understand her, or even acted as if they did not hear her.

My mother has long realized the limitations of her English as well. When I was fifteen, she used to have me call people on the phone to pretend I was she. In this guise, I was forced to ask for information or even to complain and yell at people who had been rude to her. One time it was a call to her stockbroker in New York. She had cashed out her small portfolio and it just so happened we were going to go to New York the next week, our very first trip outside California. I had to get on the phone and say in an adolescent voice that was not very convincing, "This is Mrs. Tan."

And my mother was standing in the back whispering loudly, "Why he don't send me check, already two weeks late. So mad he lie to me, losing me money."

And then I said in perfect English, "Yes, I'm getting rather concerned. You had agreed to send the check two weeks ago, but it hasn't arrived."

Then she began to talk more loudly. "What he want, I come to New York tell him front of his boss, you cheating me?" And I was trying to calm her down, make her be quiet, while telling the stockbroker, "I can't tolerate any more excuses. If I don't receive the check immediately, I am going to have to speak to your manager when I'm in New York next week." And sure enough, the following week there we were in front of this astonished stockbroker, and I was sitting there red-faced and quiet, and my mother, the real Mrs. Tan, was shouting at his boss in her impeccable broken English.

We used a similar routine just five days ago, for a situation that was far less humorous. My mother had gone to the hospital for an appointment, to find out about a benign brain tumor a CAT scan had revealed a month ago. She said she had spoken very good English, her best English, no mistakes. Still, she said, the hospital did not apologize when they said they had lost the CAT scan and she had come for nothing. She said they did not seem to have any sympathy when she told them she was anxious to know the exact diagnosis, since her husband and son had both died of brain tumors. She said they would not give her any more information until the next time and she would have to make another appointment for that. So she said she would not leave until the doctor called her daughter. She wouldn't budge. And when the doctor finally called her daughter, me, who spoke in perfect English—lo and behold—we had assurances the CAT scan would be found, promises that a conference call on Monday would be held, and apologies for any suffering my mother had gone through for a most regrettable mistake.

I think my mother's English almost had an effect on limiting my possibilities in life as well. Sociologists and linguists probably will tell you that a person's developing language skills are more influenced by peers. But I do think that the language spoken in the family, especially in immigrant families which are more insular, plays a large role in shaping the language of the child. And I believe that it affected my results on achievement tests, IQ tests, and the SAT. While my English skills were never judged as poor, compared to math, English could not be considered my strong suit. In grade school I did moderately well, getting perhaps B's, sometimes B-pluses, in English and scoring perhaps in the sixtieth or seventieth percentile on achievement tests. But those scores were not good enough to override the opinion that my true abilities lay in math and science, because in those areas I achieved A's and scored in the ninetieth percentile or higher.

This was understandable. Math is precise; there is only one correct answer. Whereas, for me at least, the answers on English tests were always a judgment call, a matter of opinion and personal experience. Those tests were constructed around items like fill-in-the-blank sentence completion, such as, "Even though Tom was _____ , Mary thought he was _____ ." And the correct answer always seemed to be the most bland combinations of thoughts, for example, "Even though Tom was shy, Mary thought he was charming," with the grammatical structure "even though" limiting the correct answer to some sort of semantic opposites, so you wouldn't get answers like, "Even though Tom was foolish, Mary thought he was ridiculous." Well, according to my mother, there were very few limitations as to what Tom could have been and what Mary might have thought of him. So I never did well on tests like that.

The same was true with word analogies, pairs of words in which you were supposed to find some sort of logical, semantic relationship—for example, *"Sunset* is to *nightfall* as _____ is to _____ ."* And here you would be presented with a list of four possible pairs, one of which showed the same kind of relationship: *red* is to *stoplight, bus* is to *arrival, chills* is to *fever, yawn* is to *boring.* Well, I could never think that way. I knew what the tests were asking, but I could not block out of my mind the images already created by the first pair, *"sunset* is to *nightfall"*—and I would see a burst of color against a darkening sky, the moon rising, the lowering of a curtain of stars. And all the other pairs of words—red, bus, stoplight, boring—just threw up a mass of confusing images, making it impossible for me to sort out something as logical as saying: "A sunset precedes nightfall" is the same as "a chill precedes a fever." The only way I would have gotten that answer right would have been to imagine an associative situation, for example, by being disobedient and staying out past sunset, catching a chill at night which turns into feverish pneumonia as punishment, which indeed did happen to me.

I have been thinking about all this lately, about my mother's English, about achievement tests. Because lately I've been asked, as a writer, why there are not more Asian Americans represented in American literature. Why are there few Asian Americans enrolled in creative writing programs? Why do so many Chinese students go into engineering? Well, these are broad sociological questions I can't begin to answer. But I have noticed in surveys—in fact, just last week—that Asian students, as a whole, always do significantly better on math achievement tests than in English. And this makes me think that there are other Asian-American students whose English spoken in the home might also be described as "broken" or "limited." And perhaps they also have teachers who are steering them away from writing and into math and science, which is what happened to me.

Fortunately, I happen to be rebellious in nature and enjoy the challenge of disproving assumptions made about me. I became an English major my first year in college, after being enrolled as pre-med. I started writing nonfiction as a freelancer the week after I was told by my former boss that writing was my worst skill and I should hone my talents toward account management.

But it wasn't until 1985 that I finally began to write fiction. And at first I wrote using what I thought to be wittily crafted sentences, sentences that would finally prove I had mastery over the English language. Here's an example from the first draft of a story that later made its way into *The Joy Luck Club*, but without this line: "That was my mental quandary in its nascent state." A terrible line, which I can hardly pronounce.

Fortunately, for reasons I won't get into today, I later decided I should envision a reader for the stories I would write. And the reader I decided upon was my mother, because these were stories about mothers. So with this reader in mind—and in fact she did read my early drafts—I began to write stories using all the Englishes I grew up with: the English I spoke to my mother, which for lack of a better term might be described as "simple"; the English she used with me, which for lack of a better term might be described as "broken"; my translation of her Chinese, which could certainly be described as "watered down"; and what I imagine to be her translation of her Chinese if she could speak in perfect English, her internal language, and for that I sought to preserve the essence, but neither an English nor a Chinese structure. I wanted to capture what language ability tests can never reveal: her intent, her passion, her imagery, the rhythms of her speech and the nature of her thoughts.

Apart from what any critic had to say about my writing, I knew I had succeeded where it counted when my mother finished reading my book and gave me her verdict: "So easy to read."

Thinking About the Text _____

1. What does Tan realize about the nature of the language she grew up with? Why does Tan choose her mother as the audience for her books?

2. Why does Tan say the term "limited English" is problematic? How have Tan and her mother overcome some of these "limits"?

3. How is Tan's tone affected by her experience with language?

Coming into Language

JIMMY SANTIAGO BACA

Jimmy Santiago Baca was born in 1952 and is of Apache Indian and Chicano descent. He was abandoned by his parents at the age of two and lived in an orphanage briefly before escaping to hide in the barrio and at relatives' houses. He ended up on the streets before being sent to prison at the age of 17 for various offences. At the age of 27, after battling illiteracy, a life on the streets, and being in and out of prison, Baca published his first collection of poetry, *Immigrants in Our Own Land*, in 1979.

On weekend graveyard shifts at St. Joseph's Hospital I worked the emergency room, mopping up pools of blood and carting plastic bags stuffed with arms, legs, and hands to the outdoor incinerator. I enjoyed the quiet, away from the screams of shotgunned, knifed, and mangled kids writhing on gurneys outside the operating rooms. Ambulance sirens shrieked and squad car lights reddened the cool nights, flashing against the hospital walls: gray—red, gray—red. On slow nights I would lock the door of the administration office, search the reference library for a book on female anatomy and, with my feet propped on the desk, leaf through the illustrations, smoking my cigarette. I was seventeen.

One night my eye was caught by a familiar-looking word on the spine of a book. The title was *450 Years of Chicano History in Pictures.* On the cover were black-and-white photos: Padre Hidalgo exhorting Mexican peasants to revolt against the Spanish dictators; Anglo vigilantes hanging two Mexicans from a tree; a young Mexican woman with rifle and ammunition belts crisscrossing her breast; César Chávez[1] and field workers marching for fair wages; Chicano railroad workers laying creosote ties; Chicanas laboring at machines in textile factories; Chicanas picketing and hoisting boycott signs.

From the time I was seven, teachers had been punishing me for not knowing my lessons by making me stick my nose in a circle chalked on the blackboard. Ashamed of not understanding and fearful of asking questions, I dropped out of school in the ninth grade. At seventeen I still didn't know how to read, but those pictures confirmed my identity. I stole the book that night, stashing it for safety under the slop sink until I got off work. Back at my boardinghouse, I showed the book to friends. All of us were amazed; this book told us we were alive. We, too, had defended ourselves with our fists against hostile Anglos, gasping for breath in fights with the policemen who outnumbered us. The book reflected back to us our struggle in a way that made us proud.

Most of my life I felt like a target in the cross hairs of a hunter's rifle. When strangers and outsiders questioned me I felt the hang-rope tighten around my neck and the trapdoor creak beneath my feet. There was nothing so humiliating as being unable to express myself, and my inarticulateness increased my sense of jeopardy, of being endangered. I felt intimidated and vulnerable, ridiculed and scorned. Behind a mask of humility, I seethed with mute rebellion.

Before I was eighteen, I was arrested on suspicion of murder after refusing to explain a deep cut on my forearm. With shocking speed I found myself handcuffed to a chain gang of inmates and bused to a holding facility to await trial. There I met men, prisoners, who read aloud to each other the works of Neruda, Paz, Sabines, Nemerov, and Hemingway.[2] Never had I felt such freedom as in that dormitory. Listening to the words of these writers, I felt that invisible threat from without lessen—my sense of teetering on a rotting plank over swamp water where famished alligators clapped their horny snouts for my blood. While I listened to the words of the poets, the alligators slumbered powerless in their lairs. Their language was the magic that could liberate me from myself, transform me into another person, transport me to other places far away.

And when they closed the books, these Chicanos, and went into their own Chicano language, they made barrio life come alive for me in the fullness of its vitality. I began to learn my own language, the bilingual words and phrases explaining to me my place in the universe. Every day I felt like the paper boy taking delivery of the latest news of the day.

Months later I was released, as I had suspected I would be. I had been guilty of nothing but shattering the windshield of my girlfriend's car in a fit of rage.

Two years passed. I was twenty now, and behind bars again. The federal marshals had failed to provide convincing evidence to extradite me to Arizona on a drug charge, but still I was being held. They had ninety days to prove I was guilty. The only evidence against me was that my girlfriend had been at the scene of the crime with my drivers license in her purse. They had to come up with something else. But there was nothing else. Eventually they negotiated a deal with the actual drug dealer, who took the stand against me. When the judge hit me with a million-dollar bail, I emptied my pockets on his booking desk: twenty-six cents.

One night in my third month in the county jail, I was mopping the floor in front of the booking desk. Some detectives had kneed an old drunk and handcuffed him to the booking bars. His shrill screams raked my nerves like a hacksaw on bone, the desperate protest of his dignity against their inhumanity. But the detectives just laughed as he tried to rise and kicked him to his knees. When they went to the bathroom to pee and the desk attendant walked to the file cabinet to pull the arrest record, I shot my arm through the bars, grabbed one of the attendant's university textbooks, and tucked it in my overalls. It was the only way I had of protesting.

It was late when I returned to my cell. Under my blanket I switched on a pen flashlight and opened the thick book at random, scanning the pages. I could hear the jailer making his rounds on the other tiers. The jangle of his keys and the sharp click of his boot heels intensified my solitude. Slowly I enunciated the words . . . p-o-n-d, ri-pple. It scared me that I had been reduced to this to find comfort. I always had thought reading a waste of time, that nothing could be gained by it. Only by action, by moving out into the world and confronting and challenging the obstacles, could one learn anything worth knowing.

Even as I tried to convince myself that I was merely curious, I became so absorbed in how the sounds created music in me and happiness, I forgot where I was. Memories began to quiver in me, glowing with a strange but familiar intimacy in which I found refuge. For a while, a deep sadness overcame me, as if I had chanced on a long-lost friend and mourned the years of separation. But soon the heartache of having missed so much of life, that had numbed me since I was a child, gave way, as if a grave illness lifted itself from me and I was cured, innocently believing in the beauty of life again. I stumblingly repeated the author's name as I fell asleep, saying it over and over in the dark: Words-worth, Words-worth.[3]

Before long my sister came to visit me, and I joked about taking her to a place called Kubla Khan and getting her a blind date with this *vato* named Coleridge[4] who lived on the seacoast and was *malías* on morphine. When I asked her to make a trip into enemy territory to buy me a grammar book, she said she couldn't. Bookstores intimidated her, because she, too, could neither read nor write.

Days later, with a stub pencil I whittled sharp with my teeth, I propped a Red Chief notebook on my knees and wrote my first words. From that moment, a hunger for poetry possessed me.

Until then, I had felt as if I had been born into a raging ocean where I swam relentlessly, flailing my arms in hope of rescue, of reaching a shoreline I never sighted. Never solid ground beneath me, never a resting place. I had lived with only the desperate hope to stay afloat; that and nothing more.

But when at last I wrote my first words on the page, I felt an island rising beneath my feet like the back of a whale. As more and more words emerged, I could finally rest: I had a place to stand for the first time in my life. The island grew, with each page, into a continent inhabited by people I knew and mapped with the life I lived.

I wrote about it all—about people I had loved or hated, about the brutalities and ecstasies of my life. And, for the first time, the child in me who had witnessed and endured unspeakable terrors cried out not just in impotent despair, but with the power of language. Suddenly, through language, through writing, my grief and my joy could be shared with anyone who would listen. And I could do this all alone; I could do it anywhere. I was no longer a captive of demons eating away at me, no longer a victim of other people's mockery and loathing, that had made me clench my fist white with rage and grit my teeth to silence. Words now pleaded back with the bleak lucidity of hurt. They were wrong, those others, and now I could say it.

Through language I was free. I could respond, escape, indulge; embrace or reject earth or the cosmos. I was launched on an endless journey without boundaries or rules, in which I could salvage the floating fragments of my past, or be born anew in the spontaneous ignition of understanding some heretofore concealed aspect of myself. Each word steamed with the hot lava juices of my primordial making, and I crawled out of stanzas dripping with birth-blood, reborn and freed from the chaos of my life. The child in the dark room of my heart, that had never been able to find or reach the light switch, flicked it on now; and I found in the room a stranger, myself, who had waited so many years to speak again. My words struck in me light-ning crackles of elation and thunderhead storms of grief.

When I had been in the county jail longer than anyone else, I was made a trustee. One morning, after a fistfight, I went to the unlocked and unoccupied office used for lawyer-client meetings, to think. The bare white room with its fluorescent tube lighting seemed to expose and illuminate my dark and worthless life. And yet, for the first time, I had something to lose—my chance to read, to write; a way to live with dignity and meaning, that had opened for me when I stole that scuffed, secondhand book about the Romantic poets. In prison, the ab-scess had been lanced.

"I will never do any work in this prison system as long as I am not allowed to get my G.E.D."[5] That's what I told the reclassification panel. The captain flicked off the tape recorder. He looked at me hard and said, "You'll never walk outta here alive. Oh, you'll work, put a copper penny on that, you'll work."

After that interview I was confined to deadlock maximum security in a subterranean dungeon, with ground-level chicken-wired windows painted gray. Twenty-three hours a day I was in that cell. I kept sane by borrowing books from the other cons on the tier. Then, just before Christmas, I received a letter from Harry, a charity house samaritan who doled out hot soup to the homeless in Phoenix. He had picked my name from a list of cons who had no one to write to them. I wrote back asking for a grammar book, and a week later received one of Mary Baker Eddy's[6] treatises on salvation and redemption, with Spanish and English on op-posing pages. Pacing my cell all day and most of each night, I grappled with grammar until I was able to write a long true-romance confession for a con to send to his pen pal. He paid me with a pack of smokes. Soon I had a thriving barter business, exchanging my poems and letters for novels, commissary pencils, and writing tablets.

One day I tore two flaps from the cardboard box that held all my belongings and punc-tured holes along the edge of each flap and along the border of a ream of state-issue paper. After I had aligned them to form a spine, I threaded the holes with a shoestring, and sketched on the cover a hummingbird fluttering above a rose. This was my first journal.

Whole afternoons I wrote, unconscious of passing time or whether it was day or night. Sunbursts exploded from the lead tip of my pencil, words that grafted me into awareness of who I was; peeled back to a burning core of bleak terror, an embryo floating in the image of water, I cracked out of the shell wide-eyed and insane. Trees grew out of the palms of my hands, the threatening otherness of life dissolved, and I became one with the air and sky, the dirt and the iron and concrete. There was no longer any distinction between the other and I.

Language made bridges of fire between me and everything I saw. I entered into the blade of grass, the basketball, the con's eye, and child's soul.

At night I flew. I conversed with floating heads in my cell, and visited strange houses where lonely women brewed tea and rocked in wicker rocking chairs listening to sad Joni Mitchell songs.

Before long I was frayed like a rope carrying too much weight, that suddenly snaps. I quit talking. Bars, walls, steel bunk, and floor bristled with millions of poem-making sparks. My face was no longer familiar to me. The only reality was the swirling cornucopia of images in my mind, the voices in the air. Mid-air a cactus blossom would appear, a snake-flame in blinding dance around it, stunning me like a guard's fist striking my neck from behind.

The prison administrators tried several tactics to get me to work. For six months, after the next monthly prison board review, they sent cons to my cell to hassle me. When the guard would open my cell door to let one of them in, I'd leap out and fight him—and get sent to thirty-day isolation. I did a lot of isolation time. But I honed my image-making talents in that sensory-deprived solitude. Finally they moved me to death row, and after that to "nut-run," the tier that housed the mentally disturbed.

As the months passed, I became more and more sluggish. My eyelids were heavy, I could no longer write or read. I slept all the time.

One day a guard took me out to the exercise field. For the first time in years I felt grass and earth under my feet. It was spring. The sun warmed my face as I sat on the bleachers watching the cons box and run, hit the handball, lift weights. Some of them stopped to ask how I was, but I found it impossible to utter a syllable. My tongue would not move, saliva drooled from the corners of my mouth. I had been so heavily medicated I could not summon the slightest gesture. Yet inside me a small voice cried out, I am fine! I am hurt now but I will come back! I am fine!

Back in my cell, for weeks I refused to eat. Styrofoam cups of urine and hot water were hurled at me. Other things happened. There were beatings, shock therapy, intimidation.

Later, I regained some clarity of mind. But there was a place in my heart where I had died. My life had compressed itself into an unbearable dread of being. The strain had been too much. I had stepped over that line where a human being has lost more than he can bear, where the pain is too intense, and he knows he is changed forever. I was now capable of killing, coldly and without feeling. I was empty, as I have never, before or since, known emptiness. I had no connection to this life.

But then, the encroaching darkness that began to envelop me forced me to re-form and give birth to myself again in the chaos. I withdrew even deeper into the world of language, cleaving the diamonds of verbs and nouns, plunging into the brilliant light of poetry's regenerative mystery. Words gave off rings of white energy, radar signals from powers beyond me that infused me with truth. I believed what I wrote, because I wrote what was true. My words did not come from books or textual formulas, but from a deep faith in the voice of my heart.

I had been steeped in self-loathing and rejected by everyone and everything—society, family, cons, God, and demons. But now I had become as the burning ember floating in darkness that descends on a dry leaf and sets flame to forests. The word was the ember and the forest was my life.

I was born a poet one noon, gazing at weeds and creosoted grass at the base of a telephone pole outside my grilled cell window. The words I wrote then sailed me out of myself, and I was transported and metamorphosed into the images they made. From the dirty brown blades of grass came bolts of electrical light that jolted loose my old self; through the top of my head that self was released and reshaped in the clump of scrawny grass. Through language I became the grass, speaking its language and feeling its green feelings and black root sensations. Earth was my mother and I bathed in sunshine. Minuscule speckles of sunlight passed through my green skin and metabolized in my blood.

Writing bridged my divided life of prisoner and free man. I wrote of the emotional butchery of prisons, and of my acute gratitude for poetry. Where my blind doubt and spontaneous trust in life met, I discovered empathy and compassion. The power to express myself was a welcome storm rasping at tendril roots, flooding my soul's cracked dirt. Writing was water that cleansed the wound and fed the parched root of my heart.

I wrote to sublimate my rage, from a place where all hope is gone, from a madness of having been damaged too much, from a silence of killing rage. I wrote to avenge the betrayals of a lifetime, to purge the bitterness of injustice. I wrote with a deep groan of doom in my blood, bewildered and dumbstruck; from an indestructible love of life, to affirm breath and laughter and the abiding innocence of things. I wrote the way I wept, and danced, and made love.

FOOTNOTES

1. **Padre Hidalgo:** Father Miguel Hidalgo y Costilla (1753–1811) began the Mexican independence movement when he led an 1810 revolt against Spanish forces in Mexico; **César Chávez** (1927–1993): Founder of the United Farm Workers of America, a labor union representing the interests of the largely Hispanic population of migrant workers.—ED.

2. Pablo **Neruda** (1904–1973): Chilean poet; Octavio **Paz** (b. 1914): Mexican poet and Nobel laureate; Jaime **Sabines** (b. 1926): Contemporary Mexican poet; Howard **Nemerov** (1920–1991): Pulitzer Prize winner and poet laureate of the United States; Ernest **Hemingway** (1899–1961): American novelist.—ED.

3. William **Wordsworth** (1770–1850): English Romantic poet.—ED.

4. Samuel Taylor **Coleridge** (1772–1834): Author of the poem "Kubla Khan," said to have been inspired by an opium dream.—ED.

5. **G.E.D.:** General Equivalency Diploma, a high-school equivalency certificate.—ED.

6. **Mary Baker Eddy** (1821–1910): Founder of the Church of Christ, Scientist.—ED.

Thinking About the Text _____

1. How does Baca come to gain a sense of identity and freedom during his prison sentence? What strategies does he use to explain his ideas?

2. What function does reading and writing serve for Baca? How does Baca's experience of reading and writing affect his narrative style (language, rhetorical appeals, tone, etc.)?

3. What is Baca's first step toward gaining a true sense of identity? How can you relate Baca's experiences to your own experiences?

How to Tame a Wild Tongue

GLORIA ANZALDÚA

Gloria Anzaldúa was born in 1942 on the Mexican border in Jesus Maria Valley, Texas. Anzaldúa self-identifies as Chicana, lesbian, and feminist. She co-edited the ground-breaking *This Bridge Called My Back* (1981), and is the author of several bilingual children's books as well as many essays. The following essay is excerpted from Anzaldúa's 1987 *Borderlands/La Frontera: The New Mestiza*, which is considered one of the most influential theoretical interpretations of the experience of being a "border woman." In this essay, Anzaldúa explores the role of language in the construction of identity, specifically her own. Through her analysis of her own experiences, Anzaldúa suggests that while language can be alienating (as in the case of the imposition of Anglo culture on Chicano/as), it can also be liberating.

"We're going to have to control your tongue," the dentist says, pulling out all the metal from my mouth. Silver bits plop and tinkle into the basin. My mouth is a motherlode.

The dentist is cleaning out my roots. I get a whiff of the stench when I gasp. "I can't cap that tooth yet, you're still draining," he says.

"We're going to have to do something about your tongue," I hear the anger rising in his voice. My tongue keeps pushing out the wads of cotton, pushing back the drills, the long thin needles. "I've never seen anything as strong or as stubborn," he says. And I think, how do you tame a wild tongue, train it to be quiet, how do you bridle and saddle it? How do you make it lie down?

*Who is to say that robbing a people of its language
is less violent than war?*

—*Ray Gwyn Smith*[1]

I remember being caught speaking Spanish at recess—that was good for three licks on the knuckles with a sharp ruler. I remember being sent to the corner of the classroom for "talking back" to the Anglo teacher when all I was trying to do was tell her how to pronounce my name. "If you want to be American, speak 'American.' If you don't like it, go back to Mexico where you belong."

"I want you to speak English. *Pa' hallar buen trabajo tienes que saber hablar el inglés bien. Qué vale toda tu educación si todavía hablas inglés con un* 'accent,'" my mother would say, mortified that I spoke English like a Mexican. At Pan American University, I and all Chicano students were required to take two speech classes. Their purpose: to get rid of our accents.

Attacks on one's form of expression with the intent to censor are a violation of the First Amendment. *El Anglo con cara de inocente nos arrancó la lengua.* Wild tongues can't be tamed, they can only be cut out.

Overcoming the Tradition of Silence

Ahogadas, escupimos el oscuro.
Peleando con nuestra propia sombra
el silencio nos sepulta.

En boca cerrada no entran moscas. "Flies don't enter a closed mouth" is a saying I kept hearing when I was a child. *Ser habladora* was to be a gossip and a liar, to talk too much. *Muchachitas bien criadas*, well-bred girls don't answer back. *Es una falta de respeto* to talk back to one's mother or father. I remember one of the sins I'd recite to the priest in the confession box the few times I went to confession: talking back to my mother, *hablar pa' 'tras, repelar. Hociona, repelona, chismosa*, having a big mouth, questioning, carrying tales are all signs of being *mal criada*. In my culture they are all words that are derogatory if applied to women—I've never heard them applied to men.

The first time I heard two women, a Puerto Rican and a Cuban, say the word "*nosotras*," I was shocked. I had not known the word existed. Chicanas use *nosotros* whether we're male or female. We are robbed of our female being by the masculine plural. Language is a male discourse.

And our tongues have become
dry   the wilderness has
dried out our tongues   and
we have forgotten speech.

—Irena Klepfisz[2]

Even our own people, other Spanish speakers *nos quieren poner candados en la boca.* They would hold us back with their bag of *reglas de academia.*

Oyé como ladra: el lenguaje de la frontera

Quien tiene boca se equivoca.

—Mexican saying

"*Pocho*, cultural traitor, you're speaking the oppressor's language by speaking English, you're ruining the Spanish language," I have been accused by various Latinos and Latinas. Chicano Spanish is considered by the purist and by most Latinos deficient, a mutilation of Spanish.

But Chicano Spanish is a border tongue which developed naturally. Change, *evolución, enriquecimiento de palabras nuevas por invención o adopción* have created variants of Chicano Spanish, *un nuevo lenguaje. Un lenguaje que corresponde a un modo de vivir.* Chicano Spanish is not incorrect, it is a living language.

For a people who are neither Spanish nor live in a country in which Spanish is the first language; for a people who live in a country in which English is the reigning tongue but who are not Anglo; for a people who cannot entirely identify with either standard (formal, Castilian) Spanish nor standard English, what recourse is left to them but to create their own language? A language which they can connect their identity to, one capable of communicating the realities and values true to themselves—a language with terms that are neither *español ni inglés*, but both. We speak a patois, a forked tongue, a variation of two languages.

Chicano Spanish sprang out of the Chicanos' need to identify ourselves as a distinct people. We needed a language with which we could communicate with ourselves, a secret language. For some of us, language is a homeland closer than the Southwest—for many Chicanos today live in the Midwest and East. And because we are a complex, heterogeneous people, we speak many languages. Some of the languages we speak are

1. Standard English

2. Working class and slang English

3. Standard Spanish

4. Standard Mexican Spanish

5. North Mexican Spanish dialect

6. Chicano Spanish (Texas, New Mexico, Arizona, and California have regional variations)

7. Tex-Mex

8. *Pachuco* (called *caló*)

My "home" tongues are the languages I speak with my sister and brothers, with my friends. They are the last five listed, with 6 and 7 being closest to my heart. From school, the media, and job situations, I've picked up standard and working class English. From Mamagrande Locha and from reading Spanish and Mexican literature, I've picked up Standard Spanish and Standard Mexican Spanish. From *los recién llegados*, Mexican immigrants, and *braceros*, I learned the North Mexican dialect. With Mexicans I'll try to speak either Standard Mexican Spanish or the North Mexican dialect. From my parents and Chicanos living in the Valley, I picked up Chicano Texas Spanish, and I speak it with my mom, younger brother (who married a Mexican and who rarely mixes Spanish with English), aunts, and older relatives.

With Chicanas from *Nuevo Mexico* or *Arizona* I will speak Chicano Spanish a little, but often they don't understand what I'm saying. With most California Chicanas I speak entirely in English (unless I forget). When I first moved to San Francisco, I'd rattle off something in Spanish, unintentionally embarrassing them. Often it is only with another Chicana *tejano* that I can talk freely.

Words distorted by English are known as anglicisms or *pochismos*. The *pocho* is an anglicized Mexican or American of Mexican origin who speaks Spanish with an accent characteristic of North Americans and who distorts and reconstructs the language according to the influence of English.[3] Tex-Mex, or Spanglish, comes most naturally to me. I may switch back and forth from English to Spanish in the same sentence or in the same word. With my sister and my brother Nune and with Chicano *tejano* contemporaries I speak in Tex-Mex.

From kids and people my own age I picked up *Pachuco*. *Pachuco* (the language of the zoot suiters) is a language of rebellion, both against Standard Spanish and Standard English. It is a secret language. Adults of the culture and outsiders cannot understand it. It is made up of slang words from both English and Spanish. *Ruca* means girl or woman, *vato* means guy or dude, *chale* means no, *simón* means yes, *churro is* sure, talk is *periquiar*, *pigionear* means petting, *que gacho* means how nerdy, *ponte águila* means watch out, death is called *la pelona*. Through lack of practice and not having others who can speak it, I've lost most of the *Pachuco* tongue.

Chicano Spanish

Chicanos, after 250 years of Spanish/Anglo colonization, have developed significant differences in the Spanish we speak. We collapse two adjacent vowels into a single syllable and sometimes shift the stress in certain words such as *maíz/maiz, cohete/cuete*. We leave out certain consonants when they appear between vowels: *lado/lao, mojada/mojao*. Chicanos from South Texas pronounce *f* as *j* as in *jue* (*fue*). Chicanos use "archaisms," words that are no longer in the Spanish language, words that have been evolved out. We say *semos, truje, haiga, ansina,* and *naiden*. We retain the "archaic" *j*, as in *jalar*, that derives from an earlier *h* (the French *halar* or the Germanic *halon* which was lost to standard Spanish in the sixteenth century), but which is still found in several regional dialects such as the one spoken in South Texas. (Due to geography, Chicanos from the Valley of South Texas were cut off linguistically from other speakers. We tend to use words that the Spaniards brought over from Medieval Spain. The majority of the Spanish colonizers in Mexico and the Southwest came from Extremadura—Hernán Cortés was one of them—and Andalucía. Andalucians pronounce *ll* like a *y*, and their *d*'s tend to be absorbed by adjacent vowels: *tirado* becomes *tirao*. They brought *el lenguaje popular, dialectos y regionalismos*.)[4]

Chicanos and other Spanish speakers also shift *ll* to *y* and *z* to *s*.[5] We leave out initial syllables, saying *tar* for *estar*, *toy* for *estoy*, *hora* for *ahora* (*cubanos* and *puertorriqueños* also leave out initial letters of some words). We also leave out the final syllable such as *pa* for *para*. The intervocalic *y*, the *ll* as in *tortilla, ella, botella*, gets replaced by *tortia* or *tortiya, ea, botea*. We add an additional syllable at the beginning of certain words: *atocar* for *tocar*, *agastar* for *gastar*. Sometimes we'll say *lavaste las vacijas*, other times *lavates* (substituting the *ates* verb endings for the *aste*).

We used anglicisms, words borrowed from English: *bola* from ball, *carpeta* from carpet, *máchina de lavar* (instead of *lavadora*) from washing machine. Tex-Mex argot, created by adding a Spanish sound at the beginning or end of an English word such as *cookiar* for cook, *watchar* for watch, *parkiar* for park, and *rapiar* for rape, is the result of the pressures on Spanish speakers to adapt to English.

We don't use the word *vosotros/as* or its accompanying verb form. We don't say *claro* (to mean yes), *imagínate*, or *me emociona*, unless we picked up Spanish from Latinas, out of a book, or in a classroom. Other Spanish-speaking groups are going through the same, or similar, development in their Spanish.

Linguistic Terrorism

Deslenguadas. Somos los del español deficiente. *We are your linguistic nightmare, your linguistic aberration, your linguistic* mestisaje, *the subject of your* burla. *Because we speak with tongues of fire we are culturally crucified. Racially, culturally, and linguistically* somos huérfanos—*we speak an orphan tongue.*

Chicanas who grew up speaking Chicano Spanish have internalized the belief that we speak poor Spanish. It is illegitimate, a bastard language. And because we internalize how our language has been used against us by the dominant culture, we use our language differences against each other.

Chicana feminists often skirt around each other with suspicion and hesitation. For the longest time I couldn't figure it out. Then it dawned on me. To be close to another Chicana is like looking into the mirror. We are afraid of what we'll see there. *Pena.* Shame. Low estimation of self. In childhood we are told that our language is wrong. Repeated attacks on our native tongue diminish our sense of self. The attacks continue throughout our lives.

Chicanas feel uncomfortable talking in Spanish to Latinas, afraid of their censure. Their language was not outlawed in their countries. They had a whole lifetime of being immersed in their native tongue; generations, centuries in which Spanish was a first language, taught in school, heard on radio and TV, and read in the newspaper.

If a person, Chicana or Latina, has a low estimation of my native tongue, she also has a low estimation of me. Often with *mexicanas y latinas* we'll speak English as a neutral language. Even among Chicanas we tend to speak English at parties or conferences. Yet, at the same time, we're afraid the other will think we're *agringadas* because we don't speak Chicano Spanish. We oppress each other trying to out-Chicano each other, vying to be the "real" Chicanas, to speak like Chicanos. There is no one Chicano language just as there is no one Chicano experience. A monolingual Chicana whose first language is English or Spanish is just as much a Chicana as one who speaks several variants of Spanish. A Chicana from Michigan or Chicago or Detroit is just as much a Chicana as one from the Southwest. Chicano Spanish is as diverse linguistically as it is regionally.

By the end of this century, Spanish speakers will comprise the biggest minority group in the United States, a country where students in high schools and colleges are encouraged to take French classes because French is considered more "cultured." But for a language to remain alive it must be used.[6] By the end of this century English, and not Spanish, will be the mother tongue of most Chicanos and Latinos.

So, if you want to really hurt me, talk badly about my language. Ethnic identity is twin skin to linguistic identity—I am my language. Until I can take pride in my language, I cannot take pride in myself. Until I can accept as legitimate Chicano Texas Spanish, Tex-Mex, and all the other languages I speak, I cannot accept the legitimacy of myself. Until I am free to write bilingually and to switch codes without having always to translate, while I still have to speak English or Spanish when I would rather speak Spanglish, and as long as I have to accommodate the English speakers rather than having them accommodate me, my tongue will be illegitimate.

I will no longer be made to feel ashamed of existing. I will have my voice: Indian, Spanish, white. I will have my serpent's tongue—my woman's voice, my sexual voice, my poet's voice. I will overcome the tradition of silence.

My fingers
move sly against your palm
Like women everywhere, we speak in code. . . .

—*Melanie Kaye/Kantrowitz*[7]

"Vistas," corridos, y comida: My Native Tongue

In the 1960s, I read my first Chicano novel. It was *City of Night* by John Rechy, a gay Texan, son of a Scottish father and a Mexican mother. For days I walked around in stunned amazement that a Chicano could write and could get published. When I read *I Am Joaquín*[8] I was surprised to see a bilingual book by a Chicano in print. When I saw poetry written in Tex-Mex for the first time, a feeling of pure joy flashed through me. I felt like we really existed as a people. In 1971, when I started teaching High School English to Chicano students, I tried to supplement the required texts with works by Chicanos, only to be reprimanded and forbidden to do so by the principal. He claimed that I was supposed to teach "American" and English literature. At the risk of being fired, I swore my students to secrecy and slipped in Chicano short stories, poems, a play. In graduate school, while working toward a Ph.D., I had to "argue" with one adviser after the other, semester after semester, before I was allowed to make Chicano literature an area of focus.

Even before I read books by Chicanos or Mexicans, it was the Mexican movies I saw at the drive-in—the Thursday night special of $1.00 a carload—that gave me a sense of belonging. "*Vámonos a las vistas*," my mother would call out and we'd all—grandmother, brothers, sister, and cousins—squeeze into the car. We'd wolf down cheese and bologna white bread sandwiches while watching Pedro Infante in melodramatic tearjerkers like *Nosotros los pobres*, the first "real" Mexican movie (that was not an imitation of European movies). I remember seeing *Cuando los hijos se van* and surmising that all Mexican movies played up the love a mother has for her children and what ungrateful sons and daughters suffer when they are not devoted to their mothers. I remember the singing-type "westerns" of Jorge Negrete and Miquel Aceves Mejía. When watching Mexican movies, I felt a sense of homecoming as well as alienation. People who were to amount to something didn't go to Mexican movies, or *bailes*, or tune their radios to *bolero, rancherita*, and *corrido* music.

The whole time I was growing up, there was *norteño* music sometimes called North Mexican border music, or Tex-Mex music, or Chicano music, or *cantina* (bar) music. I grew up listening to *conjuntos*, three- or four-piece bands made up of folk musicians playing guitar, *bajo sexto*, drums, and button accordion, which Chicanos had borrowed from the German immigrants who had come to Central Texas and Mexico to farm and build breweries. In the Rio Grande Valley, Steve Jordan and Little Joe Hernández were popular, and Flaco Jiménez was the accordion king. The rhythms of Tex-Mex music are those of the polka, also adapted from the Germans, who in turn had borrowed the polka from the Czechs and Bohemians.

I remember the hot, sultry evenings when *corridos*—songs of love and death on the Texas-Mexican borderlands—reverberated out of cheap amplifiers from the local *cantinas* and wafted in through my bedroom window.

Corridos first became widely used along the South Texas/Mexican border during the early conflict between Chicanos and Anglos. The *corridos* are usually about Mexican heroes who do valiant deeds against the Anglo oppressors. Pancho Villa's song, *"La cucaracha,"* is the most famous one. *Corridos* of John F. Kennedy and his death are still very popular in the Valley. Older Chicanos remember Lydia Mendoza, one of the great border *corrido* singers who was called *la Gloria de Tejas*. Her *"El tango negro,"* sung during the Great Depression, made her a singer of the people. The ever-present *corridos* narrated one hundred years of border history, bringing news of events as well as entertaining. These folk musicians and folk songs are our chief cultural mythmakers, and they made our hard lives seem bearable.

I grew up feeling ambivalent about our music. Country-western and rock-and-roll had more status. In the fifties and sixties, for the slightly educated and *agringado* Chicanos, there existed a sense of shame at being caught listening to our music. Yet I couldn't stop my feet from thumping to the music, could not stop humming the words, nor hide from myself the exhilaration I felt when I heard it.

There are more subtle ways that we internalize identification, especially in the forms of images and emotions. For me food and certain smells are tied to my identity, to my homeland. Woodsmoke curling up to an immense blue sky; woodsmoke perfuming my grandmother's clothes, her skin. The stench of cow manure and the yellow patches on the ground; the crack of a .22 rifle and the reek of cordite. Homemade white cheese sizzling in a pan, melting inside a folded *tortilla*. My sister Hilda's hot, spicy *menudo*, *chile colorado* making it deep red, pieces of *panza* and hominy floating on top. My brother Carito barbequing *fajitas* in the backyard. Even now and 3,000 miles away, I can see my mother spicing the ground beef, pork, and venison with *chile*. My mouth salivates at the thought of the hot steaming *tamales* I would be eating if I were home.

Si le preguntas a mi mamá, "¿Qué eres?"

*Identity is the essential core of who
we are as individuals, the conscious
experience of the self inside.*

—*Gershen Kaufman*[9]

Nosotros los Chicanos straddle the borderlands. On one side of us, we are constantly exposed to the Spanish of the Mexicans, on the other side we hear the Anglos' incessant clamoring so that we forget our language. Among ourselves we don't say *nosotros los americanos, o nosotros los españoles, o nosotros los hispanos.* We say *nosotros los mexicanos* (by *mexicanos* we do not mean citizens of Mexico; we do not mean a national identity, but a racial one). We distinguish between *mexicanos del otro lado* and *mexicanos de este lado.* Deep in our hearts we believe that being Mexican has nothing to do with which country one lives in. Being Mexican is a state of soul—not one of mind, not one of citizenship. Neither eagle nor serpent, but both. And like the ocean, neither animal respects borders.

Dime con quien andas y te diré quien eres.
(*Tell me who your friends are and I'll tell you who you are.*)

—*Mexican saying*

Si le preguntas a mi mamá, "¿Qué eres?" te dirá, "Soy mexicana." My brothers and sister say the same. I sometimes will answer "*soy mexicana*" and at others will say "*soy Chicana*" o "*soy tejana.*" But I identified as "*Raza*" before I ever identified as "*mexicana*" or "Chicana."

As a culture, we call ourselves Spanish when referring to ourselves as a linguistic group and when copping out. It is then that we forget our predominant Indian genes. We are 70–80 percent Indian.[10] We call ourselves Hispanic[11] or Spanish-American or Latin American or Latin when linking ourselves to other Spanish-speaking peoples of the Western hemisphere and when copping out. We call ourselves Mexican-American[12] to signify we are neither Mexican nor American, but more the noun "American" than the adjective "Mexican" (and when copping out).

Chicanos and other people of color suffer economically for not acculturating. This voluntary (yet forced) alienation makes for psychological conflict, a kind of dual identity—we don't identify with the Anglo-American cultural values and we don't totally identify with the Mexican cultural values. We are a synergy of two cultures with various degrees of Mexicanness or Angloness. I have so internalized the borderland conflict that sometimes I feel like one cancels out the other and we are zero, nothing, no one. *A veces no soy nada ni nadie. Pero hasta cuando no lo soy, lo soy.*

When not copping out, when we know we are more than nothing, we call ourselves Mexican, referring to race and ancestry; *mestizo* when affirming both our Indian and Spanish (but we hardly ever own our Black) ancestry; Chicano when referring to a politically aware people born and/or raised in the United States; *Raza* when referring to Chicanos; *tejanos* when we are Chicanos from Texas.

Chicanos did not know we were a people until 1965 when Cesar Chavez and the farmworkers united and *I Am Joaquín* was published and *la Raza Unida* party was formed in Texas. With that recognition, we became a distinct people. Something momentous happened to the Chicano soul—we became aware of our reality and acquired a name and a language (Chicano Spanish) that reflected that reality. Now that we had a name, some of the fragmented pieces began to fall together—who we were, what we were, how we had evolved. We began to get glimpses of what we might eventually become.

Yet the struggle of identities continues, the struggle of borders is our reality still. One day the inner struggle will cease and a true integration take place. In the meantime, *tenémos que hacer la lucha. ¿Quién está protegiendo los ranchos de mi gente? ¿Quién está tratando de cerrar la fisura entre la india y el blanco en nuestra sangre? El Chicano, si, el Chicano que anda como un ladrón en su propia casa.*

Los Chicanos, how patient we seem, how very patient. There is the quiet of the Indian about us.[13] We know how to survive. When other races have given up their tongue we've kept ours. We know what it is to live under the hammer blow of the dominant *norteamericano* culture. But more than we count the blows, we count the days the weeks the years the centuries the aeons until the white laws and commerce and customs will rot in the deserts they've created, lie bleached. *Humildes* yet proud, *quietos* yet wild, *nosotros los mexicanos-Chicanos* will walk by the crumbling ashes as we go about our business. Stubborn, persevering, impenetrable as stone, yet possessing a malleability that renders us unbreakable, we, the *mestizas* and *mestizos,* will remain.

FOOTNOTES

1. Ray Gwyn Smith, *Moorland Is Cold Country*, unpublished book.

2. Irena Klepfisz, "*Di rayze aheym/*The Journey Home," in *The Tribe of Dina: A Jewish Women's Anthology,* Melanie Kaye/Kantrowitz and Irena Klepfisz, eds. (Montpelier, VT: Sinister Wisdom Books, 1986), 49.

3. R. C. Ortega, *Dialectología Del Barrio*, trans. Hortencia S. Alwan (Los Angeles, CA: R. C. Ortega Publisher & Bookseller, 1977), 132.

4. Eduardo Hernandéz-Chávez, Andrew D. Cohen, and Anthony F. Beltramo, *El Lenguaje de los Chicanos: Regional and Social Characteristics of Language Used by Mexican Americans* (Arlington, VA: Center for Applied Linguistics, 1975), 39.

5. Hernandéz-Chávez, xvii.

6. Irena Klepfisz, "Secular Jewish Identity: Yidishkayt in America," in *The Tribe of Dina*, Kaye/Kantrowitz and Klepfisz, eds., 43.

7. Melanie Kaye/Kantrowitz, "Sign," in *We Speak in Code: Poems and Other Writings* (Pittsburgh, PA: Motheroot Publications, Inc., 1980), 85.

8. Rodolfo Gonzales, *I Am Joaquín/Yo Soy Joaquín* (New York, NY: Bantam Books, 1972). It was first published in 1967.

9. Gershen Kaufman, *Shame: The Power of Caring* (Cambridge, MA: Schenkman Books, Inc., 1980), 68.

10. John R. Chávez, *The Lost Land: The Chicano Images of the Southwest* (Albuquerque, NM: University of New Mexico Press, 1984), 88–90.

11. "Hispanic" is derived from *Hispanis* (*España*, a name given to the Iberian Peninsula in ancient times when it was a part of the Roman Empire) and is a term designated by the U.S. government to make it easier to handle us on paper.

12. The treaty of Guadalupe Hidalgo created the Mexican-American in 1848.

13. Anglos, in order to alleviate their guilt for dispossessing the Chicano, stressed the Spanish part of us and perpetrated the myth of the Spanish Southwest. We have accepted the fiction that we are Hispanic, that is Spanish, in order to accommodate ourselves to the dominant culture and its abhorrence of Indians. Chávez, 88–91.

Thinking About the Text _____

1. Why does Anzaldúa weave Spanish and English together throughout her essay? Do you believe it is her intention to exclude or include a specific audience?

2. How does Anzaldúa suggest language shapes identity? Can we assume an identity about Anzaldúa based on this suggestion?

3. How does Anzaldúa's essay parallel Rich's "Split at the Root"? Do both authors come to the same conclusion about identity?

Language Use in Family and in Society

LEE THOMAS AND LINH CAO

Lee Thomas is a teacher of linguistics at the University of Nevada, Reno. Linh Cao teaches English at Sparks High School, Sparks, Nevada. In "Language Use in Family and in Society," the authors point out that even families can be separated by language use and by changes in cultural perspectives. The article originally appeared in *English Journal*, an educational journal.

Our parents have sacrificed their lives and have paid their dues in "tears and sweat," as our grandmother used to say, in order to push us over the fence so we could attain education and success in the United States. Now that our parents have successfully pushed us over the fence, we find ourselves struggling to get back for fear of losing what we once had. This, however, is not an easy feat because language and culture so separate us, placing us each in our own worlds, both of which are filled with loneliness, loss, and great emotional and psychological pain.

Linh Cao

Looking at Linh's statement, we can see the important issues it raises. In this article, we discuss alternatives to the traditional research paper, suggesting that students can do meaningful language research within family and society. Although the work we describe here was done at the college level, it has obvious implications for secondary teaching.

Linh's family is of Vietnamese and Chinese descent. Members representing three generations of the family immigrated in 1979 to Reno, Nevada, from Vietnam as a result of the political and economic instability following the Vietnam War. The grandparents speak Hainanese (a Chinese dialect) and Vietnamese. The father of the family speaks Hainanese, Mandarin, Vietnamese, and a little English, Vietnamese being his most often used language. Linh's mother speaks Vietnamese and Hainanese and very limited English. The five children represent a wide age range, and their language experiences have differed significantly. The oldest, Linh, now 27, a high school English teacher and a graduate student in the MA Teaching English as a Second Language program at the University of Nevada, Reno, is both a participant and researcher in this study.

Linh was born in Vietnam, and her first language was Hainanese, which she speaks very little now. When she started in school, she learned Mandarin, which she also remembers little of anymore. After the Communist takeover in Vietnam in 1975, the Vietnamese government wanted to get rid of all Chinese influence and demanded that all the Chinese schools in Vietnam teach Vietnamese, at which point she learned to read and write that language. She was eight years old when the family moved to the United States. Today, she is most comfortable with English, yet she still speaks, reads, and writes Vietnamese, although her Vietnamese vocabulary does not extend too far into educational, social, or psychological domains.

Quyen,[1] now 26; Tung, 21; and Kim, 22, were also born in Vietnam. Like Linh, Quyen attended Vietnamese school and can still speak Vietnamese fairly well, and she has since improved her Mandarin and Hainanese. She accomplished this primarily through contact with schoolmates from Taiwan, Hong Kong, and Singapore. Yet she, too, is most comfortable with English. Tung and Kim were about two and three years old when they came to the US and are now exclusively comfortable in English, their Vietnamese vocabulary extending only into familial settings like food and cleanliness. Their Hainanese consists of few phrases—offering food to their grandparents or wishing them a happy new year. Communication among the siblings began to shift to English not long after they started school in the US.

Quyen and Linh communicate with Mom in Vietnamese quite comfortably, although sometimes they get stuck when they don't know or have forgotten a particular word or expression, which she provides for them when she understands what they're trying to say. With Tung and Kim, however, Mom's communication is extremely limited, their conversation being restricted primarily to "yes/no" dialogue. Quyen and Linh often end up translating. With Dad, Linh communicates in Vietnamese and intermittent English words or phrases. Quyen communicates with Dad more in English than Vietnamese, and Tung and Kim communicate with him exclusively in English.

Quoc, the youngest sibling, now 11, was born in the US. Dad decided that the family needed to speak Mandarin with Quoc in an attempt to go back to their Chinese roots. Mom and the rest of the family learned how to say Mandarin phrases such as, Have you eaten your food? Have you cleaned up after yourself? Are you sleepy? Don't make messes in the house. Don't run in the house. But their Mandarin pretty much stops there. The grandparents have had similar things to say to Quoc in Hainanese, but not much else. Starting at about two years of age, Quoc spoke Hainanese with his grandparents, Mandarin with his parents, and English with his older siblings. Since he started school, he has been speaking to his siblings primarily in English, and he has little to say to his grandparents anymore. His language with Mom and

Dad is Mandarin and English filled with much code-mixing and switching; that is, when speaking Mandarin he will use English terms and at times switch into English for extended pieces of discourse. Mom does the same due to her lack of proficiency in English and Mandarin.

Family Discourse Strategies

Given the above explanation of familial language proficiency, we might wonder how communication proceeds. The following three pieces of discourse represent some important recurring dynamics of interaction in the family. The transcription notations follow:

V	Vietnamese[2]
H	Hainanese
M	Mandarin
E	English
//	Linh's romanized phonetic transcription of Hainanese
[ ]	Linh's romanized phonetic transcription of Mandarin
( )	translations into English
Note	narration of physical movement, description, and interpretation of background information and cultural comment

Notice that first the interlocutor is noted, followed by the language(s) used. For example, Dad-E indicates that Dad is speaking, and the primary language used is English. Dad-E, V would indicate a shift from English to Vietnamese in that conversational turn.

SELECTION #1

This interlude between Mom and Tung occurs solely in Vietnamese.

Mom-V: Nề Tùng, mi thích ăn bánh canh nề, ăn đi.
(Here Tung, you like to eat this noodle dish, here, have some.)

Tung-V: Được rồi, má múc nhiều quá.
(Okay, Mom, you're giving me too much.)

Mom-V: Ăn đi chớ, mi ăn ít quá.
(Go ahead and eat, you eat too little.)

Note: Tung takes the bowl of noodles back to his desk where he eats over some papers that are spread out. He sighs and appears to be exasperated.

Mom-V:	Làm bài chi đó? Làm khó quá hả? (What homework are you doing? It's too hard, huh?)
Tung-V:	Biên cái "essay", không biết răng nói cho má nghe. (I have to write an essay. I don't know how to explain it to you.)
Mom-V:	ời . . . (Hmm . . .)

Note: Mom is silent, stands around for a bit, then leaves Tung to go back to the kitchen. In her role as mother, Mom is handicapped here with Tung. She can talk to him about food, but ultimately, food is just food. It cannot serve as the medium to reach into Tung's world of school, his worries about essay writing, how he feels about his essay topic . . . or his teacher, his friends, his delights. Yet, Mom stands, waiting for words that will not come.

In his book *Hunger of Memory*, Richard Rodriguez characterized his communication with his mother: "[She] grew restless, seemed troubled and anxious at the scarcity of words exchanged in the house. She smiled at small talk. She pried at the edges of my sentences to get me to say something more" (24). In the above discourse one sees this scenario clearly. What are Tung's options following his mother's last turn at talk? He has stated that he cannot explain his assignment to his mother. Why? First they do not share the vocabulary in Vietnamese to enter into "essay talk," that is, the elaboration of the goals or process of essay writing. Second, Tung's mother has little life experience around essay writing due to her limited education. So the conversation ends abruptly as both share only their sense of frustration.

This selection also depicts what conversation analysts call "routinized interactive exchanges." In this family, language interactions are limited to several domains, food being an important one. This converges with a cultural value attributed to food and mothers feeding children as a way of demonstrating love and care. The routine that this family has developed is for the parental figure to offer food, at times too much or an item not desired, and the child to react in a declining manner. Then a judgment is made: "Go ahead and eat. You eat too little." A routine such as this allows for talk to occur, yet it often leads to frustration, which is more clearly represented in selection #2. While this type of talk fills space, it does not allow for substantive conversation about topics important to parenting or to being a child filled with questions.

SELECTION *#2*

This interaction centers around Quoc, who has just come home from elementary school as he walks into the family room and kitchen where Grandma and Grandpa are sitting. Mom comes into the kitchen to prepare a sandwich for Quoc, while Grandma and Grandpa start asking him questions. Notice how four languages are used—Hainanese, Mandarin,

Vietnamese, and English. The grandparents introduce the topic of food in Hainanese. Quoc attempts to maintain the discourse in Hainanese, but he is constrained by his limited proficiency; he repeats the same response three times before switching in frustration to English. Mom enters, code-mixing Mandarin, Vietnamese, and English with Quoc, allowing him to contribute meaningfully in the context as she appears to comfort him.

Grandma-H: /non jia ho gai bia bo?/
(Do you want to eat this cookie?)

Quoc-H: /no bo jia/
(I don't want to eat it.)

Grandpa-H: /jia ho gai di/
(Eat this then.)

Note: Grandpa points to some Chinese pastries, gestures for Quoc to come over, and pushes the pastries toward Quoc.)

Quoc-H: /non bo jia/
(I don't want to eat it.)

Grandpa-H: /dai yieu bo hia na/
(Why not eat?)

Quoc-H: /non bo jia/
(I don't want to eat it.)

Grandma-V: Tại răng không ăn?
(What not eat?)

Note: Quoc grows increasingly irritated with the grandparents' insistence that he eat what they offer him, and stomps away, pouting, and looking sideways at Grandma.

Grandma-V: Chu cha! Hắng liết kià, hắng liết con mắt. Coi cái mặt kià. ư, sấu!
(Goodness! Look at that scornful face, look at that sideways glance. Look at that face. Humph, bad!)

Quoc-H, E: /non bo jia/   God, just leave me alone!
(I don't want to eat it.) God, just leave me alone.

Note: Quoc stomps over to the living room, sits down on the floor in front of the coffee table, pulls out his homework from his backpack, and starts working. Mom comes over with a sandwich on a plate.

Mom-M, E, V: [je shu jo go] sandwich nề.
(Quoc, you eat this sandwich here.)

Quoc-E, M: Okay, [she she, niang.]
                   Okay, (thank you, Mom.)

Mom-M, E, V: [je jo] homework hả?
                   (Quoc, you're doing homework, yes?)

Quoc-E, M: Yes, [je] have to color [jo go] map.
                   (Yes, Quoc has to color this map.)

Mom-E, M: Okay, [quai.]
                   (Okay, good.)

Here, using four languages, a rich set of assumptions involving cultural expectations of the roles of the family around the theme of respect are played out in a routinized interaction. Conflict arises around the food theme, and the conflict remains unresolved. The grandparents address Quoc as if he were three or four, using oversimplified Hainanese. This is the level of Quoc's Hainanese proficiency, yet, as we are aware from conversation with him, he knows that this kind of talk treats him as though he were still a toddler, and he feels diminished not receiving the respect from his grandparents for the fact that he is, after all, eleven. He becomes irritated with the grandparents and acts this out through his stomping away, his pouting, and his sideways glance. Respect, of course, works both ways. The grandmother perceives Quoc's behavior as highly disrespectful, as it would be in Asian culture, where respect for elders must consistently be demonstrated, and children must not be seen as challenging the authority or position of an elder (Ima and Kheo 156–57). Quoc's mother most likely does not interfere in the interaction between Quoc and his grandparents for exactly the same reason: She does not want to be seen as siding with her child in the conflict and not respecting her elders.

Quoc's irritation here on one level is due to the fact that he cannot explain to his grandparents why he doesn't want the pastries they offer. Maybe he doesn't like their taste, maybe he's waiting for the sandwich his mother is making. He has no way, no language to express this other than English, and he does finally revert to English in his frustration. Yet the grandparents do not speak English. Quoc is trapped in this situation through both language and cultural constraints. His Asian culture requires that he show respect to his grandparents, but he doesn't possess the language skills necessary to decline an offer with the subtlety required to show respect. This example is reminiscent of a story recounted by Lilly Wong-Fillmore in her article "When Learning a Second Language Means Losing the First." She tells of the outcome when a Korean grandfather visited his grandchildren in the US. The US family had stopped speaking Korean in the home, and when the children addressed their grandfather in Korean, they made errors in the morphological markings required to indicate respect. They were physically punished for their disrespectful language. Language failed them.

SELECTION #3

This interaction is carried out in Vietnamese and English as Mom, Dad, Tung, Kim, and Linh plan a visit to China and Vietnam.

Dad-E: Linh, you guy look at the calendar. You gotta talk about what you guy wanna do in China . . .

Mom-V: Ông ni, làm cái chi mà ổng cứ nói tiến
Anh với máy đứa ni không à.
(This man, why does he speak English with the kids so much these days!)

Dad-E: You gotta have plan, otherwise you guy fight where you wanna go.

Note: Dad takes calendar off the wall in the family room, moves over to the kitchen table where Linh is sitting, watching Mom cook and fuss with some pots and pans. Tung and Kim are in the adjacent family room watching some talk show on TV and laughing to themselves, not really taking Dad seriously.

Linh-V: Tính thì tính. Má cua nề. Ngày ni mình ở đay đi Los, ngày ni lên máy bay đi Trung Quốc, ngày tới Quảng Châu, rồi đi Hải Nam ở máy ngày?
(All right, let's plan. Mom, come look. This day we go to Los Angeles, this day we get on a plane and fly to China, this day we get to Quang Zhou, then we go to Hai Nam for how many days?)

Mom-V: Thì ở Hải Nam một tuần, rồi đi Việt Nam . . . ngày ni ở Quảng Châu đi Sài Gòn , rồi đi Đà Nẵng rồi mới dề Tam Kỳ dược. ở Tam Kỳ, máy ngày, bốn năm ngày, rồi ra lại Đà Nẵng rồi ra Sài Gòn. ở Sài Gòn đi máy bay qua lại Quảng Châu, hay là đi Hồng Kông nửa?
(Well, we'll stay in Hai Nan for one week, then we'll go to Viet Nam. This day, we'll go to Sai Gon from Quang Zhou, then we'll go to Da Nang and then we can go to Tam Ky. We'll stay in Tam Ky for four, five days, then back out to Da Nang and Sai Gon to return to Quang Zhou, or do we go to Hong Kong?)

Note: At this point, Tung moves from the TV into the kitchen to get some food off the stove. Mom gets up from the kitchen table to get the food for Tung, and Linh continues looking at the calendar.

Tung-V: Thôi má, dược rồi.
(Okay, Mom, that's enough.)

Mom-V: Thăng ni, ăn có sí à . . .
(This boy, You eat just a tiny bit . . .)

Dad-V:	Lìn, mi tính, thì tính mà mi phải hỏi hai đứa nửa, coi thử hẳng họp ý không á.
	(Linh, you can plan, but you have to ask those two, to see if they agree.)
Linh-E:	Okay you guys, come look at this and see if you think it's okay.
Tung-E:	Whatever's fine with me.
Kim-E:	Hey, I wanna go to Beijing . . . I told my friends I'd meet them there . . .
Dad-V, E:	Đó, tháy chửa! I told you guy, you gotta talk it out and plan ahead.
	(See, look at that!) I told you guy, you gotta talk it out and plan ahead.

This interaction in English and Vietnamese dramatically points to an important role older siblings often play in an immigrant family during language loss and shift. Note how Linh mediates between the parents and younger siblings. She plays not only a role of translator of language, she indeed must take on a unique authority role which all must rely on. The authority on a superficial level seems to come from her linguistic ability, yet what is given over to her is partially parental authority. This role of "go-between" presents even more of a dilemma when the individual assuming the role is young, such as a child in elementary school. How can parents comfortably give over to children their parenting roles?

In such a case, psychologically, second language (L2) domination over the first language (L1) could cause parents to feel that they have lost authority because they now depend on their children to translate (Ima and Kheo 155–56). In Southeast Asian cultures, parents' roles are generally authoritative in nature, and parents have the last word. In a role reversal, where children receive information first and then transfer this information to parents, parents begin to take a secondary role in decision making. They also feel that they no longer control their children's destiny, especially in school and in major academic decisions such as going to college. In this family, once Linh entered high school, she read course and graduation requirements, chose classes on her own, and later gave advice to Quyen, Kim, and Tung when they entered high school. When parental signatures were required, the parents signed off at the "X." Linh recalls trying to explain to them what they were signing, but they were constrained in two ways. First, none of the languages they shared with Linh had been developed to a level by all of them to meet the expressive needs for discussing the deeper issues of education. Second, their own low level of education prevented shared understanding of the concepts, and specifically the American education system was very foreign to them. She remembers them often shaking their heads sighing, "I don't know, you do what you think is good." Once Linh and her siblings entered college, the parents' loss of control became even more overwhelming to all involved.

Many of the tensions created by language loss in this family can be seen in the educational domain. The awkwardness of a school open house or awards ceremony that resulted from the parents' limited language and the children playing "go-between" in parent-teacher dialogue eventually led to the children not informing the parents of the activities. They felt embarrassed that their parents did not know English or the American culture very well. Interestingly, the children recognize that they have contributed to their parents' powerlessness, putting them into a secondary position of decision making. As so many immigrant children before them, as new Americans, they have distanced themselves from their parents.

As Linh says:

Our parents might hear about how difficult some classes and subjects may be or how many hours we must invest in homework, but they can seldom understand what it is to have to write an essay, or to analyze a novel for its thematic values, or to perform a biology experiment, or to take the SAT test, or to apply for college. Their only consolation is that we're doing "something academic," but because they know so little about American schooling, it could very well be something else altogether (e.g. drugs, crimes, gang activity). How do we even begin to discuss our feelings with our parents when all that we have been able to say to them is what revolves around food, cleanliness, going to and from school and work? How do we begin to discuss our indecision about the best plan of study to pursue in college or what will make us happy in life? We never learned how.

With respect to playing the role of "go-between" she says:

For L2 and L1 proficient children, there is an added burden of having to mediate/facilitate relationship and interaction between L2 proficient siblings and parents proficient in the L1 only or with limited L2 proficiency. Mom and Dad often ask Quyen and me about what Tung and Kim are doing in school, what they plan to study, what careers they plan to pursue, and basically, who they are as people. Quyen and I do our best, but we often ask ourselves if this is right. Shouldn't parents have the right to know their own children rather than having to learn about them through others?

Conclusion

Today in the United States the public is mistakenly of the opinion that immigrant families resist learning English. The reality is that English is being acquired very rapidly and that family languages are being lost (Cho and Krashen 37). The discourse examples presented here reflect how this plays out in everyday communication in one typical immigrant family undergoing language shift and loss, demonstrating subtractive bilingualism, that is, losing one language while acquiring another. The result for this family, as we believe is also the case for so many families, is one of frustration, confusion, and isolation.

The difficulties in maintaining communication in immigrant families when heritage languages are not maintained increases as the children move toward English monolingualism. It is important that we consider the dynamics of this transition as we design English language programs that will support the desire of a public quite uninformed about the process of language acquisition and much less about language shift and loss. As people demand less assistance and demonstrate less tolerance for heritage language maintenance, English teachers may increasingly be the only contact students will have with teachers of language. It will be English teachers who teach them whether there is tolerance for other languages. These teachers will model to all students what they believe language is, how it should be used, how it is used to exclude some in a society, and how language policies discriminate. It is really a critical moment in the teaching of English for us to expand the English curriculum to a "language" curriculum to teach about the role of language in people's lives and touch on general sociolinguistic phenomena. The topics of bilingualism, dialects, language policy, and the history of languages in the United States are all filled with opportunities for student research about what language is and how it affects people's lives. We don't need to wait until students are in universities, as we have done for so long, to have them investigate these topics.

What we teach, research, and model about language affects public attitudes about it. Ethnographic studies such as the one undertaken here, looking at how language is used in particular settings, can be used to explore language use in other settings such as classrooms or meetings. Investigating language use in legal and medical settings with ethnographic techniques is fascinating for students. They can also develop projects looking at language use of unique groups like high school cliques or clubs to gain understanding of language and social interaction. What they will quickly find is that research opportunities about language are all around them just waiting to be explored.

FOOTNOTES

1. The names of the siblings have been changed.
2. Written Vietnamese reflects Linh's vernacular central Vietnamese accent.

REFERENCES

Cho, Grace, and Stephen Krashen. "The Negative Consequences of Heritage Language Loss and Why We Should Care." *Heritage Language Development*. Eds. Stephen Krashen, Lucy Tse, and Jeff McQuillan. Culver City, CA: Language Education Associates, 1998. 31–39.

Ima, Kenji, and Phinga-Evelyn Kheo. "The Crying Father and My Father Doesn't Love Me: Selective Observations and Reflections on Southeast Asians and Special Education." *Integrating Language and Learning for Inclusion: An Asian/Pacific Focus*. Ed. Li-Rong Lilly Cheng. San Diego: Singular Publishing Group, 1995.

Rodriguez, Richard. *Hunger of Memory*. Boston: David R. Godine, 1982.

Wong-Fillmore, Lilly. "When Learning a Second Language Means Losing the First." *Early Childhood Research Quarterly* 6 (1991): 323–46.

Thinking About the Text _____

1. What do Thomas and Cao try to get across with this text? What are their perspectives on language use?

2. Describe the voice/tone of this piece of writing. Is it different from what might be expected in a scholarly article? How so? Why might the authors have made this choice?

3. Think about your own family and the language conventions used in your family. What research topics might come from a close examination of language within your family or community?

A Kind of Love

ANDREI CODRESCU

Andrei Codrescu is a 56-year-old Romanian born American poet, screen-writer, novelist, essayist and NPR correspondent. He wrote and starred in the documentary film ROAD SCHOLAR, and is currently the editor of the literary journal "Exquisite Corpse." He teaches at Louisiana State University in Baton Rouge.

There are two kinds of love I can think of right off the bat. One kind is the kind I call Stat Love, which is the kind you study and discuss, the kind of love that thrives on facts and statistics. The sum total of what you know about the beloved is the beloved, except that there is always more to learn and more to know. If you're in Stat Love, you are her public defender, the messenger of her qualities, the trumpeter of her records, the fan of her history. She is the ideal, and you are the pest.

The other kind of love is the Roomy kind. You know little about her and want to know even less. You simply want to be in her presence, inhale her atmosphere, be in the room she creates around you, lose yourself, be entranced. Not only do you not know her stats, you don't even know yours any more. She has put you in a magic space-time, a place made possible only by exaltation. This is the kind of love I have for baseball, which is a good excuse for ignorance.

I saw my first game at Memorial Stadium in Baltimore in the spring of 1979. The Orioles were playing the Angels. I was much taken at the time with the literalism of sports headlines, and I was amused at the idea of birds fighting angels. I also liked bears squashing padres, and different-color socks going at it. As my friend Jeff Miller used to say: "Ouch, ouch go the little padres." Rodger Kamenetz, a friend of mine, took me and my son Lucian to this game and I didn't understand anything. Both Rodger and my son filled me in on fine points, but I couldn't tell who was scoring, when and what was happening. The sport went against any idea of ball games I ever had. The week after that week I went to a game all by myself. Rodger asked me what the score was. "Nothing to nothing," I said. He laughed. The score, plainly in the morning paper, had been 12 zip.

I was involved at the time in a struggle to get my citizenship, and I was having an epic battle with the immigration department. I had the weird feeling that I wouldn't get my citizenship until I learned baseball, and that's exactly what happened. The first game I went to and understood from start to finish was the Birds and the Tigers in the summer of 1981. The Tigers are another favorite of mine for various mythical reasons having to do with Detroit in 1967, and the delirium and riots of 1968. And as soon as I understood that game, something popped in me, the pod opened and the nouveau American I always was suddenly emerged. And of course, I got my citizenship, the Orioles won the pennant in a spectacular series where Eddie Murray hit a home run on the bottom of the ninth with the bases loaded, and at the citizenship party at my house my friends gave me a baseball signed by all of them in a little ceremony. The party lasted all night. I take that ball wherever I go; it's moved with me to Louisiana, where they don't even have major league baseball. There are Saints here, but they are football saints, not the same at all. With citizenship and a baseball signed by all my friends—my son has one signed by Sandy Koufax—I started to understand large tracts of American writing that had been closed to me until then. Things like Fielding Dawson's stories and the esthetics of the Black Mountain of school poetry and painting. The whole late fifties, early sixties art movements that established America as the leader in painting—abstract expressionism, pop art and the rest, were all secretly and not so secretly cornball attempts at a vision of America in a state of baseball.

Baseball is very literary. There are well-known writings on baseball, from Dawson to Malamud, but there is something else. Both baseball and poetry begin in childhood. They are mirror images in a way. Baseball is the active form and poetry the contemplative. Now a poet like Edgar Allan Poe, whose grave is on the way to Memorial Stadium in Baltimore, wouldn't have liked baseball. He was an aristocrat who hated the masses; he preferred the night to the day. He loved silence and despised crowds. Which is ironic, because Baltimore's rough democracy did him in. He was killed by vote salesmen, hoods hired by the local pols. On the other hand, it isn't entirely inappropriate for this city to love both their poet and their baseball. There is a lyrical link between the two. When the cheers of the crowd carry on the wind and wash over his grave, Poe can dream that the crowd is cheering for him. He wouldn't be wrong. They are cheering a ball being set suddenly free, which is very much like a poem freed from its poet.

Poe isn't the only marker on the way to Memorial Stadium. There is also the place, near the Peabody Institute, where Freud first came when he came to America. The occasion was the founding of the American Psychoanalytical Society. This too is significant. Freud, who said so much about everything, would have said wonderful things about baseball too. Speaking of Houdini, "the last great mother lover," E. L. Doctorow said that when Freud came to America, mother love died forever. I wonder if baseball, which is always mentioned in the same breath with mother and apple pie, could have withstood the force of *Herr Doktor*'s critique. Would apple pie? Probably. Freud would have taken to baseball the way he took to cocaine. Mid-European intellectuals have an *organ* for baseball.

Before I saw baseball, I never knew a sport where people didn't worry about the ball all the time. In soccer there is constant competition for the ball—the identity of the player is defined by his possession of the ball. He *is* when he is touching the ball.

In baseball there is a different relation between ball and players, and consequently, between game and spectators. The ball is allowed more personality, it is permitted distance. It is stalked rather than gang raped. It is also a dance between two men—a Spanish dance. It is a corrida, a bullfight. The pitcher is a toreador—he stands and acts like one—the batter is the charging bull. The ball is the toreador's life—issuing out of him as an eternal tease to the brute power of the bat. It is a battle between spirit and flesh, between two different kinds of cunning, a cultivated one and a natural one, between civilization and nature.

There is some evidence that baseball was brought to America by Romanians. Transylvanian shepherds play a primitive form of stick ball called *oina* that resembles baseball. Some Romanian officers visited Cooperstown and showed the natives. Even if *oina* isn't exactly baseball, there is a Latin connection. The many Spanish players that give the game its contemporary salsa may claim an Aztec lineage. The Aztecs too played something like baseball. Some of the major-league players of Central American origin instinctively combine the style of the corrida with the existential seriousness of the Aztec game—the ceremonial ball game. In the Aztec game of pelota the winning team was put to death. It was a great honor to be made into an instant god. The game was played with hips and knees only; you were not allowed to use hands or feet. There were two stone bases or goalposts, a large stone horseshoe and a parrot with a small hole in it, called a *pama*. The *hatcha*, or the court, sloped down between stone walls. The spectators were arrayed along the top. The game had cosmic and ritual significance, no doubt. In any case, it was serious, just as the corrida is serious. In modern baseball, that seriousness is a matter only of certain moments. The moment just before the pitch, for instance, when everything is in suspense. The world becomes very mysterious at that point.

I hear too that a ball pitched at a speed higher than fifty miles hour cannot be seen. The last batter capable of seeing high-speed balls was Ted Williams, whose batting average in 1941 was over .400. So it is a truly mystical game. The batter has to know somehow where the ball is, and hit it before it gets there. A good batter can bat with his eyes closed, using the mystical sense. The high rate of failure with the bat would be unallowable in any other sport. Seven out of ten! A basketball player with that kind of failure rate would be inconceivable. Baseball's high rate of failure makes it a game of extraordinary tolerance. What's more, the players are arranged according to what might happen in the field. *Anything* might happen, except what *does* happen. So in addition to great tolerance for failure, baseball is a game of possibilities. That's the American ideal par excellence, it says so on Miss Liberty. Send me your failures, I'll make them possible.

There is something in the game that goes with the American landscape. Its essence is waiting, not rushing. There is a streak of patience, almost stoicism in it. Likewise the great prairies, the Western ranges. People rush across these, of course, but they find themselves overwhelmed. Even the fiercest gold rushers soon found themselves stilled, overwhelmed by the land. America has not yet been made human. The land is still the true power. The geology. Space, as Olson said, is the central fact of man in North America. Baseball has an understanding of American space. The lulls in the action, when the spectators can eat hot dogs or sushi, drink beer and converse, are large reprieves, islands of wonder. The whole cosmos can bear down in the pauses between action, and does. When the end of the world comes, whole stadiums will be spirited straight into the sky in the space between two pitches somewhere around the fourth inning in a steady, even game.

The language of the game is interesting. You can think of the pauses as caesuras, breaks between the lines. As a poem the game is composed of a number of short lines representing the pitches. The number of lines per batter form a stanza. Then there is a space. Sometimes the stanzas become breathless, rushing full paragraphs that build rapidly on each other until the poem-inning explodes. The poem lives for this sudden blossoming out of prosodic regularity. Should someone make a computer analysis of baseball prosody, I believe that they would come up with something close to the prosody of some great American lyrical epic, Whitman's *Leaves of Grass*, let's say, or Doc Williams's *Paterson*. Of course we could be surprised by its coming out like the *Popol Vuh*, the Mayan epic, or Bernal Diaz's *Conquest of Mexico*, or even *Don Quixote*. Prosody is funny. The game is definitely an epic though, formed of many lyrical moments dependent on silences for their effectiveness. An unfolding story punctuated by brief emotional swellings. Football is a pure narrative, a straight short story on the C&W theme of "How long can you hold on to something everyone wants?" Football is a linear short story that aims straight for narrative continuity and a thumping climax. Soccer is all lyricism without any relief from the intensity. The ball is oversexed, the players overexcited.

The sexuality of baseball is different. Both men and women like the game. Football is mostly a men's game, a straining against the massed flesh of the world to achieve a difficult penetration. It is direct and genital. Baseball is courtly, there is a lot of romancing of the ball in it, teasing, coyness, missed opportunities, ground gained and regained. The bat-penis is teased and teased by the ball-egg. The teasing is meant to elicit maximum potency, the batter's terrifying best that will send the ball out of the ballpark. Out of sight.

In this sense, the game is predominantly female. It is played on the body of a woman—the diamond—symbolic of the body of mother earth. The initiative belongs to the pitcher, who is the servant of the egg, the yielder of the tease. Like the toreador he is often so exaggeratedly macho that he is positively hieratic, impossible, artificial. He is a highly skilled drone, tending to the work of the queen. A palace minister who knows the ins and outs of his mistress's will.

There is a direct and personal rivalry between him and the batter. Although they are both men, the batter represents only himself and his masculinity. The pitcher is responsible for the egg, and for the form of the game. The kinds of things pitchers sometimes do to batters, like hitting them with the ball, have to do with the frustration of being a hired hand—albeit a metaphysical one—facing a free man. In reality they are both doing the bidding of the feminine: one intimately, the other cosmically. Overtly and covertly. The overall plan is union: freeing the ball. Orgasm (scoring), of course, is the goal of all sports, but some sports have weak, attenuated orgasms—like golf (WASP orgasm), while others, like soccer, have demotic, indiscriminate slumgasms. Baseborgasm is soaring, dignified, serious, roomy. And there is time for a snack between the convulsions.

Baseball crowds are also different. They are summery, picnicky, beer soaked, light. Those gruesome rushes of collective aggression in football are missing. I love to sit slightly high in the stands, letting the mood of the crowd flow through me when the home team is winning. In Romania, I was not allowed any communion with the masses. There, the division between guys with glasses and guys with muscles is unbreachable. There is nothing more terrifying than walking up the street as a postgame soccer crowd walks toward you when the home team lost the game. You have glasses, you are Jewish, you have on a lycée uniform, there is only one of you and the whole history of intellectual, class and racial persecution is about to bear down on you. The individual and the mass. All the alienated existentialism we provincial Eastern European Jews invented, along with modern literature, comes from that immense fear of seeing that crowd advance toward you. I realized that the reason I'd never gone to a baseball game before 1979 is that I abhor crowds. They scare me. When they stand up as one, tens of thousands of them, screaming, I thank God they are crying for a ball not for the blood of Jews. But the feeling is similar, and the adrenaline the same. What must it have been like to be a Jew disguised as a German at one of Hitler's rallies? I don't want to think about it. But my fears were allayed, if not totally put to rest. There were all kinds at the game: Jews, guys with glasses, housewives in shorts. Goodwill and hot dogs prevailed. Of course, there are warlike sections like the one Wild Bill Hagy used to sit in, but those beer-bellied brutes just don't like suits. There is a big difference between that and muddled politics. I don't like suits either. One might make a case for the innocence of American political conventions and the ignorance of the electorate as corollaries of baseball, but that would be stretching it. Baseball is cornball all right, but it is not simple.

Thinking About the Text _____

1. What does Codrescu mean when he says, "And as soon as I understood [baseball], something popped out in me, the pod opened and the noveau American I always was suddenly emerged"?

2. Which rhetorical appeals does Codrescu employ? How do they strengthen his essay?

3. How does baseball help Codrescu "understand large tracts of American writing"? What is his main purpose in the essay and why does he choose a symbolic tool to illustrate this?

The Debate Has Been Miscast From the Start

HENRY LOUIS GATES

Henry Louis Gates, Jr. was born in 1950 in Keyser, WV. Gates was recognized early on by an English instructor at Potomac State Community College, who encouraged his student to transfer to Yale University. Gates graduated from that institution with highest honors in 1973. He then went on to receive his M.A. in 1974 and Ph.D. in 1979 from Clare College, Cambridge. After receiving his Ph.D., Gates began teaching at Yale but moved quickly from his position there to a full professorship at Cornell to an endowed chair at Duke. In 1991, he became the W. E. B. DuBois Professor of the Humanities at Harvard and head of its Afro-American Studies program. Gates is one of the most controversial and respected scholars in the field of African-American studies. Gates has published several books, including *Signifying Monkey* (1989), *Loose Cannons* (1992), and *Colored People* (1993).

What is multiculturalism and why are they saying such terrible things about it?

We've been told that it threatens to fragment American culture into a warren of ethnic enclaves, each separate and inviolate. We've been told that it menaces the Western tradition of literature and the arts. We've been told that it aims to politicize the school curriculum, replacing honest historical scholarship with a "feel good" syllabus designed solely to bolster the self-esteem of minorities. The alarm has been sounded, and many scholars and educators—liberals as well as conservatives—have responded to it. After all, if multiculturalism is just a pretty name for ethnic chauvinism, who needs it?

But I don't think that's what multiculturalism is—at least, I don't think that's what it ought to be. And because the debate has been miscast from the beginning, it may be worth setting the main issues straight.

To both proponents and antagonists, multiculturalism represents—either refreshingly or frighteningly—a radical departure. Like most claims for cultural novelty, this one is more than a little exaggerated. For the challenges of cultural pluralism—and the varied forms of official resistance to it—go back to the very founding of our republic.

In the university today, it must be admitted, the challenge has taken on a peculiar inflection. But the underlying questions are time-tested. What does it mean to be an American? Must academic inquiry be subordinated to the requirements of national identity? Should scholarship and education reflect our actual diversity, or should they, rather, forge a communal identity that may not yet have been achieved?

For answers, you can, of course, turn to the latest jeremiad on the subject from, say, George Will, Dinesh D'Souza, or Roger Kimball. But in fact these questions have always occasioned lively disagreement among American educators. In 1917, William Henry Hulme decried "the insidious introduction into our scholarly relations of the political propaganda of a wholly narrow, selfish, and vicious nationalism and false patriotism." His opponents were equally emphatic in their beliefs. "More and more clearly," Fred Lewis Pattee ventured in 1919, "is it seen now that the American soul, the American conception of democracy, Americanism, should be made prominent in our school curriculums, as a guard against the rising spirit of experimental lawlessness." Sound familiar?

Given the political nature of the debate over education and the national interest, the conservative penchant for charging the multiculturalists with "politics" is a little perplexing. For conservative critics, to their credit, have never hesitated to provide a political defense of what they consider to be the "traditional" curriculum: The future of the republic, they argue, depends on the inculcation of proper civic virtues. What these virtues are is a matter of vehement dispute. But to imagine a curriculum untouched by political concerns is to imagine—as no one does—that education can take place in a vacuum.

So where's the beef? Granted, multiculturalism is no panacea for our social ills. We're worried when Johnny can't read. We're worried when Johnny can't add. But shouldn't we be worried, too, when Johnny tramples gravestones in a Jewish cemetery or scrawls racial epithets on a dormitory wall? And it's because we've entrusted our schools with the fashioning of a democratic polity that education has never been exempt from the kind of debate that marks every other aspect of American political life.

Perhaps this isn't altogether a bad thing. As the political theorist Amy Gutmann has argued: "In a democracy, political disagreement is not something that we should generally seek to avoid. Political controversies over our educational problems are a particularly important source of social progress because they have the potential for educating so many citizens."

And while I'm sympathetic to what Robert Nisbet once dubbed the "academic dogma"—the ideal of knowledge for its own sake—I also believe that truly humane learning, unblinkered by the constraints of narrow ethnocentrism, can't help but expand the limits of human understanding and social tolerance. Those who fear that "Balkanization" and social fragmentation lie this way have got it exactly backward. Ours is a world that already is fissured by nationality, ethnicity, race, and gender. And the only way to transcend those divisions—to forge, for once, a civic culture that respects both differences and commonalities—is through education that seeks to comprehend the diversity of human culture. Beyond the hype and the high-flown rhetoric is a pretty homely truth: There is no tolerance without respect—and no respect without knowledge.

The historical architects of the university always understood this. As Cardinal Newman wrote more than a century ago, the university should promote "the power of viewing many things at once as one whole, of referring them severally to their true place in the universal system, of understanding their respective values, and determining their mutual dependence." In just this vein, the critic Edward Said has recently suggested that "our model for academic freedom should therefore be the migrant or traveler: for if, in the real world outside the academy, we must need be ourselves and only ourselves, inside the academy we should be able to discover and travel among other selves, other identities, other varieties of the human adventure. But, most essentially, in this joint discovery of self and other, it is the role of the academy to transform what might be conflict, or context, or assertion into reconciliation, mutuality, recognition, creative interaction."

But if multiculturalism represents the culmination of an age-old ideal—the dream known, in the 17th century, as *mathesis universalis*—why has it been the target of such ferocious attacks? On this point, I'm often reminded of a wonderfully wicked piece of 19th-century student doggerel about Benjamin Jowett, the great Victorian classicist and master of Balliol College, Oxford:

Here stand I, my name is Jowett,
If there's knowledge, then I know it;
I am the master of this college,
What I know not, is not knowledge.

Of course, the question of how we determine what is worth knowing is now being raised with uncomfortable persistence. So that in the most spirited attacks on multiculturalism in the academy today, there's a nostalgic whiff of the old sentiment: We are the masters of this college; what we know not is not knowledge.

I think this explains the conservative desire to cast the debate in terms of the West vs. the Rest. And yet that's the very opposition that the pluralist wants to challenge. Pluralism sees cultures as porous, dynamic, and interactive, rather than the fixed property of particular ethnic groups. Thus the idea of a monolithic, homogeneous "West" itself comes into question (nothing new here: Literary historians have pointed out that the very concept of "Western culture" may date back only to the 18th century). But rather than mourning the loss of some putative ancestral purity, we can recognize what's valuable, resilient, even cohesive, in the hybrid and variegated nature of our modernity.

Genuine multiculturalism is not, of course, everyone's cup of tea. Vulgar cultural nationalists—like Allan Bloom or Leonard Jeffries—correctly identify it as the enemy. These polemicists thrive on absolute partitions: between "civilization" and "barbarism," between "black" and "white," between a thousand versions of Us and Them. But they are whistling in the wind.

For whatever the outcome of the culture wars in the academy, the world we live in is multicultural already. Mixing and hybridity is the rule, not the exception. As a student of African-American culture, of course, I've come to take this kind of cultural palimpsest for granted. Duke Ellington, Miles Davis, John Coltrane have influenced popular musicians the world over. Wynton Marsalis is as comfortable with Mozart as he is with jazz; Anthony Davis writes operas in a musical idiom that combines Bartok with the blues.

In dance, Judith Jamison, Alvin Ailey, Katherine Dunham all excelled at "Western" cultural forms, melding these with African-American styles to produce performances that were neither, and both. In painting, Romare Bearden and Jacob Lawrence, Martin Puryear and Augusta Savage learned to paint and sculpt by studying Western masters, yet each has pioneered the constructs of a distinctly African-American visual art.

And in literature, of course, the most formally complex and compelling black writers—such as Jean Toomer, Sterling Brown, Langston Hughes, Zora Hurston, Richard Wright, Ralph Ellison, James Baldwin, and Gwendolyn Brooks—have always blended forms of Western literature with African-American vernacular and written traditions. Then, again, even a vernacular form such as the spiritual took for its texts the King James version of the Old and New Testaments. Toni Morrison's master's thesis was on Virginia Woolf and Faulkner; Rita Dove is as comfortable with German literature as she is with the blues.

Indeed, the greatest African-American art can be thought of as an exploration of that hyphenated space between the African and the American. As James Baldwin once reflected during his long European sojourn, "I would have to appropriate these white centuries, I would have to make them mine. I would have to accept my special attitude, my special place in this scheme, otherwise I would have no place in any scheme."

"Pluralism," the American philosopher John Dewey insisted early in this century, "is the greatest philosophical idea of our times." But he recognized that it was also the greatest problem of our times: "How are we going to make the most of the new values we set on variety, difference, and individuality—how are we going to realize their possibilities in every field, and at the same time not sacrifice that plurality to the cooperation we need so much?" It has the feel of a scholastic conundrum: How can we negotiate between the one and the many?

Today, the mindless celebration of difference has proven as untenable as that bygone model of monochrome homogeneity. If there is an equilibrium to be struck, there's no guarantee we will ever arrive at it. The worst mistake we can make, however, is not to try.

Thinking About the Text _____

1. Gates contrasts multiculturalism with "ethnic chauvinism": according to Gates, what is the difference? Why does he think we've confused the two?

2. What does Gates say are the "time-tested" questions underlying cultural pluralism "since the founding of our republic"? How does he think politics informs the debate around multiculturalism in education?

3. What does Gates mean by "the West vs. the Rest"? How does his use of language influence the way you read the rest of the piece?

Discrimination Is a Virtue

ROBERT KEITH MILLER

"Discrimination Is a Virtue" is an essay focusing on the misuse of the word discrimination and how its misuse reflects on our society's tendency to pretend differences do not exist. Miller broadens his scope from the misuse of the word to how failure to recognize such differences in society affects issues of mental health and politics.

When I was a child, my grandmother used to tell me a story about a king who had three daughters and decided to test their love. He asked each of them "How much do you love me?" The first replied that she loved him as much as all the diamonds and pearls in the world. The second said that she loved him more than life itself. The third replied "I love you as fresh meat loves salt."

This answer enraged the king; he was convinced that his youngest daughter was making fun of him. So he banished her from his realm and left all of his property to her elder sisters.

As the story unfolded it became clear, even to a 6-year-old, that the king had made a terrible mistake. The two older girls were hypocrites, and as soon as they had profited from their father's generosity, they began to treat him very badly. A wiser man would have realized that the youngest daughter was the truest. Without attempting to flatter, she said, in effect, "We go together naturally; we are a perfect team."

Years later, when I came to read Shakespeare, I realized that my grandmother's story was loosely based upon the story of King Lear, who put his daughters to a similar test and did not know how to judge the results. Attempting to save the king from the consequences of his foolishness, a loyal friend pleads, "Come sir, arise, away! I'll teach you differences." Unfortunately, the lesson comes too late. Because Lear could not tell the difference between true love and false, he loses his kingdom and eventually his life.

We have a word in English which means "the ability to tell differences." That word is *discrimination*. But within the last 30 years, this word has been so frequently misused that an entire generation has grown up believing that "discrimination" means "racism." People are always proclaiming that "discrimination" is something that should be done away with. Should that ever happen, it would prove to be our undoing.

Discrimination means discernment; it means the ability to perceive the truth, to use good judgment and to profit accordingly. The *Oxford English Dictionary* traces this understanding of the word back to 1648 and demonstrates that for the next 300 years, "discrimination" was a virtue, not a vice. Thus, when a character in a nineteenth-century novel makes a happy marriage, Dickens has another character remark, "It does credit to your discrimination that you should have found such a very excellent young woman."

Of course, "the ability to tell differences" assumes that differences exist, and this is unsettling for a culture obsessed with the notion of equality. The contemporary belief that discrimination is a vice stems from the compound *discriminate against*. What we need to remember, however, is that some things deserve to be judged harshly: we should not leave our kingdoms to the selfish and the wicked.

Discrimination is wrong only when someone or something is discriminated against because of prejudice. But to use the word in this sense, as so many people do, is to destroy its true meaning. If you discriminate against something because of general preconceptions rather than particular insights, then you are not discriminating—bias has clouded the clarity of vision which discrimination demands.

One of the great ironies of American life is that we manage to discriminate in the practical decisions of daily life, but usually fail to discriminate when we make public policies. Most people are very discriminating when it comes to buying a car, for example, because they realize that cars have differences. Similarly, an increasing number of people have learned to discriminate in what they eat. Some foods are better than others—and indiscriminate eating can undermine one's health.

Yet in public affairs, good judgment is depressingly rare. In many areas which involve the common good, we see a failure to tell differences.

Consider, for example, some of the thinking behind modern education. On the one hand, there is a refreshing realization that there are differences among children, and some children—be they gifted or handicapped—require special education. On the other hand, we are politically unable to accept the consequences of this perception. The trend in recent years has been to group together students of radically different ability. We call this process "mainstreaming," and it strikes me as a characteristically American response to the discovery of differences: we try to pretend that differences do not matter.

Similarly, we try to pretend that there is little difference between the sane and the insane. A fashionable line of argument has it that "everybody is a little mad" and that few mental patients deserve long-term hospitalization. As a consequence of such reasoning, thousands of seriously ill men and women have been evicted from their hospital beds and returned to what is euphemistically called "the community"—which often means being left to sleep on city streets, where confused and helpless people now live out of paper bags as the direct result of our refusal to discriminate.

Or to choose a final example from a different area: how many recent elections reflect thoughtful consideration of the genuine differences among candidates? Benumbed by television commercials that market aspiring officeholders as if they were a new brand of toothpaste or hair spray, too many Americans vote with only a fuzzy understanding of the issues in question. Like Lear, we seem too eager to leave the responsibility of government to others and too ready to trust those who tell us whatever we want to hear.

So as we look around us, we should recognize that "discrimination" is a virtue which we desperately need. We must try to avoid making unfair and arbitrary distinctions, but we must not go to the other extreme and pretend that there are no distinctions to be made. The ability to make intelligent judgments is essential both for the success of one's personal life and for the functioning of society as a whole. Let us be open-minded by all means, but not so open-minded that our brains fall out.

Thinking About the Text _____

1. Find examples of words that have been used in ways other than their definitions. Provide some examples of correct and incorrect usages. Why do you think such words have been used improperly?

2. Comment on Miller's idea that political correctness has clouded not only our judgment but also made us a society fearful to speak freely.

3. Given the title, "Discrimination is a Virtue," did your preconceptions of what the essay was going to be about change after (or during) reading the essay? Does this hold to Miller's idea? Why or why not?

Learning the Language

RICHARD RODRIGUEZ

Richard Rodriguez was born in Sacramento, California, in 1944 to Mexican-American immigrants. Although unable to speak English when he entered elementary school in Sacramento, Rodriguez graduated from Stanford University, received a Master's degree from Columbia University, and studied English Renaissance literature as a graduate student at the University of California, Berkeley, and the Warburg Institute, London. Rodriguez left academic life abruptly, however, because of his belief that the several offers he received for university-level teaching positions were the result of affirmative action. After leaving academia, Rodriguez published several books, including two autobiographical works, *Hunger of Memory: The Education of Richard Rodriguez* (1982) and *Days of Obligation: An Argument with My Mexican Father* (1992). His writings have also appeared in *American Scholar, New Republic, Wall Street Journal, Los Angeles Times, Harper's,* and *Washington Post.*

I remember to start with that day in Sacramento—a California now nearly thirty years past—when I first entered a classroom, able to understand some fifty stray English words.

The third of four children, I had been preceded to a neighborhood Roman Catholic school by an older brother and sister. But neither of them had revealed very much about their classroom experiences. Each afternoon they returned, as they left in the morning, always together, speaking in Spanish as they climbed the five steps of the porch. And their mysterious books, wrapped in shopping-bag paper, remained on the table next to the door, closed firmly behind them.

An accident of geography sent me to a school where all my classmates were white, many the children of doctors and lawyers and business executives. All my classmates certainly must have been uneasy on that first day of school—as most children are uneasy—to find themselves apart from their families in the first institution of their lives. But I was astonished.

The nun said, in a friendly but oddly impersonal voice, 'Boys and girls, this is Richard Rodriguez.' (I heard her sound out: *Rich-heard Road-ree-guess*.) It was the first time I had heard anyone name me in English. 'Richard,' the nun repeated more slowly, writing my name down in her black leather book. Quickly I turned to see my mother's face dissolve in a watery blur behind the pebbled glass door.

Many years later there is something called bilingual education—a scheme proposed in the late 1960s by Hispanic-American social activists, later endorsed by a congressional vote. It is a program that seeks to permit non-English-speaking children, many from lower-class homes, to use their family language as the language of school. (Such is the goal its supporters announce.) I heard them and am forced to say no: It is not possible for a child—any child— ever to use his family's language in school. Not to understand this is to misunderstand the public uses of schooling and to trivialize the nature of intimate life—a family's 'language.'

Memory teaches me what I know of these matters; the boy reminds the adult. I was a bilingual child, a certain kind—socially disadvantaged—the son of working-class parents, both Mexican immigrants.

In the early years of my boyhood, my parents coped very well in America. My father had steady work. My mother managed at home. They were nobody's victims. Optimism and ambition led them to a house (our home) many blocks from the Mexican south side of town. We lived among *gringos* and only a block from the biggest, whitest houses. It never occurred to my parents that they couldn't live wherever they chose. Nor was the Sacramento of the fifties bent on teaching them a contrary lesson. My mother and father were more annoyed than intimidated by those two or three neighbors who tried initially to make us unwelcome. ('Keep your brats away from my sidewalk!') But despite all they achieved, perhaps because they had so much to achieve, any deep feeling of ease, the confidence of 'belonging' in public was withheld from them both. They regarded the people at work, the faces in crowds, as very distant from us. They were the others, *los gringos*. That term was interchangeable in their speech with another, even more telling, *los americanos*.

I grew up in a house where the only regular guests were my relations. For one day, enormous families of relatives would visit and there would be so many people that the noise and the bodies would spill out to the backyard and front porch. Then, for weeks, no one came by. (It was usually a salesman who rang the doorbell.) Our house stood apart. A gaudy yellow in a row of white bungalows. We were the people with the noisy dog. The people who raised pigeons and chickens. We were the foreigners on the block. A few neighbors smiled and waved. We waved back. But no one in the family knew the names of the old couple who lived next door; until I was seven years old, I did not know the names of the kids who lived across the street.

In public, my father and mother spoke a hesitant, accented, not always grammatical English. And they would have to strain—their bodies tense—to catch the sense of what was rapidly said by *los gringos*. At home they spoke Spanish. The language of their Mexican past sounded in counterpoint to the English of public society. The words would come quickly, with ease. Conveyed through those sounds was the pleasing, soothing, consoling reminder of being at home.

During those years when I was first conscious of hearing, my mother and father addressed me only in Spanish; in Spanish I learned to reply. By contrast, English (*inglés*), rarely heard in the house, was the language I came to associate with *gringos*. I learned my first words of English overhearing my parents speak to strangers. At five years of age, I knew just enough English for my mother to trust me on errands to stores one block away. No more.

I was a listening child, careful to hear the very different sounds of Spanish and English. Wide-eyed with hearing, I'd listen to sounds more than words. First, there were English (*gringo*) sounds. So many words were still unknown that when the butcher or the lady at the drugstore said something to me, exotic polysyllabic sounds would bloom in the midst of their sentences. Often, the speech of people in public seemed to me very loud, booming with confidence. The man behind the counter would literally ask, 'What can I do for you?' But by being so firm and so clear, the sound of his voice said that he was a *gringo*; he belonged in public society.

I would also hear then the high nasal notes of middle-class American speech. The air stirred with sound. Sometimes, even now, when I have been traveling abroad for several weeks, I will hear what I heard as a boy. In hotel lobbies or airports, in Turkey or Brazil, some Americans will pass, and suddenly I will hear it again—the high sound of American voices. For a few seconds I will hear it with pleasure, for it is now the sound of *my* society—a reminder of home. But inevitably—already on the flight headed for home—the sound fades with repetition. I will be unable to hear it anymore.

When I was a boy, things were different. The accent of *los gringos* was never pleasing nor was it hard to hear. Crowds at Safeway or at bus stops would be noisy with sound. And I would be forced to edge away from the chirping chatter above me.

I was unable to hear my own sounds, but I knew very well that I spoke English poorly. My words could not stretch far enough to form complete thoughts. And the words I did speak I didn't know well enough to make into distinct sounds. (Listeners would usually lower their heads, better to hear what I was trying to say.) But it was one thing for *me* to speak English with difficulty. It was more troubling for me to hear my parents speak in public: their high-whining vowels and guttural consonants; their sentences that got stuck with 'ch' and 'ah' sounds; the confused syntax; the hesitant rhythm of sounds so different from the way *gringos* spoke. I'd notice, moreover, that my parents' voices were softer than those of *gringos* we'd meet.

I am tempted now to say that none of this mattered. In adulthood I am embarrassed by childhood fears. And, in a way, it didn't matter very much that my parents could not speak English with ease. Their linguistic difficulties had no serious consequences. My mother and father made themselves understood at the county hospital clinic and at government offices. And yet, in another way, it mattered very much—it was unsettling to hear my parents struggle with English. Hearing them, I'd grow nervous, my clutching trust in their protection and power weakened.

There were many times like the night at a brightly lit gasoline station (a blaring white memory) when l stood uneasily, hearing my father. He was talking to a teenaged attendant. I do not recall what they were saying, but I cannot forget the sounds my father made as he spoke. At one point his words slid together to form one word—sounds as confused as the threads of blue and green oil in the puddle next to my shoes. His voice rushed through what he had left to say. And, toward the end, reached falsetto notes, appealing to his listener's understanding. I looked away to the lights of passing automobiles. I tried not to hear anymore. But I heard only too well the calm, easy tones in the attendant's reply. Shortly afterward, walking toward home with my father, I shivered when he put his hand on my shoulder. The very first chance that I got, I evaded his grasp and ran on ahead into the dark, skipping with feigned boyish exuberance.

But then there was Spanish. *Español*: my family's language. *Español*: the language that seemed to me a private language. I'd hear strangers on the radio and in the Mexican Catholic church across town speaking in Spanish, but I couldn't really believe that Spanish was a public language, like English. Spanish speakers, rather, seemed related to me, for I sensed that we shared—through our language—the experience of feeling apart from *los gringos*. It was thus a ghetto Spanish that I heard and I spoke. Like those whose lives are bound by a barrio, I was reminded by Spanish of my separateness from *los otros, los gringos* in power. But more intensely than for most barrio children—because I did not live in a barrio—Spanish seemed to me the language of home. (Most days it was only at home that I'd hear it.) It became the language of joyful return.

A family member would say something to me and I would feel myself specially recognized. My parents would say something to me and I would feel embraced by the sounds of their words. Those sounds said: *I am speaking with ease in Spanish. I am addressing you in words I never use with* los gringos. *I recognize you as someone special, close, like no one outside. You belong with us. In the family.*

(*Ricardo.*)

At the age of five, six, well past the time when most other children no longer easily notice the difference between sounds uttered at home and words spoken in public, I had a different experience. I lived in a world magically compounded of sounds. I remained a child longer than most; I lingered too long, poised at the edge of language—often frightened by the sounds of *los gringos*, delighted by the sounds of Spanish at home. I shared with my family a language that was startlingly different from that used in the great city around us.

For me there were none of the gradations between public and private society so normal to a maturing child. Outside the house was public society; inside the house was private. Just opening or closing the screen door behind me was an important experience. I'd rarely leave home all alone or without reluctance. Walking down the sidewalk, under the canopy of tall trees, I'd warily notice the—suddenly—silent neighborhood kids who stood warily watching me. Nervously, I'd arrive at the grocery store to hear there the sounds of the *gringo*—foreign to me—reminding me that in this world so big, I was a foreigner. But then I'd return. Walking back toward our house, climbing the steps from the sidewalk, when the front door was open in summer, I'd hear voices beyond the screen door talking in Spanish. For a second or two, I'd stay, linger there, listening. Smiling, I'd hear my mother call out, saying in Spanish (words): 'Is that you, Richard?' All the while her sounds would assure me: *You are home now; come closer; inside. With us.*

'*Si*,' I'd reply.

Once more inside the house I would resume (assume) my place in the family. The sounds would dim, grow harder to hear. Once more at home, I would grow less aware of that fact. It required, however, no more than the blurt of the doorbell to alert me to listen to sounds all over again. The house would turn instantly still while my mother went to the door. I'd hear her hard English sounds. I'd wait to hear her voice return to soft-sounding Spanish, which assured me, as surely as did the clicking tongue of the lock on the door, that the stranger was gone.

Plainly, it is not healthy to hear such sounds so often. It is not healthy to distinguish public words from private sounds so easily. I remained cloistered by sounds, timid and shy in public, too dependent on voices at home. And yet it needs to be emphasized: I was an extremely happy child at home. I remember many nights when my father would come back from work, and I'd hear him call out to my mother in Spanish, sounding relieved. In Spanish, he'd sound light and free notes he never could manage in English. Some nights I'd jump up just at hearing his voice. With *mis hermanos* I would come running into the room where he was with my mother. Our laughing (so deep was the pleasure!) became screaming. Like others who know the pain of public alienation, we transformed the knowledge of our public separateness and made it consoling—the reminder of intimacy. *We are speaking now the way we never speak out in public. We are alone—together*, voices sounded, surrounded to tell me. Some nights, no one seemed willing to loosen the hold sounds had on us. At dinner, we invented new words. (Ours sounded Spanish, but made sense only to us.) We pieced together new words by taking, say, an English verb and giving it Spanish endings. My mother's instructions at bedtime would be lacquered with mock-urgent tones. Or a word like *si* would become, in several notes, able to convey added measures of feeling. Tongues explored the edges of words, especially the fat vowels. And we happily sounded that military drum roll, the twirling roar of the Spanish *r*. Family language: my family's sounds. The voices of my parents and sisters and brother. Their voices insisting: *You belong here. We are family members. Related. Special to one another. Listen!* Voices singing and sighing, rising, straining, then surging, teeming with pleasure that bursts syllables into fragments of laughter. At times it seemed there was steady quiet only when, from another room, the rustling whispers of my parents faded and I moved closer to sleep.

Supporters of bilingual education today imply that students like me miss a great deal by not being taught in their family's language. What they seem not to recognize is that, as a socially disadvantaged child, I considered Spanish to be a private language. What I needed to learn in school was that I had the right—and the obligation—to speak the public language of *los gringos*. The odd truth is that my first-grade classmates could have become bilingual, in the conventional sense of that word, more easily than I. Had they been taught (as upper-middle-class children are often taught early) a second language like Spanish or French, they could have regarded it simply as that: another public language. In my case such bilingualism could not have been so quickly achieved. What I did not believe was that I could speak a single public language.

Without question, it would have pleased me to hear my teachers address me in Spanish when I entered the classroom. I would have felt much less afraid. I would have trusted them and responded with ease. But I would have delayed—for how long postponed?—having to learn the language of public society. I would have evaded—and for how long could I have afforded to delay?—learning the great lesson of school, that I had a public identity.

Fortunately my teachers were unsentimental about their responsibility. What they understood was that I needed to speak a public language. So their voices would search me out, asking me questions. Each time I'd hear them, I'd look up in surprise to see a nun's face frowning at me. I'd mumble, not really meaning to answer. The nun would persist. 'Richard, stand up. Don't look at the floor. Speak up. Speak to the entire class, not just to me!' But I couldn't believe that the English language was mine to use. (In part, I did not want to believe it.) I continued to mumble. I resisted the teacher's demands. (Did I somehow suspect that once I learned the public language my pleasing family life would be changed?) Silent, waiting for the bell to sound, I remained dazed, diffident, afraid.

Because I wrongly imagined that English was intrinsically a public language and Spanish an intrinsically private one, I easily noted the difference between classroom language and the language of home. At school, words were directed to a general audience of listeners. ('Boys and girls.') Words were meaningfully ordered. And the point was not self-expression alone but to make oneself understood by many others. The teacher quizzed: 'Boys and girls, why do we use that word in this sentence? Could we think of a better word to use there? Would the sentence change its meaning if the words were differently arranged? And wasn't there a better way of saying much the same thing?' (I couldn't say. I wouldn't try to say.)

Three months. Five. Half a year passed. Unsmiling, ever watchful, my teachers noted my silence. They began to connect my behavior with the difficult progress my older sister and brother were making. Until one Saturday morning three nuns arrived at the house to talk to our parents. Stiffly, they sat on the blue living room sofa. From the doorway of another room, spying the visitors, I noted the incongruity—the clash of two worlds, the faces and the voices of school intruding upon the familiar setting of home. I overheard one voice gently wondering, 'Do your children speak only Spanish at home, Mrs. Rodriguez?' While another voice added, 'That Richard especially seems so timid and shy.'

That Rich-heard!

With great tact the visitors continued, 'Is it possible for you and your huband to encourage your children to practice their English when they are home?' Of course, my parents complied. What would they not do for their children's well-being? And how could they have questioned the Church's authority which those women represented. . . . The moment after the visitors left, the change was observed, '*Ahora,* speak to us *en inglés,*' my father and mother united to tell us.

At first, it seemed a kind of game. After dinner each night, the family gathered to practice 'our' English. (It was still then *inglés,* a language foreign to us, so we felt drawn as strangers to it.) Laughing, we would try to define words we could not pronounce. We played with strange English sounds, often overanglicizing our pronunciations. And we filled the smiling gaps of our sentences with familiar Spanish sounds. But that was cheating, somebody shouted. Everyone laughed. In school, meanwhile, like my brother and sister, I was required to attend a daily tutoring session. I needed a full year of special attention. I also needed my teachers to keep my attention from straying in class by calling out, *Rich-heard*—their English voices slowly prying loose my ties to my other name, its three notes, *Ri-car-do*. Most of all I needed to hear my mother and father speak to me in a moment of seriousness in broken— suddenly heartbreaking—English. The scene was inevitable: One Saturday morning I entered the kitchen where my parents were talking in Spanish. I did not realize that they were talking in Spanish however until, at the moment they saw me, I heard their voices change to speak English. Those *gringo* sounds they uttered startled me. Pushed me away. In that moment of trivial misunderstanding and profound insight, I felt my throat twisted by unsounded grief. I turned quickly and left the room. But I had no place to escape to with Spanish. (The spell was broken.) My brother and sisters were speaking English in another part of the house.

Again and again in the days following, increasingly angry, I was obliged to hear my mother and father: 'Speak to us *en inglés*.' *(Speak.)* Only then did I determine to learn classroom English. Weeks after, it happened: One day in school I raised my hand to volunteer an answer. I spoke out in a loud voice. And I did not think it remarkable when the entire class understood. That day, I moved very far from the disadvantaged child I had been only days earlier. The belief, the calming assurance that I belonged in public, had at last taken hold.

Shortly after, I stopped hearing the high and low sounds of *los gringos*. A more and more confident speaker of English, I didn't trouble to listen to *how* strangers sounded, speaking to me. And there simply were too many English-speaking people in my day for me to hear American accents anymore. Conversations quickened. Listening to persons who sounded eccentrically pitched voices, I usually noted their sounds for an initial few seconds before I concentrated on *what* they were saying. Conversations became content-full. Transparent. Hearing someone's *tone* of voice—angry or questioning or sarcastic or happy or sad—I didn't distinguish it from the words it expressed. Sound and word were thus tightly wedded. At the end of a day I was often bemused, always relieved to realize how 'silent,' though crowded with words, my day in public had been. (This public silence measured and quickened the change in my life.)

At last, seven years old, I came to believe what had been technically true since my birth: I was an American citizen.

But the special feeling of closeness at home was diminished by then. Gone was the desperate, urgent, intense feeling of being at home; rare was the experience of feeling myself individualized by family intimates. We remained a loving family, but one greatly changed. No longer so close; no longer bound tight by the pleasing and troubling knowledge of our public separateness. Neither my older brother nor sister rushed home after school anymore. Nor did I. When I arrived home there would often be neighborhood kids in the house. Or the house would be empty of sounds.

The silence at home, however, was finally more than a literal silence. Fewer words passed between parent and child, but more profound was the silence that resulted from my inattention to sounds. At about the time I no longer bothered to listen with care to the sounds of English in public, I grew careless about listening to the sounds family members made when they spoke. Most of the time I heard someone speaking at home and didn't distinguish his sounds from the words people uttered in public. I didn't even pay much attention to my parents' accented and ungrammatical speech. At least not at home. Only when I was with them in public would I grow alert to their accents. Though, even then, their sounds caused me less and less concern. For I was increasingly confident of my own public identity.

I would have been happier about my public success had I not sometimes recalled what it had been like earlier, when my family had conveyed its intimacy through a set of conveniently private sounds. Sometimes in public, hearing a stranger, I'd hark back to my past. A Mexican farmworker approached me downtown to ask directions to somewhere. '*¿Hijito . . . ?*' he said. And his voice summoned deep longing. Another time, standing beside my mother in the visiting room of a Carmelite convent, before the dense screen which rendered the nuns shadowy figures, I heard several Spanish-speaking nuns—their busy, singsong overlapping voices— assure us that yes, yes, we were remembered, all our family was remembered in their prayers. (Their voices echoed faraway family sounds.) Another day, a dark-faced old woman—her hand light on my shoulder—steadied herself against me as she boarded a bus. She murmured something I couldn't quite comprehend. Her Spanish voice came near, like the face of a never-before-seen relative in the instant before I was kissed. Her voice, like so many of the Spanish voices I'd heard in public, recalled the golden age of my youth. Hearing Spanish then, I continued to be a careful, if sad, listener to sounds. Hearing a Spanish-speaking family walking behind me, I turned to look. I smiled for an instant, before my glance found the Hispanic-looking faces of strangers in the crowd going by.

Today I hear bilingual educators say that children lose a degree of 'individuality' by becoming assimilated into public society. (Bilingual schooling was popularized in the seventies, that decade when middle-class ethnics began to resist the process of assimilation—the American melting pot.) But the bilingualists simplistically scorn the value and necessity of assimilation. They do not seem to realize that there are two ways a person is individualized. So they do not realize that while one suffers a diminished sense of *private* individuality by becoming assimilated into public society, such assimilation makes possible the achievement of *public* individuality.

The bilingualists insist that a student should be reminded of his difference from others in mass society, his heritage. But they equate mere separateness with individuality. The fact is that only in private—with intimates—is separateness from the crowd a prerequisite for individuality. (An intimate draws me apart, tells me that I am unique, unlike all others.) In public, by contrast, full individuality is achieved, paradoxically, by those who are able to consider themselves members of the crowd. Thus it happened for me: Only when I was able to think of myself as an American, no longer an alien in *gringo* society, could I seek the rights and opportunities necessary for full public individuality. The social and political advantages I enjoy as a man result from the day that I came to believe that my name, indeed, is *Rich-heard Road-ree-guess*. It is true that my public society today is often impersonal. (My public society is usually mass society.) Yet despite the anonymity of the crowd and despite the fact that the individuality I achieve in public is often tenuous—because it depends on my being one in a crowd—I celebrate the day I acquired my new name. Those middle-class ethnics who scorn assimilation seem to me filled with decadent self-pity, obsessed by the burden of public life. Dangerously, they romanticize public separateness and they trivialize the dilemma of the socially disadvantaged.

Thinking About the Text _____

1. How does Rodriguez distinguish between "private language" and "public language"?

2. Why does Rodriguez believe that it is important for bilingual children to learn the language of public society? What do they gain and/or lose in learning this language?

3. How does Rodriguez establish his ethos throughout this essay? Is his use of this rhetorical appeal effective in conveying his position on the issue of bilingual education?

Bilingual Education:
The Key to Basic Skills

ANGELO GONZALEZ

Angelo Gonzalez is affiliated with ASPIRA, an organization that promotes awareness regarding issues related to Hispanic Americans. This piece originally appeared in the New York Times Educational Supplement and looks closely at the positive effects of bilingual education.

If we accept that a child cannot learn unless taught through the language he speaks and understands; that a child who does not speak or understand English must fall behind when English is the dominant medium of instruction; that one needs to learn English so as to be able to participate in an English-speaking society; that self-esteem and motivation are necessary for effective learning; that rejection of a child's native language and culture is detrimental to the learning process: then any necessary effective educational program for limited or no English-speaking ability must incorporate the following:

- Language arts and comprehensive reading programs taught in the child's native language.

- Curriculum content areas taught in the native language to further comprehension and academic achievement.

- Intensive instruction in English.

- Use of materials sensitive to and reflecting the culture of children within the program.

Most Important Goal

The mastery of basic reading skills is the most important goal in primary education since reading is the basis for much of all subsequent learning. Ordinarily, these skills are learned at home. But where beginning reading is taught in English, only the English-speaking child profits from these early acquired skills that are prerequisites to successful reading development. Reading programs taught in English to children with Spanish as a first language waste their acquired linguistic attributes and also impede learning by forcing them to absorb skills of reading simultaneously with a new language.

Both local and national research data provide ample evidence for the efficacy of well-implemented programs. The New York City Board of Education Report on Bilingual Pupil Services for 1982–83 indicated that in all areas of the curriculum—English, Spanish and mathematics—and at all grade levels, students demonstrated statistically significant gains in tests of reading in English and Spanish and in math. In all but two of the programs reviewed, the attendance rates of students in the program, ranging from 86 to 94 percent, were higher than those of the general school population. Similar higher attendance rates were found among students in high school bilingual programs.

At Yale University, Kenji Hakuta, a linguist, reported recently on a study of working-class Hispanic students in the New Haven bilingual program. He found that children who were the most bilingual, that is, who developed English without the loss of Spanish, were brighter in both verbal and nonverbal tests. Over time, there was an increasing correlation between English and Spanish—a finding that clearly contradicts the charge that teaching in the home language is detrimental to English. Rather the two languages are interdependent within the bilingual child, reinforcing each other.

Essential Contribution

As Jim Cummins of the Ontario Institute for Studies in Education has argued, the use and development of the native language makes an essential contribution to the development of minority children's subject-matter knowledge and academic learning potential. In fact, at least three national data bases—the National Assessment of Educational Progress, National Center for Educational Statistics-High School and Beyond Studies, and the Survey of Income and Education—suggest that there are long-term positive effects among high school students who have participated in bilingual-education programs. These students are achieving higher scores on tests of verbal and mathematics skills.

These and similar findings buttress the argument stated persuasively in the recent joint recommendation of the Academy for Educational Development and the Hazen Foundation, namely, that America needs to become a more multilingual nation and children who speak a non-English language are a national resource to be nurtured in school.

Unfortunately, the present Administration's educational policies would seem to be leading us in the opposite direction. Under the guise of protecting the common language of public life in the United States, William J. Bennett, the Secretary of Education, unleashed a frontal attack on bilingual education. In a major policy address, he engaged in rhetorical distortions about the nature and effectiveness of bilingual programs, pointing only to unnamed negative research findings to justify the Administration's retrenchment efforts.

Arguing for the need to give local school districts greater flexibility in determining appropriate methodologies in serving limited-English proficient students, Mr. Bennett fails to realize that, in fact, districts serving large numbers of language-minority students, as is the case in New York City, do have that flexibility. Left to their own devices in implementing legal mandates, many school districts have performed poorly at providing services to all entitled language-minority students.

A Harsh Reality

The harsh reality in New York City for language-minority students was documented comprehensively last month by the Educational Priorities Panel. The panel's findings revealed that of the 113,831 students identified as being limited in English proficiency, as many as 44,000 entitled students are not receiving any bilingual services. The issue at hand is, therefore, not one of choice but rather violation of the rights of almost 40 percent of language-minority children to equal educational opportunity. In light of these findings the Reagan Administration's recent statements only serve to exacerbate existing inequities in the American educational system for linguistic-minority children. Rather than adding fuel to a misguided debate, the Administration would serve these children best by insuring the full funding of the 1984 Bilingual Education Reauthorization Act as passed by the Congress.

Thinking About the Text _____

1. Explain the structure of this essay. What techniques does the author use to make that structure apparent?

2. How is an appeal to logos, or logic, employed in this argument? Is this an effective choice, and does this choice make the argument a compelling one?

3. In looking at style, is this essay written at a formal or informal level? How does the style of this piece compare to the style used by Rodriguez and others?

Section 3

Construction of Social Reality

We are all members of a larger society. The United States, for example, can be considered a society of individuals, groups, communities, and cultures who interact with each other on a more or less frequent basis. We talk about the social realities we are faced with, about what it means to live in the United States or in other countries and to be a member of a majority or minority group. And similar to constructing our communities and constructing language, we also construct social reality to fit our world views and perspectives. bell hooks, in "A Revolution of Values: The Promise of Multicultural Change," introduces us to a social reality based in the idea of freedom and justice for all people, but still floundering to find a way to use these ideas in everyday interactions. Dinesh D'Souza, in "The Visigoths in Tweed," opposes hooks' argument for multiculturalism and laments the loss of Western learning in favor of multiculturalism. Leslie Marmon Silko points out in "The Border Patrol State" that the United States constructs the identity of undocumented immigrants by calling them "illegal aliens," dehumanizing and demonizing them. The following two articles, "Body Ritual Among the Nacirema," by Horace M. Miner, and "Shakespeare in the Bush," by Laura Bohannan, present interesting perspectives on the social realties of two cultural groups. The final selection, Ralph Ellison's "Prologue" from *Invisible Man* is an additional manifestation of social realities that are not based on freedom and justice for all but that are mired in racist ideologies which are still a part of society's values.

When you read this section, think about what your social reality is. Also think about how your social reality shifts in different situations, and how you project your own ideas of justice, freedom, equality, brother/sisterhood on those around you.

- Ask a friend or family member what they consider to be "success" or "failure." Compare their ideas with your own. Why are your ideas similar to theirs? Why are your ideas different?

- Think about a time when you lived in an environment/community where you felt out of place. What strategies did you use to become more familiar with your surroundings? How did your ideas about the community change over time?

- Look closely at these lines:

Give me your tired, your poor,
Your huddled masses yearning to breathe free,
The wretched refuse of your teeming shore.
Send these, the homeless, tempest-tossed to me.
I lift my lamp beside the golden door.

What are the promises made in these lines? Based on your experiences, have these promises come true for immigrants to the United States?

A Revolution of Values: The Promise of Multicultural Change

BELL HOOKS

bell hooks was born Gloria Jean Watkins in 1952 in Hopkinsville, Kentucky. hooks chose as a pen name the lower case version of her great-grandmother's name, the forthright Bell Hooks. Her list of works include *Ain't I a Woman* (1984), *Talking Back* (1988), and *Teaching to Transgress* (1994). In 1991, hooks was presented the Before Columbus Foundation's American Book Award for *Yearning* (1990). Most recently she has published *Communion: Female Search for Love* (2002). In the following essay hooks examines the role of cultural diversity in education and suggests a radical pedagogical change.

Two summers ago I attended my twentieth high school reunion. It was a last-minute decision. I had just finished a new book. Whenever I finish a work, I always feel lost, as though a steady anchor has been taken away and there is no sure ground under my feet. During the time between ending one project and beginning another, I always have a crisis of meaning. I begin to wonder what my life is all about and what I have been put on this earth to do. It is as though immersed in a project I lose all sense of myself and must then, when the work is done, rediscover who I am and where I am going. When I heard that the reunion was happening, it seemed just the experience to bring me back to myself, to help in the process of rediscovery. Never having attended any of the past reunions, I did not know what to expect. I did know that this one would be different. For the first time we were about to have a racially integrated reunion. In past years, reunions had always been segregated. White folks had their reunion on their side of town and black folks had a separate reunion.

None of us was sure what an integrated reunion would be like. Those periods in our adolescent lives of racial desegregation had been full of hostility, rage, conflict, and loss. We black kids had been angry that we had to leave our beloved all-black high school, Crispus Attucks, and be bussed halfway cross town to integrate white schools. We had to make the journey and thus bear the responsibility of making desegregation a reality. We had to give up the familiar and enter a world that seemed cold and strange, not our world, not our school. We were certainly on the margin, no longer at the center, and it hurt. It was such an unhappy time. I still remember my rage that we had to awaken an hour early so that we could be bussed to school before the white students arrived. We were made to sit in the gymnasium and wait. It was believed that this practice would prevent outbreaks of conflict and hostility since it removed the possibility of social contact before classes began. Yet, once again, the burden of this transition was placed on us. The white school was desegregated, but in the classroom, in the cafeteria, and in most social spaces racial apartheid prevailed. Black and white students who considered ourselves progressive rebelled against the unspoken racial taboos meant to sustain white supremacy and racial apartheid even in the face of desegregation. The white folks never seemed to understand that our parents were no more eager for us to socialize with them than they were to socialize with us. Those of us who wanted to make racial equality a reality in every area of our life were threats to the social order. We were proud of ourselves, proud of our willingness to transgress the rules, proud to be courageous.

Part of a small integrated clique of smart kids who considered ourselves "artists," we believed we were destined to create outlaw culture where we would live as Bohemians forever free; we were certain of our radicalness. Days before the reunion, I was overwhelmed by memories and shocked to discover that our gestures of defiance had been nowhere near as daring as they had seemed at the time. Mostly, they were acts of resistance that did not truly challenge the status quo. One of my best buddies during that time was white and male. He had an old gray Volvo that I loved to ride in. Every now and then he would give me a ride home from school if I missed the bus—an action which angered and disturbed those who saw us. Friendship across racial lines was bad enough, but across gender it was unheard of and dangerous. (One day, we found out just how dangerous when grown white men in a car tried to run us off the road.) Ken's parents were religious. Their faith compelled them to live out a belief in racial justice. They were among the first white folks in our community to invite black folks to come to their house, to eat at their table, to worship together with them. As one of Ken's best buddies, I was welcome in their house. After hours of discussion and debate about possible dangers, my parents agreed that I could go there for a meal. It was my first time eating together with white people. I was 16 years old. I felt then as though we were making history, that we were living the dream of democracy, creating a culture where equality, love, justice, and peace would shape America's destiny.

After graduation, I lost touch with Ken even though he always had a warm place in my memory. I thought of him when meeting and interacting with liberal white folks who believed that having a black friend meant that they were not racist, who sincerely believed that they were doing us a favor by extending offers of friendly contact for which they felt they should be rewarded. I thought of him during years of watching white folks play at unlearning racism but walking away when they encountered obstacles, rejection, conflict, pain. Our high school friendship had been forged not because we were black and white but because we shared a similar take on reality. Racial difference meant that we had to struggle to claim the integrity of that bonding. We had no illusions. We knew there would be obstacles, conflict, and pain. In white supremacist capitalist patriarchy—words we never used then—we knew we would have to pay a price for this friendship, that we would need to possess the courage to stand up for our belief in democracy, in racial justice, in the transformative power of love. We valued the bond between us enough to meet the challenge.

Days before the reunion, remembering the sweetness of that friendship, I felt humbled by the knowledge of what we give up when we are young, believing that we will find something just as good or better someday, only to discover that not to be so. I wondered just how it could be that Ken and I had ever lost contact with one another. Along the way I had not found white folks who understood the depth and complexity of racial injustice, and who were as willing to practice the art of living a nonracist life, as folks were then. In my adult life I have seen few white folks who are really willing to go the distance to create a world of racial equality—white folks willing to take risks, to be courageous, to live against the grain. I went to the reunion hoping that I would have a chance to see Ken face-to-face, to tell him how much I cherished all that we had shared, to tell him—in words which I never dared to say to any white person back then—simply that I loved him.

Remembering this past, I am most struck by our passionate commitment to a vision of social transformation rooted in the fundamental belief in a radically democratic idea of freedom and justice for all. Our notions of social change were not fancy. There was no elaborate postmodern political theory shaping our actions. We were simply trying to change the way we went about our everyday lives so that our values and habits of being would reflect our commitment to freedom. Our major concern then was ending racism. Today, as I witness the rise in white supremacy, the growing social and economic apartheid that separates white and black, the haves and the have-nots, men and women, I have placed alongside the struggle to end racism a commitment to ending sexism and sexist oppression, to eradicating systems of class exploitation. Aware that we are living in a culture of domination, I ask myself now, as I did more than twenty years ago, what values and habits of being reflect my/our commitment to freedom.

In retrospect, I see that in the last twenty years I have encountered many folks who say they are committed to freedom and justice for all even though the way they live, the values and habits of being they institutionalize daily, in public and private rituals, help maintain the culture of domination, help create an unfree world. In the book *Where Do We Go From Here? Chaos or Community*, Martin Luther King, Jr., told the citizens of this nation, with prophetic insight, that we would be unable to go forward if we did not experience a "true revolution of values." He assured us that

> the stability of the large world house which is ours will involve a revolution of values to accompany the scientific and freedom revolutions engulfing the earth. We must rapidly begin the shift from a "thing"-oriented society to a "person"-oriented society. When machines and computers, profit motives and property rights are considered more important than people, the giant triplets of racism, materialism and militarism are incapable of being conquered. A civilization can flounder as readily in the face of moral and spiritual bankruptcy as it can through financial bankruptcy.

Today, we live in the midst of that floundering. We live in chaos, uncertain about the possibility of building and sustaining community. The public figures who speak the most to us about a return to old-fashioned values embody the evils King describes. They are most committed to maintaining systems of domination—racism, sexism, class exploitation, and imperialism. They promote a perverse vision of freedom that makes it synonymous with materialism. They teach us to believe that domination is "natural," that it is right for the strong to rule over the weak, the powerful over the powerless. What amazes me is that so many people claim not to embrace these values and yet our collective rejection of them cannot be complete since they prevail in our daily lives.

These days, I am compelled to consider what forces keep us from moving forward, from having that revolution of values that would enable us to live differently. King taught us to understand that if "we are to have peace on earth" that "our loyalties must transcend our race, our tribe, our class, and our nation." Long before the word "multiculturalism" became fashionable, he encouraged us to "develop a world perspective." Yet, what we are witnessing today in our everyday life is not an eagerness on the part of neighbors and strangers to develop a world perspective but a return to narrow nationalism, isolationism, and xenophobia. These shifts are usually explained in New Right and neoconservative terms as attempts to bring order to the chaos, to return to an (idealized) past. The notion of family evoked in these discussions is one in which sexist roles are upheld as stabilizing traditions. Nor surprisingly, this vision of family life is coupled with a notion of security that suggests we are always most safe with people of our same group, race, class, religion, and so on. No matter how many statistics on domestic violence, homicide, rape, and child abuse indicate that, in fact, the idealized patriarchal family is not a "safe" space, that those of us who experience any form of assault are more likely to be victimized by those who are like us rather than by some mysterious strange outsiders, these conservative myths persist. It is apparent that one of the primary reasons we have not experienced a revolution of values is that a culture of domination necessarily promotes addiction to lying and denial.

That lying takes the presumably innocent form of many white people (and even some black folks) suggesting that racism does not exist anymore, and that conditions of social equality are solidly in place that would enable any black person who works hard to achieve economic self-sufficiency. Forget about the fact that capitalism requires the existence of a mass underclass of surplus labor. Lying takes the form of mass media creating the myth that the feminist movement has completely transformed society, so much so that the politics of patriarchal power have been inverted and that men, particularly white men, just like emasculated black men, have become the victims of dominating women. So, it goes, all men (especially black men) must pull together (as in the Clarence Thomas hearings) to support and reaffirm patriarchal domination. Add to this the widely held assumptions that blacks, other minorities, and white women are taking jobs from white men, and that people are poor and unemployed because they want to be, and it becomes most evident that part of our contemporary crisis is created by a lack of meaningful access to truth. That is to say, individuals are not just presented untruths, but are told them in a manner that enables most effective communication. When this collective cultural consumption of and attachment to misinformation is coupled with the layers of lying individuals do in their personal lives, our capacity to face reality is severely diminished as is our will to intervene and change unjust circumstances.

If we examine critically the traditional role of the university in the pursuit of truth and the sharing of knowledge and information, it is painfully clear that biases that uphold and maintain white supremacy, imperialism, sexism, and racism have distorted education so that it is no longer about the practice of freedom. The call for a recognition of cultural diversity, a rethinking of ways of knowing, a deconstruction of old epistemologies, and the concomitant demand that there be a transformation in our classrooms, in how we teach and what we teach, has been a necessary revolution—one that seeks to restore life to a corrupt and dying academy.

When everyone first began to speak about cultural diversity, it was exciting. For those of us on the margins (people of color, folks from working class backgrounds, gays, and lesbians, and so on) who had always felt ambivalent about our presence in institutions where knowledge was shared in ways that reinscribed colonialism and domination, it was thrilling to think that the vision of justice and democracy that was at the very heart of the civil rights movement would be realized in the academy. At last, there was the possibility of a learning community, a place where difference could be acknowledged, where we would finally all understand, accept, and affirm that our ways of knowing are forged in history and relations of power. Finally, we were all going to break through collective academic denial and acknowledge that the education most of us had received and were giving was not and is never politically neutral. Though it was evident that change would not be immediate, there was tremendous hope that this process we had set in motion would lead to a fulfillment of the dream of education as the practice of freedom.

Many of our colleagues were initially reluctant participants in this change. Many folks found that as they tried to respect "cultural diversity" they had to confront the limitations of their training and knowledge, as well as a possible loss of "authority." Indeed, exposing certain truths and biases in the classroom often created chaos and confusion. The idea that the classroom should always be a "safe," harmonious place was challenged. It was hard for individuals to fully grasp the idea that recognition of difference might also require of us a willingness to see the classroom change, to allow for shifts in relations between students. A lot of people panicked. What they saw happening was not the comforting "melting pot" idea of cultural diversity, the rainbow coalition where we would all be grouped together in our difference, but everyone wearing the same have-a-nice-day smile. This was the stuff of colonizing fantasy, a perversion of the progressive vision of cultural diversity. Critiquing this longing in a recent interview, "Critical Multiculturalism and Democratic Schooling" (in the *International Journal of Educational Reform)*, Peter McLaren asserted:

> *Diversity that somehow constitutes itself as a harmonious ensemble of benign cultural spheres is a conservative and liberal model of multiculturalism that, in my mind, deserves to be jettisoned because, when we try to make culture an undisturbed space of harmony and agreement where social relations exist within cultural forms of uninterrupted accords we subscribe to a form of social amnesia in which we forget that all knowledge is forged in histories that are played out in the field of social antagonisms.*

Many professors lacked strategies to deal with antagonisms in the classroom. When this fear joined with the refusal to change that characterized the stance of an old (predominantly white male) guard it created a space for disempowered collective backlash.

All of a sudden, professors who had taken issues of multiculturalism and cultural diversity seriously were backtracking, expressing doubts, casting votes in directions that would restore biased traditions or prohibit changes in faculty and curricula that were to bring diversity of representation and perspective. Joining forces with the old guard, previously open professors condoned tactics (ostracization, belittlement, and so on) used by senior colleagues to dissuade junior faculty members from making paradigm shifts that would lead to change. In one of my Toni Morrison seminars, as we went around our circle voicing critical reflections on Morrison's language, a sort of classically white, blondish, J. Crew coed shared that one of her other English professors, an older white man (whose name none of us wanted her to mention), confided that he was so pleased to find a student still interested in reading literature—words—the language of texts and "not that race and gender stuff." Somewhat amused by the assumption he had made about her, she was disturbed by his conviction that conventional ways of critically approaching a novel could not coexist in classrooms that also offered new perspectives.

I then shared with the class my experience of being at a Halloween party. A new white male colleague, with whom I was chatting for the first time, went on a tirade at the mere mention of my Toni Morrison seminar, emphasizing that *Song of Solomon* was a weak rewrite of Hemingway's *For Whom the Bell Tolls.* Passionately full of disgust for Morrison he, being a Hemingway scholar, seemed to be sharing the often-heard concern that black women writers/thinkers are just poor imitations of "great" white men. Not wanting at that moment to launch into Unlearning Colonialism, Divesting of Racism and Sexism 101, I opted for the strategy taught to me by that in-denial-of-institutionalized-patriarchy, self-help book *Women Who Love Too Much.* I just said, "Oh!" Later, I assured him that I would read *For Whom the Bell Tolls* again to see if I would make the same connection. Both these seemingly trivial incidents reveal how deep-seated is the fear that any de-centering of Western civilizations, of the white male canon, is really an act of cultural genocide.

Some folks think that everyone who supports cultural diversity wants to replace one dictatorship of knowing with another, changing one set way of thinking for another. This is perhaps the gravest misperception of cultural diversity. Even though there are those overly zealous among us who hope to replace one set of absolutes with another, simply changing content, this perspective does not accurately represent progressive visions of the way commitment to cultural diversity can constructively transform the academy. In all cultural revolutions there are periods of chaos and confusion, times when grave mistakes are made. If we fear mistakes, doing things wrongly, constantly evaluating ourselves, we will never make the academy a culturally diverse place where scholars and the curricula address every dimension of that difference.

As backlash swells, as budgets are cut, as jobs become even more scarce, many of the few progressive interventions that were made to change the academy, to create an open climate for cultural diversity are in danger of being undermined or eliminated. These threats should not be ignored. Nor should our collective commitment to cultural diversity change because we have not yet devised and implemented perfect strategies for them. To create a culturally diverse academy, we must commit ourselves fully. Learning from other movements for social change, from civil rights and feminist liberation efforts, we must accept the protracted nature of our struggle and be willing to remain both patient and vigilant. To commit ourselves to the work of transforming the academy so that it will be a place where cultural diversity informs every aspect of our learning, we must embrace struggle and sacrifice. We cannot be easily discouraged. We cannot despair when there is conflict. Our solidarity must be affirmed by shared belief in a spirit of intellectual openness that celebrates diversity, welcomes dissent, and rejoices in collective dedication to truth.

Drawing strength from the life and work of Martin Luther King, Jr., I am often reminded of his profound inner struggle when he felt called by his religious beliefs to oppose the war in Vietnam. Fearful of alienating conservative bourgeois supporters, and of alienating the black church, King meditated on a passage from Romans, chapter 12, verse 2, which reminded him of the necessity of dissent, challenge and change: "Be not conformed to this world but be ye transformed by the renewal of your minds." All of us in the academy and in the culture as a whole are called to renew our minds if we are to transform educational institutions—and society—so that the way we live, teach, and work can reflect our joy in cultural diversity, our passion for justice, and our love of freedom.

Thinking About the Text _____

1. How does recalling her high school reunion situate hooks as an authority on education? Is the strategy effective?

2. What does hooks believe about the integration of cultural diversity into higher education? How does she support her argument? What does she think many of her colleagues believe? How has "antagonism in the classroom" affected such debates?

3. Why does hooks invoke Martin Luther King, Jr. in her essay? How does this affect her position?

The Visigoths in Tweed

DINESH D'SOUZA

Dinesh D'Souza was born in 1961 in Bombay, India. He immigrated to the United States in 1978 and graduated from Dartmouth College in 1983. D'Souza has worked as editor of several conservative magazines, including *Dartmouth Review, Prospect,* and *Policy Review.* He has also worked as an assistant domestic policy advisor in the Ronald Reagan administration. D'Souza has published several books on conservative issues, including *Illiberal Education: The Politics of Race and Sex on Campus* (1991) and, in collaboration with Alvin J. Schmidt, *The Menace of Multiculturalism: Trojan Horse in America* (1997).

"I am a male wasp who attended and succeeded at Choate (preparatory) school, Yale College, Yale Law School, and Princeton Graduate School. Slowly but surely, however, my life-long habit of looking, listening, feeling, and thinking as honestly as possible has led me to see that white, male-dominated, western European culture is the most destructive phenomenon in the known history of the planet.

"[This Western culture] is deeply hateful of life and committed to death; therefore, it is moving rapidly toward the destruction of itself and most other life forms on earth. And truly it deserves to die. . . . We have to face our own individual and collective responsibility for what is happening—our greed, brutality, indifference, militarism, racism, sexism, blindness. . . . Meanwhile, everything we have put into motion continues to endanger us more every day."

This bizarre outpouring, so reminiscent of the "confessions" from victims of Stalin's show trials, appeared in a letter to *Mother Jones* magazine and was written by a graduate of some of our finest schools. But the truth is that the speaker's anguish came not from any balanced assessment but as a consequence of exposure to the propaganda of the new barbarians who have captured the humanities, law, and social science departments of so many of our universities. It should come as no surprise that many sensitive young Americans reject the system that has nurtured them. At Duke University, according to the *Wall Street Journal*, professor Frank Lentricchia in his English course shows the movie *The Godfather* to teach his students that organized crime is "a metaphor for American business as usual."

Yes, a student can still get an excellent education—among the best in the world—in computer technology and the hard sciences at American universities. But liberal arts students, including those attending Ivy League schools, are very likely to be exposed to an attempted brainwashing that deprecates Western learning and exalts a neo-Marxist ideology promoted in the name of multiculturalism. Even students who choose hard sciences must often take required courses in the humanities, where they are almost certain to be inundated with an anti-Western, anticapitalist view of the world.

Each year American society invests $160 billion in higher education, more per student than any nation in the world except Denmark. A full 45 percent of this money comes from the federal, state, and local governments. No one can say we are starving higher education. But what are we getting for our money, at least so far as the liberal arts are concerned?

A fair question? It might seem so, but in university circles it is considered impolite because it presumes that higher education must be accountable to the society that supports it. Many academics think of universities as intellectual enclaves, insulated from the vulgar capitalism of the larger culture.

Yet, since the academics constantly ask for more money, it seems hardly unreasonable to ask what they are doing with it. Honest answers are rarely forthcoming. The general public sometimes gets a whiff of what is going on—as when Stanford alters its core curriculum in the classics of Western civilization—but it knows very little of the systematic and comprehensive change sweeping higher education.

An academic and cultural revolution has overtaken most of our 3,535 colleges and universities. It's a revolution to which most Americans have paid little attention. It is a revolution imposed upon the students by a university elite, not one voted upon or even discussed by the society at large. It amounts, according to University of Wisconsin-Madison Chancellor Donna Shalala, to "a basic transformation of American higher education in the name of multiculturalism and diversity."

The central thrust of this "basic transformation" involves replacing traditional core curricula—consisting of the great works of Western culture—with curricula flavored by minority, female, and Third World authors.

Here's a sample of the viewpoint represented by the new curriculum. Becky Thompson, a sociology and women's studies professor, in a teaching manual distributed by the American Sociological Association, writes: "I begin my course with the basic feminist principle that in a racist, classist, and sexist society we have all swallowed oppressive ways of being, whether intentionally or not. Specifically, this means that it is not open to debate whether a white student is racist or a male student is sexist. He/she simply is."

Professors at several colleges who have resisted these regnant dogmas about race and gender have found themselves the object of denunciation and even university sanctions. Donald

Kagan, dean of Yale College, says: "I was a student during the days of Joseph McCarthy, and there is less freedom now than there was then."

As in the McCarthy period, a particular group of activists has cowed the authorities and bent them to its will. After activists forcibly occupied his office, President Lattie Coor of the University of Vermont explained how he came to sign a sixteen-point agreement establishing, among other things, minority faculty hiring quotas. "When it became clear that the minority students with whom I had been discussing these issues wished to pursue negotiations *in the context of occupied offices* . . . I agreed to enter negotiations." As frequently happens in such cases, Coor's "negotiations" ended in a rapid capitulation by the university authorities.

At Harvard, historian Stephan Thernstrom was harangued by student activists and accused of insensitivity and bigotry. What was his crime? His course included a reading from the journals of slave owners, and his textbook gave a reasonable definition of affirmative action as "preferential treatment" for minorities. At the University of Michigan, renowned demographer Reynolds Farley was assailed in the college press for criticizing the excesses of Marcus Garvey and Malcolm X; yet the administration did not publicly come to his defense.

University leaders argue that the revolution suggested by these examples is necessary because young Americans must be taught to live in and govern a multiracial and multicultural society. Immigration from Asia and Latin America, combined with relatively high minority birth rates, is changing the complexion of America. Consequently, in the words of University of Michigan President James Duderstadt, universities must "create a model of how a more diverse and pluralistic community can work for our society."

No controversy, of course, about benign goals such as pluralism or diversity, but there is plenty of controversy about how these goals are being pursued. Although there is no longer a Western core curriculum at Mount Holyoke or Dartmouth, students at those schools must take a course in non-Western or Third World culture. Berkeley and the University of Wisconsin now insist that every undergraduate enroll in ethnic studies, making this virtually the only compulsory course at those schools.

If American students were truly exposed to the richest elements of other cultures, this could be a broadening and useful experience. A study of Chinese philosophers such as Confucius or Mencius would enrich students' understanding of how different peoples order their lives, thus giving a greater sense of purpose to their own. Most likely, a taste of Indian poetry such as Rabindranath Tagore's *Gitanjali* would increase the interest of materially minded young people in the domain of the spirit. An introduction to Middle Eastern history would prepare the leaders of tomorrow to deal with the mounting challenge of Islamic culture. It would profit students to study the rise of capitalism in the Far East.

But the claims of the academic multiculturalists are largely phony. They pay little attention to the Asian or Latin American classics. Rather, the non-Western or multicultural curriculum reflects a different agenda. At Stanford, for example, Homer, Plato, Dante, Machiavelli, and Locke are increasingly scarce. But often their replacements are not non-Western classics. Instead the students are offered exotic topics such as popular religion and healing in Peru, Rastafarian poetry, and Andean music.

What do students learn about the world from the books they are required to read under the new multicultural rubric? At Stanford one of the non-Western works assigned is *I, Rigoberta Menchú*, subtitled "An Indian Woman in Guatemala."

The book is hardly a non-Western classic. Published in 1983, *I, Rigoberta Menchú* is the story of a young woman who is said to be a representative voice of the indigenous peasantry. Representative of Guatemalan Indian culture? In fact, Rigoberta met the Venezuelan feminist to whom she narrates this story at a socialist conference in Paris, where, presumably, very few of the Third World's poor travel. Moreover, Rigoberta's political consciousness includes the adoption of such politically correct causes as feminism, homosexual rights, socialism, and Marxism. By the middle of the book she is discoursing on "bourgeois youths" and "Molotov cocktails," not the usual terminology of Indian peasants. One chapter is titled "Rigoberta Renounces Marriage and Motherhood," a norm that her tribe could not have adopted and survived.

If Rigoberta does not represent the convictions and aspirations of Guatemalan peasants, what is the source of her importance and appeal? The answer is that Rigoberta seems to provide independent Third World corroboration for Western left-wing passions and prejudices. She is a mouthpiece for a sophisticated neo-Marxist critique of Western society, all the more powerful because it seems to issue not from some embittered American academic but from a Third World native. For professors nourished on the political activism of the late 1960s and early 1970s, texts such as *I, Rigoberta Menchú* offer a welcome opportunity to attack capitalism and Western society in general in the name of teaching students about the developing world.

We learn in the introduction of *I, Rigoberta Menchú* that Rigoberta is a quadruple victim. As a person of color, she has suffered racism. As a woman, she has endured sexism. She lives in South America, which is—of course—a victim of North American colonialism. She is also an Indian, victimized by Latino culture within Latin America.

One of the most widely used textbooks in so-called multicultural courses is *Multi-Cultural Literacy*, published by Graywolf Press in St. Paul, Minnesota. The book ignores the *The Tale of Genji*, the Upanishads and Vedas, the Koran and Islamic commentaries. It also ignores such brilliant contemporary authors as Jorge Luis Borges, V.S. Naipaul, Octavio Paz, Naguib Mahfonz, and Wole Soyinka. Instead it offers thirteen essays of protest, including Michele Wallace's autobiographical "Invisibility Blues" and Paula Gunn Allen's "Who Is Your Mother? The Red Roots of White Feminism."

One student I spoke with at Duke University said he would not study *Paradise Lost* because John Milton was a Eurocentric white male sexist. At the University of Michigan, a young black woman who had converted to Islam refused to believe that the prophet Muhammad owned slaves and practiced polygamy. She said she had taken courses on cultural diversity and the courses hadn't taught her that.

One of the highlights of this debate on the American campus was a passionate statement delivered a few years ago by Stanford undergraduate William King, president of the Black Student Union, who argued the benefits of the new multicultural curriculum before the faculty senate of the university. Under the old system, he said, "I was never taught . . . the fact that

Socrates, Herodotus, Pythagoras, and Solon studied in Egypt and acknowledged that much of their knowledge of astronomy, geometry, medicine, and building came from the African civilization in and around Egypt. [I was never taught] that the Hippocratic oath acknowledges the Greeks' 'father of medicine,' Imhotep, a black Egyptian pharaoh whom they called Aesculapius. . . . I was never informed when it was found that the 'very dark and wooly haired' Moors in Spain preserved, expanded, and reintroduced the classical knowledge that the Greeks had collected, which led to the 'renaissance.' . . . I read the Bible without knowing Saint Augustine looked black like me, that the Ten Commandments were almost direct copies from the 147 Negative Confessions of Egyptian initiates. . . . I didn't learn Toussaint L'Ouverture's defeat of Napoleon in Haiti directly influenced the French Revolution, or that the Iroquois Indians in America had a representative democracy which served as a model for the American system."

This statement drew wild applause and was widely quoted. The only trouble is that much of it is untrue. There is no evidence that Socrates, Pythagoras, Herodotus, and Solon studied in Egypt, although Herodotus may have traveled there. Saint Augustine was born in North Africa, but his skin color is unknown, and in any case he could not have been mentioned in the Bible; he was born over 350 years after Christ. Viewing King's speech at my request, Bernard Lewis, an expert on Islamic and Middle Eastern culture at Princeton, described it as "a few scraps of truth amidst a great deal of nonsense."

Why does multicultural education, in practice, gravitate toward such myths and half-truths? To find out why, it is necessary to explore the complex web of connections that the academic revolution generates among admissions policies, life on campus, and the curriculum.

American universities typically begin with the premise that in a democratic and increasingly diverse society the composition of their classes should reflect the ethnic distribution of the general population. Many schools officially seek "proportional representation," in which the percentage of applicants admitted from various racial groups roughly approximates the ratio of those groups in society at large.

Thus universities routinely admit black, Hispanic, and American Indian candidates over better-qualified white and Asian American applicants. As a result of zealously pursued affirmative action programs, many selective colleges admit minority students who find it extremely difficult to meet demanding academic standards and to compete with the rest of the class. This fact is reflected in the dropout rates of blacks and Hispanics, which are more than 50 percent higher than those of whites and Asians. At Berkeley a study of students admitted on a preferential basis between 1978 and 1982 concluded that nearly 70 percent failed to graduate within five years.

For affirmative action students who stay on campus, a common strategy of dealing with the pressures of university life is to enroll in a distinctive minority organization. Among such organizations at Cornell University are Lesbian, Gay & Bisexual Coalition; La Asociacion Latina; National Society of Black Engineers; Society of Minority Hoteliers; Black Students United; and Simba Washanga.

Although the university brochures at Cornell and elsewhere continue to praise integration and close interaction among students from different backgrounds, the policies practiced at these schools actually encourage segregation. Stanford, for example, has "ethnic theme houses" such as the African house called Ujaama. And President Donald Kennedy has said that one of his educational objectives is to "support and strengthen ethnic theme houses." Such houses make it easier for some minority students to feel comfortable but help to create a kind of academic apartheid.

The University of Pennsylvania has funded a black yearbook, even though only 6 percent of the student body is black and all other groups appeared in the general yearbook. Vassar, Dartmouth, and the University of Illinois have allowed separate graduation activities and ceremonies for minority students. California State University at Sacramento has just established an official "college within a college" for blacks.

Overt racism is relatively rare at most campuses, yet minorities are told that bigotry operates in subtle forms such as baleful looks, uncorrected stereotypes, and "institutional racism"—defined as the underrepresentation of blacks and Hispanics among university trustees, administrators, and faculty.

Other groups such as feminists and homosexuals typically get into the game, claiming their own varieties of victim status. As Harvard political scientist Harvey Mansfield bluntly puts it, "White students must admit their guilt so that minority students do not have to admit their incapacity."

Even though universities regularly accede to the political demands of victim groups, their appeasement gestures do not help black and Hispanic students get a genuine liberal arts education. They do the opposite, giving the apologists of the new academic orthodoxy a convenient excuse when students admitted on a preferential basis fail to meet academic standards. At this point student activists and administrators often blame the curriculum. They argue that it reflects a "white male perspective" that systematically depreciates the views and achievements of other cultures, minorities, women, and homosexuals.

With this argument, many minority students can now explain why they had such a hard time with Milton in the English department, Publius in political science, and Heisenberg in physics. Those men reflected white male aesthetics, philosophy, and science. Obviously, non-white students would fare much better if the university created more black or Latino or Third World courses, the argument goes. This epiphany leads to a spate of demands: Abolish the Western classics, establish new departments such as Afro-American Studies and Women's Studies, hire minority faculty to offer distinctive black and Hispanic "perspectives."

Multicultural or non-Western education on campus frequently glamorizes Third World cultures and omits inconvenient facts about them. In fact, several non-Western cultures are caste-based or tribal, and often disregard norms of racial equality. In many of them feminism is virtually nonexistent, as indicated by such practices as dowries, widow-burning, and genital mutilation; and homosexuality is sometimes regarded as a crime or mental disorder requiring punishment. These nasty aspects of the non-Western cultures are rarely mentioned in the new courses. Indeed, Bernard Lewis of Princeton argues that while slavery and the subjugation of women have been practiced by all known civilizations, the West at least has an active and effective movement for the abolition of such evils.

Who is behind this academic revolution, this contrived multiculturalism? The new curriculum directly serves the purposes of a newly ascendant generation of young professors, weaned in the protest culture of the late 1960s and early 1970s. In a frank comment, Jay Parini, who teaches English at Middlebury College, writes "After the Vietnam War, a lot of us didn't just crawl back into our library cubicles. We stepped into academic positions. . . . Now we have tenure, and the work of reshaping the university has begun in earnest."

The goal that Parini and others like him pursue is the transformation of the college classroom from a place of learning to a laboratory of indoctrination for social change. Not long ago most colleges required that students learn the basics of the physical sciences and mathematics, the rudiments of economics and finance, and the fundamental principles of American history and government. Studies by the National Endowment for the Humanities show that this coherence has disappeared from the curriculum. As a result, most universities are now graduating students who are scientifically and culturally impoverished, if not illiterate.

At the University of Pennsylvania, Houston Baker, one of the most prominent black academics in the country, denounces reading and writing as oppressive technologies and celebrates such examples of oral culture as the rap group N.W.A. (Niggers With Attitude). One of the group's songs is about the desirability of killing policemen. Alison Jaggar, who teaches women's studies at the University of Colorado, denounces the traditional nuclear family as a "cornerstone of women's oppression" and anticipates scientific advances enabling men to carry fetuses in their bodies so that child-bearing responsibilities can be shared between the sexes. Duke professor Eve Sedgwick's scholarship is devoted to unmasking what she terms the heterosexual bias in Western culture, a project that she pursues through papers such as "Jane Austen and the Masturbating Girl" and "How To Bring Your Kids Up Gay."

Confronted by racial tension and Balkanization on campus, university leaders usually announce that, because of a resurgence of bigotry, "more needs to be done." They press for redoubled preferential recruitment of minority students and faculty, funding for a new Third World or Afro-American center, mandatory sensitivity education for whites, and so on. The more the university leaders give in to the demands of minority activists, the more they encourage the very racism they are supposed to be fighting. Surveys indicate that most young people today hold fairly liberal attitudes toward race, evident in their strong support for the civil rights agenda and for interracial dating. However, these liberal attitudes are sorely tried by the demands of the new orthodoxy: many undergraduates are beginning to rebel against what they perceive as a culture of preferential treatment and double standards actively fostered by university policies.

Can there be a successful rolling back of this revolution, or at least of its excesses? One piece of good news is that blatant forms of racial preference are having an increasingly tough time in the courts, and this has implications for university admissions policies. The Department of Education is more vigilant than it used to be in investigating charges of discrimination against whites and Asian Americans. With help from Washington director Morton Halperin, the American Civil Liberties Union has taken a strong stand against campus censorship.

Popular magazines such as *Newsweek* and *New York* have poked fun at "politically correct" speech. At Tufts University, undergraduates embarrassed the administration into backing down on censorship by putting up taped boundaries designating areas of the university to be "free speech zones," "limited speech zones," and "Twilight Zones."

Even some scholars on the political left are now speaking out against such dogmatism and excess. Eugene Genovese, a Marxist historian and one of the nation's most respected scholars of slavery, argues that "too often we find that education has given way to indoctrination. Good scholars are intimidated into silence, and the only diversity that obtains is a diversity of radical positions." More and more professors from across the political spectrum are resisting the politicization and lowering of standards. At Duke, for example, sixty professors, led by political scientist James David Barber, a liberal Democrat, have repudiated the extremism of the victims' revolution. To that end they have joined the National Association of Scholars, a Princeton, New Jersey-based group devoted to fairness, excellence, and rational debate in universities.

But these scholars need help. Resistance on campus to the academic revolution is outgunned and sorely needs outside reinforcements. Parents, alumni, corporations, foundations, and state legislators are generally not aware that they can be very effective in promoting reform. The best way to encourage reform is to communicate in no uncertain terms to university leadership and, if necessary, to use financial incentives to assure your voice is heard. University leaders do their best to keep outsiders from meddling or even finding out what exactly is going on behind the tall gates, but there is little doubt that they would pay keen attention to the views of the donors on whom they depend. By threatening to suspend donations if universities continue harmful policies, friends of liberal learning can do a lot. In the case of state-funded schools, citizens and parents can pressure elected representatives to ask questions and demand more accountability from the taxpayer-supported academics.

The illiberal revolution can be reversed only if the people who foot the bills stop being passive observers. Don't just write a check to your alma mater; that's an abrogation of responsibility. Keep abreast of what is going on and don't be afraid to raise your voice and even to close your wallet in protest. Our Western, free-market culture need not provide the rope to hang itself.

Thinking About the Text _____

1. What is D'Souza's purpose in writing this essay? What rhetorical strategies does he use to persuade his audience?

2. How, according to D'Souza, do political correctness and the creation of more multicultural curricula within America's colleges and universities encourage racism and segregation? How does D'Souza's argument relate to other works we have read?

3. Why does D'Souza say, "the claims of the academic multiculturalists are largely phony?" How does he support this argument? How effective are his strategies?

The Border Patrol State

LESLIE MARMON SILKO

Leslie Marmon Silko was born in 1948 of mixed Laguna, Mexican, and white ancestry and was raised on the Laguna Pueblo Reservation in New Mexico. Silko graduated from the University of New Mexico in 1969. She published *Laguna Woman*, her first book of poetry, in 1974. In 1977, Silko published the novel, *Ceremony*, which brought her widespread acclaim as one of the most accomplished Native American writers of her generation. Silko has since published a number of works, including novels, essays, and poetry. Her stories and poetry have been widely anthologized. She has also been on the faculties of the University of New Mexico and the University of Arizona.

I used to travel the highways of New Mexico and Arizona with a wonderful sensation of absolute freedom as I cruised down the open road and across the vast desert plateaus. On the Laguna Pueblo reservation, where I was raised, the people were patriotic despite the way the U.S. government had treated Native Americans. As proud citizens, we grew up believing the freedom to travel was our inalienable right, a right that some Native Americans had been denied in the early twentieth century. Our cousin old Bill Pratt used to ride his horse three hundred miles overland from Laguna, New Mexico, to Prescott, Arizona, every summer to work as a fire lookout.

In school in the 1950s, we were taught that our right to travel from state to state without special papers or threat of detainment was a right that citizens under Communist and totalitarian governments did not possess. That wide open highway told us we were U.S. citizens; we were free . . .

Not so long ago, my companion Gus and I were driving south from Albuquerque, returning to Tucson after a book promotion for the paperback edition of my novel *Almanac of the Dead.* I had settled back and gone to sleep while Gus drove, but I was awakened when I felt the car slowing to a stop. It was nearly midnight on New Mexico State Road 26, a dark, lonely stretch of two-lane highway between Hatch and Deming. When I sat up, I saw the headlights and emergency flashers of six vehicles—Border Patrol cars and a van were blocking both lanes of the highway. Gus stopped the car and rolled down the window to ask what was wrong. But the closest Border Patrolman and his companion did not reply; instead, the first agent ordered us to "step out of the car." Gus asked why, but his question seemed to set them off. Two more Border Patrol agents immediately approached our car, and one of them snapped, "Are you looking for trouble?" as if he would relish it.

I will never forget that night beside the highway. There was an awful feeling of menace and violence straining to break loose. It was clear that the uniformed men would be only too happy to drag us out of the car if we did not speedily comply with their request (asking a question is tantamount to resistance, it seems). So we stepped out of the car and they motioned for us to stand on the shoulder of the road. The night was very dark, and no other traffic had come down the road since we had been stopped. All I could think about was a book I had read—*Nunca Más*—the official report of a human rights commission that investigated and certified more than twelve thousand "disappearances" during Argentina's "dirty war" in the late 1970s.

The weird anger of these Border Patrolmen made me think about descriptions in the report of Argentine police and military officers who became addicted to interrogation, torture, and the murder that followed. When the military and police ran out of political suspects to torture and kill, they resorted to the random abduction of citizens off the streets. I thought how easy it would be for the Border Patrol to shoot us and leave our bodies and car beside the highway, like so many bodies found in these parts and ascribed to drug runners.

Two other Border Patrolmen stood by the white van. The one who had asked if we were looking for trouble ordered his partner to "get the dog," and from the back of the van another patrolman brought a small female German shepherd on a leash. The dog apparently did not heel well enough to suit him, and the handler jerked the leash. They opened the doors of our car and pulled the dog's head into it, but I saw immediately from the expression in her eyes that the dog hated them and that she would not serve them. When she showed no interest in the inside of our car, they brought her around back to the trunk, near where we were standing. They half-dragged her up into the trunk, but still she did not indicate any stowed-away human beings or illegal drugs.

Their mood got uglier; the officers seemed outraged that the dog could not find any contraband, and they dragged her over to us and commanded her to sniff our legs and feet. To my relief, the strange violence the Border Patrol agents had focused on us now seemed shifted to the dog. I no longer felt so strongly that we would be murdered. We exchanged looks—the dog and I. She was afraid of what they might do, just as I was. The dog's handler jerked the leash sharply as she sniffed us, as if to make her perform better, but the dog refused to accuse us; she had an innate dignity that did not permit her to serve the murderous impulses of those men. I can't forget the expression in the dog's eyes; it was as if she were embarrassed to be associated with them. I had a small amount of medicinal marijuana in my purse that night, but she refused to expose me. I am not partial to dogs, but I will always remember the small German shepherd that night.

Unfortunately, what happened to me is an everyday occurrence here now. Since the 1980s, on top of greatly expanding border checkpoints, the Immigration and Naturalization Service and the Border Patrol have implemented policies that interfere with the rights of U.S. citizens to travel freely within our borders. INS agents now patrol all interstate highways and roads that lead to or from the U.S.-Mexico border in Texas, New Mexico, Arizona. and California. Now, when you drive east from Tucson on Interstate 10 toward El Paso, you encounter an INS check station outside Las Cruces, New Mexico. When you drive north from Las Cruces up Interstate 25, two miles north of the town of Truth or Consequences, the highway is blocked with orange emergency barriers, and all traffic is diverted into a two-lane Border Patrol checkpoint—ninety-five miles north of the U.S.-Mexico border.

I was detained once at Truth or Consequences, despite my and my companion's Arizona driver's licenses. Two men, both Chicanos, were detained at the same time, despite the fact that they too presented ID and spoke English without the thick Texas accents of the Border Patrol agents. While we were stopped, we watched as other vehicles—whose occupants were white—were waved through the checkpoint. White people traveling with brown people, however, can expect to be stopped on suspicion they work with the sanctuary movement, which shelters refugees. White people who appear to be clergy, those who wear ethnic clothing or jewelry, and women with very long hair or very short hair (they could be nuns) are also frequently detained; white men with beards or men with long hair are likely to be detained, too, because Border Patrol agents have profiles of "those sorts" of white people who may help political refugees. (Most of the political refugees from Guatemala and El Salvador are Native American or mestizo because the indigenous people of the Americas have continued to resist efforts by invaders to displace them from their ancestral lands.) Alleged increases in illegal immigration by people of Asian ancestry mean that the Border Patrol now routinely detains anyone who appears to be Asian or part Asian, as well.

Once your car is diverted from the interstate highway into the checkpoint area, you are under the control of the Border Patrol, which in practical terms exercises a power that no highway patrol or city patrolman possesses: they are willing to detain anyone, for no apparent reason. Other law-enforcement officers need a shred of probable cause in order to detain someone. On the books. so does the Border Patrol; but on the road, it's another matter. They'll order you to stop your car and step out; then they'll ask you to open the trunk. If you ask why or request a search warrant, you'll be told that they'll have to have a dog sniff the car before they can request a search warrant, and the dog might not get there for two or three hours. The search warrant might require an hour or two past that. They make it clear that if you force them to obtain a search warrant for the car, they will make you submit to a strip search as well.

Traveling in the open, though, the sense of violation can be even worse. Never mind high-profile cases like that of former Border Patrol agent Michael Elmer, acquitted of murder by claiming self-defense, despite admitting that as an officer he shot an illegal immigrant in the back and then hid the body, which remained undiscovered until another Border Patrolman reported the event. (Last month, Elmer was convicted of reckless endangerment in a separate incident, for shooting at least ten rounds from his M-16 too close to a group of immigrants as they were crossing illegally into Nogales in March 1992.) Never mind that in El Paso, a high school football coach driving a vanload of his players in full uniform was pulled over on the freeway and a Border Patrol agent put a cocked revolver to his head. (The football coach was Mexican-American, as were most of the players in his van; the incident eventually caused a federal judge to issue a restraining order against the Border Patrol.) We've a mountain of personal experiences like that that never make the newspapers. A history professor at UCLA told me she had been traveling by train from Los Angeles to Albuquerque twice a month doing research. On each of her trips, she had noticed that the Border Patrol agents were at the station in Albuquerque scrutinizing the passengers. Since she is six feet tall and of Irish and German ancestry, she was not particularly concerned. Then one day when she stepped off the train in Albuquerque, two Border Patrolmen accosted her, wanting to know what she was doing, and why she was traveling between Los Angeles and Albuquerque twice a month. She presented identification and an explanation deemed suitable by the agents and was allowed to go about her business.

Just the other day, I mentioned to a friend that I was writing this article and he told me about his seventy-three-year-old father, who is half Chinese and had set out alone by car from Tucson to Albuquerque the week before. His father had become confused by road construction and missed a turnoff from Interstate 10 to Interstate 25; when he turned around and circled back, he missed the turnoff a second time. But when he looped back for yet another try, Border Patrol agents stopped him and forced him to open his trunk. After they satisfied themselves that he was not smuggling Chinese immigrants, they sent him on his way. He was so rattled by the event that he had to be driven home by his daughter.

This is the police state that has developed in the southwestern United States since the 1980s. No person, no citizen, is free to travel without the scrutiny of the Border Patrol. In the city of South Tucson, where 80 percent of the respondents were Chicano or Mexicano, a joint research project by the University of Wisconsin and the University of Arizona recently concluded that one out of every five people there had been detained, mistreated verbally or nonverbally, or questioned by INS agents in the past two years.

Manifest Destiny may lack its old grandeur of theft and blood—"lock the door" is what it means now, with racism a trump card to be played again and again, shamelessly, by both major political parties. "Immigration," like "street crime" and "welfare fraud" is a political euphemism that refers to people of color. Politicians and media people talk about "illegal aliens" to dehumanize and demonize undocumented immigrants, who are for the most part people of color. Even in the days of Spanish and Mexican rule, no attempts were made to interfere with the flow of people and goods from south to north and north to south. It is the U.S. government that has continually attempted to sever contact between tribal people north of the border and those to the south.

Now that the "Iron Curtain" is gone, it is ironic that the U.S. government and its Border Patrol are constructing a steel wall ten feet high to span sections of the border with Mexico. While politicians and multinational corporations extol the virtues of NAFTA and free trade (in goods, not flesh), the ominous curtain is already up in a six-mile section at the border crossing at Mexicali; two miles are being erected but are not yet finished at Naco; and at Nogales, sixty miles south of Tucson, the steel wall has been all rubber-stamped and awaits construction, likely to begin in March. Like the pathetic multimillion-dollar antidrug border surveillance balloons that were continually deflated by high winds and made only a couple of meager interceptions before they blew away, the fence along the border is a theatrical prop, a bit of pork for contractors. Border entrepreneurs have already used blowtorches to cut passageways through the fence to collect "tolls" and are doing a brisk business. Back in Washington, the INS announces a $300 million computer contract to modernize its record keeping and Congress passes a crime bill that shunts $255 million to the INS for 1995, $181 million earmarked for border control, which is to include seven hundred new partners for the men who stopped Gus and me in our travels, and the history professor, and my friend's father, and as many as they could from South Tucson.

It is no use; borders haven't worked, and they won't work, not now, as the indigenous people of the Americas reassert their kinship and solidarity with one another. A mass migration is already under way; its roots are not simply economic. The Uto-Aztecan languages are spoken as far north as Taos Pueblo near the Colorado border, all the way south to Mexico City. Before the arrival of the Europeans, the indigenous communities throughout this region not only conducted commerce; the people shared cosmologies, and oral narratives about the Maize Mother, the Twin Brothers, and their grandmother, Spider Woman, as well as Quetzalcoatl, the benevolent snake. The great human migration within the Americas cannot be stopped; human beings are natural forces of the earth, just as rivers and winds are natural forces.

Deep down the issue is simple: the so-called Indian Wars from the days of Sitting Bull and Red Cloud have never really ended in the Americas. The Indian people of southern Mexico, of Guatemala, and those left in El Salvador, too, are still fighting for their lives and for their land against the cavalry patrols sent out by the governments of those lands. The Americas are Indian country, and the "Indian problem" is not about to go away.

One evening at sundown, we were stopped in traffic at a railroad crossing in downtown Tucson while a freight train passed us, slowly gaining speed as it headed north to Phoenix. In the twilight I saw the most amazing sight: dozens of human beings, mostly young men, were riding the train; everywhere, on flatcars, inside open boxcars, perched on top of boxcars, hanging off ladders on tank cars and between boxcars. I couldn't count fast enough, but I saw fifty or sixty people headed north. They were dark young men, Indian and mestizo; they were smiling and a few of them waved at us in our cars. I was reminded of the ancient story of Aztlán, told by the Aztecs but known in other Uto-Aztecan communities as well. Aztlán is the beautiful land to the north, the origin place of the Aztec people. I don't remember how or why the people left Aztlán to journey farther south, but the old story says that one day, they will return.

Thinking About the Text ⎯⎯⎯⎯⎯⎯⎯⎯

1. How does Silko construct social reality in this piece? What are the issues faced by different cultural and ethnic groups?

2. What strategies does Silko use to convey her opinions about the Border Patrol? How
   effective are these strategies?

3. What is the structure of Silko's essay? How does her choice of structure aid in achieving
   her purpose in writing it?

Body Ritual Among the Nacirema

HORACE M. MINER

Horace Miner was born in St. Paul, Minnesota, in May of 1912 and grew up in Lexington, Kentucky. He attended the University of Munich and the University of Kentucky. Miner became fascinated with archeology and accepted a job as the museum curator at the Museum of Anthropology in Kentucky. He continued his study in anthropology at the University of Chicago. In 1947, Miner became an Associate Professor of Sociology and Anthropology at the University of Michigan and was on the Executive Committee of the Sociology Department for twenty-eight years (1951–1979). Miner died in November 1993 after a bout with Alzheimer's. "Nacerima" is Miner's most noted work. The essay views American culture from a non-American point of view while focusing on the misrepresentation of culture.

The anthropologist has become so familiar with the diversity of ways in which different peoples behave in similar situations that he is not apt to be surprised by even the most exotic customs. In fact, if all of the logically possible combinations of behavior have not been found somewhere in the world, he is apt to suspect that they must be present in some yet undescribed tribe. The point has, in fact, been expressed with respect to clan organization by Murdock (1949:71). In this light, the magical beliefs and practices of the Nacirema present such unusual aspects that it seems desirable to describe them as an example of the extremes to which human behavior can go.

From *American Anthropologist*, V. 58, N956 by Horace M. Miner.

Professor Linton first brought the ritual of the Nacirema to the attention of anthropologists twenty years ago (1936:326), but the culture of this people is still very poorly understood. They are a North American group living in the territory between the Canadian Cree, the Yaqui and Tarahumare of Mexico, and the Carib and Arawak of the Antilles. Little is known of their origin, although tradition states that they came from the east. According to Nacirema mythology, their nation was originated by a culture hero, Notgnihsaw, who is otherwise known for two great feats of strength—the throwing of a piece of wampum across the river Pa-To-Mac and the chopping down of a cherry tree in which the Spirit of Truth resided.

Nacirema culture is characterized by a highly developed market economy which has evolved in a rich natural habitat. While much of the people's time is devoted to economic pursuits, a large part of the fruits of these labors and a considerable portion of the day are spent in ritual activity. The focus of this activity is the human body, the appearance and health of which loom as a dominant concern in the ethos of the people. While such a concern is certainly not unusual, its ceremonial aspects and associated philosophy are unique.

The fundamental belief underlying the whole system appears to be that the human body is ugly and that its natural tendency is to debility and disease. Incarcerated in such a body, man's only hope is to avert these characteristics through the use of the powerful influences of ritual and ceremony. Every household has one or more shrines devoted to this purpose. The more powerful individuals in the society have several shrines in their houses and, in fact, the opulence of a house is often referred to in terms of the number of such ritual centers it possesses. Most houses are of wattle and daub construction, but the shrine rooms of the more wealthy are walled with stone. Poorer families imitate the rich by applying pottery plaques to their shrine walls.

While each family has at least one such shrine, the rituals associated with it are not family ceremonies but are private and secret. The rites are normally only discussed with children, and then only during the period when they are being initiated into these mysteries. I was able, however, to establish sufficient rapport with the natives to examine these shrines and to have the rituals described to me.

The focal point of the shrine is a box or chest which is built into the wall. In this chest are kept the many charms and magical potions without which no native believes he could live. These preparations are secured from a variety of specialized practitioners. The most powerful of these are the medicine men, whose assistance must be rewarded with substantial gifts. However, the medicine men do not provide the curative potions for their clients, but decide what the ingredients should be and then write them down in an ancient and secret language. This writing is understood only by the medicine men and by the herbalists who, for another gift, provide the required charm.

The charm is not disposed of after it has served its purpose, but is placed in the charm-box of the household shrine. As these magical materials are specific for certain ills, and the real or imagined maladies of the people are many, the charm-box is usually full to overflowing. The magical packets are so numerous that people forget what their purposes were and fear to use them again. While the natives are very vague on this point, we can only assume that the idea in retaining all the old magical materials is that their presence in the charm-box, before which the body rituals are conducted, will in some way protect the worshipper.

Beneath the charm-box is a small font. Each day every member of the family, in succession, enters the shrine room, bows his head before the charm-box, mingles different sorts of holy water in the font, and proceeds with a brief rite of ablution. The holy waters are secured from the Water Temple of the community, where the priests conduct elaborate ceremonies to make the liquid ritually pure.

In the hierarchy of magical practitioners, and below the medicine men in prestige, are specialists whose designation is best translated "holy-mouth-men." The Nacirema have an almost pathological horror of and fascination with the mouth, the condition of which is believed to have a supernatural influence on all social relationships. Were it not for the rituals of the mouth, they believe that their teeth would fall out, their gums bleed, their jaws shrink, their friends desert them, and their lovers reject them. They also believe that a strong relationship exists between oral and moral characteristics. For example, there is a ritual ablution of the mouth for children which is supposed to improve their moral fiber.

The daily body ritual performed by everyone includes a mouth-rite. Despite the fact that these people are so punctilious about care of the mouth, this rite involves a practice which strikes the uninitiated stranger as revolting. It was reported to me that the ritual consists of inserting a small bundle of hog hairs into the mouth, along with certain magical powders, and then moving the bundle in a highly formalized series of gestures.

In addition to the private mouth-rite, the people seek out a holy-mouth-man once or twice a year. These practitioners have an impressive set of paraphernalia, consisting of a variety of augers, awls, probes, and prods. The use of these objects in the exorcism of the evils of the mouth involves almost unbelievable ritual torture of the client. The holy-mouth-man opens the client's mouth and, using the above mentioned tools, enlarges any holes which decay may have created in the teeth. Magical materials are put into these holes. If there are no naturally occurring holes in the teeth, large sections of one or more teeth are gouged out so that the supernatural substance can be applied. In the client's view, the purpose of these ministrations is to arrest decay and to draw friends. The extremely sacred and traditional character of the rite is evident in the fact that the natives return to the holy-mouth-men year after year, despite the fact that their teeth continue to decay.

It is to be hoped that, when a thorough study of the Nacirema is made, there will be careful inquiry into the personality structure of these people. One has but to watch the gleam in the eye of a holy-mouth-man, as he jabs an awl into an exposed nerve, to suspect that a certain amount of sadism is involved. If this can be established, a very interesting pattern emerges, for most of the population shows definite masochistic tendencies. It was to these that Professor Linton referred in discussing a distinctive part of the daily body ritual which is performed only by men. This part of the rite involves scraping and lacerating the surface of the face with a sharp instrument. Special women's rites are performed only four times during each lunar month, but what they lack in frequency is made up in barbarity. As part of this ceremony, women bake their heads in small ovens for about an hour. The theoretically interesting point is that what seems to be a preponderantly masochistic people have developed sadistic specialists.

The medicine men have an imposing temple, or *latipso*, in every community of any size. The more elaborate ceremonies required to treat very sick patients can only be performed at this temple. These ceremonies involve not only the thaumaturge but a permanent group of vestal maidens who move sedately about the temple chambers in distinctive costume and headdress.

The *latipso* ceremonies are so harsh that it is phenomenal that a fair proportion of the really sick natives who enter the temple ever recover. Small children whose indoctrination is still incomplete have been known to resist attempts to take them to the temple because "that is where you go to die." Despite this fact, sick adults are not only willing but eager to undergo the protracted ritual purification, if they can afford to do so. No matter how ill the supplicant or how grave the emergency, the guardians of many temples will not admit a client if he cannot give a rich gift to the custodian. Even after one has gained admission and survived the ceremonies, the guardians will not permit the neophyte to leave until he makes still another gift.

The supplicant entering the temple is first stripped of all his or her clothes. In everyday life the Nacirema avoids exposure of his body and its natural functions. Bathing and excretory acts are performed only in the secrecy of the household shrine, where they are ritualized as part of the body-rites. Psychological shock results from the fact that body secrecy is suddenly lost upon entry into the *latipso*. A man, whose own wife has never seen him in an excretory act, suddenly finds himself naked and assisted by a vestal maiden while he performs his natural functions into a sacred vessel. This sort of ceremonial treatment is necessitated by the fact that the excreta are used by a diviner to ascertain the course and nature of the client's sickness. Female clients, on the other hand, find their naked bodies are subjected to the scrutiny, manipulation, and prodding of the medicine men.

Few supplicants in the temple are well enough to do anything but lie on their hard beds. The daily ceremonies, like the rites of the holy-mouth-men, involve discomfort and torture. With ritual precision, the vestals awaken their miserable charges each dawn and roll them about on their beds of pain while performing ablutions, in the formal movements of which the maidens are highly trained. At other times they insert magic wands in the supplicant's mouth or force him to eat substances which are supposed to be healing. From time to time the medicine men come to their clients and jab magically treated needles into their flesh. The fact that these temple ceremonies may not cure, and may even kill the neophyte, in no way decreases the people's faith in the medicine men.

There remains one other kind of practitioner, known as a "listener." This witch-doctor has the power to exorcise the devils that lodge in the heads of people who have been bewitched. The Nacirema believe that parents bewitch their own children. Mothers are particularly suspected of putting a curse on children while teaching them the secret body rituals. The counter-magic of the witch-doctor is unusual in its lack of ritual. The patient simply tells the "listener" all his troubles and fears, beginning with the earliest difficulties he can remember. The memory displayed by the Nacirema in these exorcism sessions is truly remarkable. It is not uncommon for the patient to bemoan the rejection he felt upon being weaned as a babe, and a few individuals even see their troubles going back to the traumatic effects of their own birth.

In conclusion, mention must be made of certain practices which have their base in native aesthetics but which depend upon the pervasive aversion to the natural body and its functions. There are ritual fasts to make fat people thin and ceremonial feasts to make thin people fat. Still other rites are used to make women's breasts larger if they are small, and smaller if they are large. General dissatisfaction with breast shape is symbolized in the fact that the ideal form is virtually outside the range of human variation. A few women afflicted with almost inhuman hyper-mammary development are so idolized that they make a handsome living by simply going from village to village and permitting the natives to stare at them for a fee.

Reference has already been made to the fact that excretory functions are ritualized, routinized, and relegated to secrecy. Natural reproductive functions are similarly distorted. Intercourse is taboo as a topic and scheduled as an act. Efforts are made to avoid pregnancy by the use of magical materials or by limiting intercourse to certain phases of the moon. Conception is actually very infrequent. When pregnant, women dress so as to hide their condition. Parturition takes place in secret, without friends or relatives to assist, and the majority of women do not nurse their infants.

Our review of the ritual life of the Nacirema has certainly shown them to be a magic-ridden people. It is hard to understand how they have managed to exist so long under the burdens which they have imposed upon themselves. But even such exotic customs as these take on real meaning when they are viewed with the insight provided by Malinowski when he wrote (1948:70):

> *Looking from far and above, from our high places of safety in the developed civilization, it is easy to see all the crudity and irrelevance of magic. But without its power and guidance early man could not have mastered his practical difficulties as he has done, nor could man have advanced to the higher stages of civilization.*

REFERENCES CITED

Ralph Linton, *The Study of Man*, D. Appleton-Century Co., New York, 1936.

Bronislaw Malinowski, *Magic, Science, and Religion*, The Free Press, Glencoe, 1948.

George P. Murdock, *Social Structure*, The Macmillan Co., New York, 1949.

Thinking About the Text _____

1. What is Miner's attitude towards the community of the Nacirema? How is it represented in the essay?

2. Look at a seemingly familiar cultural practice and deconstruct it (take it apart piece by piece). How can you explain this practice to an outsider to your culture?

3. Write a paragraph about the cultural rituals you have in life (dating, participation in sports, obtaining a driver's license, etc.) How are these rituals important to your daily lifestyle?

Shakespeare in the Bush

LAURA BOHANNON

Bohannon's piece, "Shakespeare in the Bush," is influenced by her background as an anthropologist. She discusses the social reality of a cultural group—African bushmen—and their reaction to Shakespeare.

Just before I left Oxford for the Tiv in West Africa, conversation turned to the season at Stratford. "You Americans," said a friend, "often have difficulty with Shakespeare. He was, after all, a very English poet, and one can easily misinterpret the universal by misunderstanding the particular."

I protested that human nature is pretty much the same the whole world over; at least the general plot and motivation of the greater tragedies would always be clear—everywhere—although some details of custom might have to be explained and difficulties of translation might produce other slight changes. To end an argument we could not conclude, my friend gave me a copy of *Hamlet* to study in the African bush: it would, he hoped, lift my mind above its primitive surroundings, and possibly I might, by prolonged meditation, achieve the grace of correct interpretation.

It was my second field trip to that African tribe, and I thought myself ready to live in one of its remote sections—an area difficult to cross even on foot. I eventually settled on the hillock of a very knowledgeable old man, the head of a homestead of some hundred and forty people, all of whom were either his close relatives or their wives and children. Like the other elders of the vicinity, the old man spent most of his time performing ceremonies seldom seen these days in the more accessible parts of the tribe. I was delighted. Soon there would be three months of enforced isolation and leisure, between the harvest that takes place just before the rising of the swamps and the clearing of new farms when the water goes down. Then, I thought, they would have even more time to perform ceremonies and explain them to me.

I was quite mistaken. Most of the ceremonies demanded the presence of elders from several homesteads. As the swamps rose, the old men found it too difficult to walk from one homestead to the next, and the ceremonies gradually ceased. As the swamps rose even higher, all activities but one came to an end. The women brewed beer from maize and millet. Men, women, and children sat on their hillocks and drank it.

People began to drink at dawn. By midmorning the whole homestead was singing, dancing, and drumming. When it rained, people had to sit inside their huts: there they drank and sang or they drank and told stories. In any case, by noon or before, I either had to join the party or retire to my own hut and my books. "One does not discuss serious matters when there is beer. Come, drink with us." Since I lacked their capacity for the thick native beer, I spent more and more time with *Hamlet*. Before the end of the second month, grace descended on me. I was quite sure that *Hamlet* had only one possible interpretation, and that one universally obvious.

Early every morning, in the hope of having some serious talk before the beer party, I used to call on the old man at his reception hut—a circle of posts supporting a thatched roof above a low mud wall to keep out wind and rain. One day I crawled through the low doorway and found most of the men of the homestead sitting huddled in their ragged cloths on stools, low plank beds, and reclining chairs, warming themselves against the chill of the rain around a smoky fire. In the center were three pots of beer. The party had started.

The old man greeted me cordially. "Sit down and drink." I accepted a large calabash full of beer, poured some into a small drinking gourd, and tossed it down. Then I poured some more into the same gourd for the man second in seniority to my host before I handed my calabash over to a young man for further distribution. Important people shouldn't ladle beer themselves.

"It is better like this," the old man said, looking at me approvingly and plucking at the thatch that had caught in my hair. "You should sit and drink with us more often. Your servants tell me that when you are not with us, you sit inside your hut looking at a paper."

The old man was acquainted with four kinds of "papers": tax receipts, bride price receipts, court fee receipts, and letters. The messenger who brought him letters from the chief used them mainly as a badge of office, for he always knew what was in them and told the old man. Personal letters for the few who had relatives in the government or mission stations were kept until someone went to a large market where there was a letter writer and reader. Since my arrival, letters were brought to me to be read. A few men also brought me bride price receipts, privately, with requests to change the figures to a higher sum. I found moral arguments were of no avail, since in-laws are fair game, and the technical hazards of forgery difficult to explain to an illiterate people. I did not wish them to think me silly enough to look at any such papers for days on end, and I hastily explained that my "paper" was one of the "things of long ago" of my country.

"Ah," said the old man. "Tell us."

I protested that I was not a storyteller. Storytelling is a skilled art among them; their standards are high, and the audiences critical—and vocal in their criticism. I protested in vain.

This morning they wanted to hear a story while they drank. They threatened to tell me no more stories until I told them one of mine. Finally, the old man promised that no one would criticize my style "for we know you are struggling with our language." "But," put in one of the elders, "you must explain what we do not understand, as we do when we tell you our stories." Realizing that here was my chance to prove *Hamlet* universally intelligible, I agreed.

The old man handed me some more beer to help me on with my storytelling. Men filled their long wooden pipes and knocked coals from the fire to place in the pipe bowls; then, puffing contentedly, they sat back to listen. I began in the proper style, "Not yesterday, not yesterday, but long ago, a thing occurred. One night three men were keeping watch outside the homestead of the great chief, when suddenly they saw the former chief approach them."

"Why was he no longer their chief?"

"He was dead," I explained. "That is why they were troubled and afraid when they saw him."

"Impossible," began one of the elders, handing his pipe on to his neighbor, who interrupted, "Of course it wasn't the dead chief. It was an omen sent by a witch. Go on."

Slightly shaken, I continued. "One of these three was a man who knew things"—the closest translation for scholar, but unfortunately, it also meant witch. The second elder looked triumphantly at the first. "So he spoke to the dead chief saying, 'Tell us what we must do so you may rest in your grave,' but the dead chief did not answer. He vanished, and they could see him no more. Then the man who knew things—his name was Horatio—said this event was the affair of the dead chief's son, Hamlet."

There was a general shaking of heads round the circle. "Had the dead chief no living brothers? Or was this son the chief?"

"No," I replied. "That is, he had one living brother who became the chief when the elder brother died."

The old men muttered: such omens were matters for chiefs and elders, not for youngsters; no good could come of going behind a chief's back; clearly Horatio was not a man who knew things.

"Yes, he was," I insisted, shooing a chicken away from my beer. "In our country the son is next to the father. The dead chief's younger brother had become the great chief. He had also married his elder brother's widow only about a month after the funeral."

"He did well," the old man beamed and announced to the others, "I told you that if we knew more about Europeans, we would find they really were very like us. In our country also," he added to me, "the younger brother marries the elder brother's widow and becomes the father of his children. Now, if your uncle, who married your widowed mother, is your father's full brother, then he will be a real father to you. Did Hamlet's father and uncle have one mother?"

His question barely penetrated my mind; I was too upset and thrown too far off balance by having one of the most important elements of *Hamlet* knocked straight out of the picture. Rather uncertainly I said that I thought they had the same mother, but I wasn't sure—the story didn't say. The old man told me severely that these genealogical details made all the difference and that when I got home I must ask the elders about it. He shouted out the door to one of his younger wives to bring his goatskin bag.

Determined to save what I could of the mother motif, I took a deep breath and began again. "The son Hamlet was very sad because his mother had married again so quickly. There was no need for her to do so, and it is our custom for a widow not to go to her next husband until she has mourned for two years."

"Two years is too long," objected the wife, who had appeared with the old man's battered goatskin bag. "Who will hoe your farms for you while you have no husband?"

"Hamlet," I retorted without thinking, "was old enough to hoe his mother's farms him-self. There was no need for her to remarry." No one looked convinced. I gave up. "His mother and the great chief told Hamlet not to be sad, for the great chief himself would be a father to Hamlet. Furthermore, Hamlet would be the next chief: therefore he must stay to learn the things of a chief. Hamlet agreed to remain, and all the rest went off to drink beer."

While I paused, perplexed at how to render Hamlet's disgusted soliloquy to an audience convinced that Claudius and Gertrude had behaved in the best possible manner, one of the younger men asked me who had married the other wives of the dead chief.

"He had no other wives," I told him.

"But a chief must have many wives! How else can he brew beer and prepare food for all his guests?"

I said firmly that in our country even chiefs had only one wife, that they had servants to do their work, and that they paid them from tax money.

It was better, they returned, for a chief to have many wives and sons who would help him hoe his farms and feed his people; then everyone loved the chief who gave much and took nothing—taxes were a bad thing.

I agreed with the last comment, but for the rest fell back on their favorite way of fobbing off my questions: "That is the way it is done, so that is how we do it."

I decided to skip the soliloquy. Even if Claudius was here thought quite right to marry his brother's widow, there remained the poison motif, and I knew they would disapprove of frat-ricide. More hopefully I resumed, "That night Hamlet kept watch with the three who had seen his dead father. The dead chief again appeared, and although the others were afraid, Hamlet followed his dead father off to one side. When they were alone, Hamlet's dead father spoke."

"Omens can't talk!" The old man was emphatic.

"Hamlet's dead father wasn't an omen. Seeing him might have been an omen, but he was not." My audience looked as confused as I sounded. "It *was* Hamlet's dead father. It was a thing we call a 'ghost.'" I had to use the English word, for unlike many of the neighboring tribes, these people didn't believe in the survival after death of any individuating part of the personality.

"What is a 'ghost?' An omen?"

"No, a 'ghost' is someone who is dead but who walks around and can talk, and people can hear him and see him but not touch him."

They objected. "One can touch zombis."

"No, no! It was not a dead body the witches had animated to sacrifice and eat. No one else made Hamlet's dead father walk. He did it himself."

"Dead men can't walk," protested my audience as one man.

I was quite willing to compromise. "A 'ghost' is the dead man's shadow."

But again they objected. "Dead men cast no shadows."

"They do in my country," I snapped.

The old man quelled the babble of disbelief that arose immediately and told me with that insincere, but courteous, agreement one extends to the fancies of the young, ignorant, and superstitious, "No doubt in your country the dead can also walk without being zombis." From the depths of his bag he produced a withered fragment of kola nut, bit off one end to show it wasn't poisoned, and handed me the rest as a peace offering.

"Anyhow," I resumed, "Hamlet's dead father said that his own brother, the one who became chief, had poisoned him. He wanted Hamlet to avenge him. Hamlet believed this in his heart, for he did not like his father's brother." I took another swallow of beer. "In the country of the great chief, living in the same homestead, for it was a very large one, was an important elder who was often with the chief to advise and help him. His name was Polonius. Hamlet was courting his daughter, but her father and her brother . . . [I cast hastily about for some tribal analogy] warned her not to let Hamlet visit her when she was alone on her farm, for he would be a great chief and so could not marry her."

"Why not?" asked the wife, who had settled down on the edge of the old man's chair. He frowned at her for asking stupid questions and growled, "They lived in the same homestead."

"That was not the reason," I informed them. "Polonius was a stranger who lived in the homestead because he helped the chief, not because he was a relative."

"Then why couldn't Hamlet marry her?"

"He could have," I explained, "but Polonius didn't think he would. After all, Hamlet was a man of great importance who ought to marry a chief's daughter, for in his country a man could have only one wife. Polonius was afraid that if Hamlet made love to his daughter, then no one else would give a high price for her."

"That might be true," remarked one of the shrewder elders, "but a chief's son would give his mistress's father enough presents and patronage to more than make up the difference. Polonius sounds like a fool to me."

"Many people think he was," I agreed. "Meanwhile Polonius sent his son Laertes off to Paris to learn the things of that country, for it was the homestead of a very great chief indeed. Because he was afraid that Laertes might waste a lot of money on beer and women and gambling, or get into trouble by fighting, he sent one of his servants to Paris secretly, to spy out what Laertes was doing. One day Hamlet came upon Polonius's daughter Ophelia. He behaved so oddly he frightened her. Indeed"—I was fumbling for words to express the dubious quality of Hamlet's madness—"the chief and many others had also noticed that when Hamlet talked one could understand the words but not what they meant. Many people thought that he had become mad." My audience suddenly became much more attentive. "The great chief wanted to know what was wrong with Hamlet, so he sent for two of Hamlet's age mates [school friends would have taken long explanation] to talk to Hamlet and find out what troubled his heart. Hamlet, seeing that they had been bribed by the chief to betray him, told them nothing. Polonius, however, insisted that Hamlet was mad because he had been forbidden to see Ophelia, whom he loved."

"Why," inquired a bewildered voice, "should anyone bewitch Hamlet on that account?"

"Bewitch him?"

"Yes, only witchcraft can make anyone mad, unless, of course, one sees the beings that lurk in the forest."

I stopped being a storyteller, took out my notebook and demanded to be told more about these two causes of madness. Even while they spoke and I jotted notes, I tried to calculate the effect of this new factor on the plot. Hamlet had not been exposed to the beings that lurk in the forest. Only his relatives in the male line could bewitch him. Barring relatives not mentioned by Shakespeare, it had to be Claudius who was attempting to harm him. And, of course, it was.

For the moment I staved off questions by saying that the great chief also refused to believe that Hamlet was mad for the love of Ophelia and nothing else. "He was sure that something much more important was troubling Hamlet's heart."

"Now Hamlet's age mates," I continued, "had brought with them a famous storyteller. Hamlet decided to have this man tell the chief and all his homestead a story about a man who had poisoned his brother because he desired his brother's wife and wished to be chief himself. Hamlet was sure the great chief could not hear the story without making a sign if he was indeed guilty, and then he would discover whether his dead father had told him the truth."

The old man interrupted, with deep cunning, "Why should a father lie to his son?" he asked.

I hedged: "Hamlet wasn't sure that it really was his dead father." It was impossible to say anything, in that language, about devil-inspired visions.

"You mean," he said, "it actually was an omen, and he knew witches sometimes send false ones. Hamlet was a fool not to go to one skilled in reading omens and divining the truth in the first place. A man-who-sees-the-truth could have told him how his father died, if he really had been poisoned, and if there was witchcraft in it; then Hamlet could have called the elders to settle the matter."

The shrewd elder ventured to disagree. "Because his father's brother was a great chief, one-who-sees-the-truth might therefore have been afraid to tell it. I think it was for that reason that a friend of Hamlet's father—a witch and an elder—sent an omen so his friend's son would know. Was the omen true?"

"Yes," I said, abandoning ghosts and the devil; a witch-sent omen it would have to be. "It was true, for when the storyteller was telling his tale before all the homestead, the great chief rose in fear. Afraid that Hamlet knew his secret he planned to have him killed."

The stage set of the next bit presented some difficulties of translation. I began cautiously. "The great chief told Hamlet's mother to find out from her son what he knew. But because a woman's children are always first in her heart, he had the important elder Polonius hide behind a cloth that hung against the wall of Hamlet's mother's sleeping hut. Hamlet started to scold his mother for what she had done."

There was a shocked murmur from everyone. A man should never scold his mother.

"She called out in fear, and Polonius moved behind the cloth. Shouting, 'A rat!' Hamlet took his machete and slashed through the cloth." I paused for dramatic effect. "He had killed Polonius!"

The old men looked at each other in supreme disgust. "That Polonius truly was a fool and knew nothing! What child would not know enough to shout, 'It's me!'" With a pang, I remembered that these people are ardent hunters, always armed with bow, arrow, and machete; at the first rustle in the grass an arrow is aimed and ready, and the hunter shouts "Game!" If no human voice answers immediately, the arrow speeds on its way. Like a good hunter Hamlet had shouted, "A rat!"

I rushed in to save Polonius's reputation. "Polonius did speak. Hamlet heard him. But he thought it was the chief and wished to kill him to avenge his father. He had meant to kill him earlier that evening. . . ." I broke down, unable to describe to these pagans, who had no belief in individual afterlife, the difference between dying at one's prayers and dying "unhousell'd, disappointed, unaneled."

This time I had shocked my audience seriously. "For a man to raise his hand against his father's brother and the one who has become his father—that is a terrible thing. The elders ought to let such a man be bewitched."

I nibbled at my kola nut in some perplexity, then pointed out that after all the man had killed Hamlet's father.

"No," pronounced the old man, speaking less to me than to the young men sitting behind the elders. "If your father's brother has killed your father, you must appeal to your father's age mates; *they* may avenge him. No man may use violence against his senior relatives." Another thought struck him. "But if his father's brother had indeed been wicked enough to bewitch Hamlet and make him mad that would be a good story indeed, for it would be his fault that Hamlet, being mad, no longer had any sense and thus was ready to kill his father's brother."

There was a murmur of applause. *Hamlet* was again a good story to them, but it no longer seemed quite the same story to me. As I thought over the coming complications of plot and motive, I lost courage and decided to skim over dangerous ground quickly.

"The great chief," I went on, "was not sorry that Hamlet had killed Polonius. It gave him a reason to send Hamlet away, with his two treacherous age mates, with letters to a chief of a far country, saying that Hamlet should be killed. But Hamlet changed the writing on their papers, so that the chief killed his age mates instead." I encountered a reproachful glare from one of the men whom I had told undetectable forgery was not merely immoral but beyond human skill. I looked the other way.

"Before Hamlet could return, Laertes came back for his father's funeral. The great chief told him Hamlet had killed Polonius. Laertes swore to kill Hamlet because of this, and because his sister Ophelia, hearing her father had been killed by the man she loved, went mad and drowned in the river."

"Have you already forgotten what we told you?" The old man was reproachful. "One cannot take vengeance on a madman; Hamlet killed Polonius in his madness. As for the girl, she not only went mad, she was drowned. Only witches can make people drown. Water itself can't hurt anything. It is merely something one drinks and bathes in."

I began to get cross. "If you don't like the story, I'll stop."

The old man made soothing noises and himself poured me some more beer. "You tell the story well, and we are listening. But it is clear that the elders of your country have never told you what the story really means. No, don't interrupt! We believe you when you say your marriage customs are different, or your clothes and weapons. But people are the same everywhere; therefore, there are always witches and it is we, the elders, who know how witches work. We told you it was the great chief who wished to kill Hamlet, and now your own words have proved us right. Who were Ophelia's male relatives?"

"There were only her father and her brother." Hamlet was clearly out of my hands.

"There must have been many more; this also you must ask of your elders when you get back to your country. From what you tell us, since Polonius was dead, it must have been Laertes who killed Ophelia, although I do not see the reason for it."

We had emptied one pot of beer, and the old men argued the point with slightly tipsy interest. Finally one of them demanded of me, "What did the servant of Polonius say on his return?"

With difficulty I recollected Reynaldo and his mission. "I don't think he did return before Polonius was killed."

"Listen," said the elder, "and I will tell you how it was and how your story will go, then you may tell me if I am right. Polonius knew his son would get into trouble, and so he did. He had many fines to pay for fighting, and debts from gambling. But he had only two ways of getting money quickly. One was to marry off his sister at once, but it is difficult to find a man who will marry a woman desired by the son of a chief. For if the chief's heir commits adultery with your wife, what can you do? Only a fool calls a case against a man who will someday be his judge. Therefore Laertes had to take the second way: he killed his sister by witchcraft, drowning her so he could secretly sell her body to the witches."

I raised an objection. "They found her body and buried it. Indeed Laertes jumped into the grave to see his sister once more—so, you see, the body was truly there. Hamlet, who had just come back, jumped in after him."

"What did I tell you?" The elder appealed to the others. "Laertes was up to no good with his sister's body. Hamlet prevented him, because the chief's heir, like a chief, does not wish any other man to grow rich and powerful. Laertes would be angry, because he would have killed his sister without benefit to himself. In our country he would try to kill Hamlet for that reason. Is this not what happened?"

"More or less," I admitted. "When the great chief found Hamlet was still alive, he encouraged Laertes to try to kill Hamlet and arranged a fight with machetes between them. In the fight both the young men were wounded to death. Hamlet's mother drank the poisoned beer that the chief meant for Hamlet in case he won the fight. When he saw his mother die of poison, Hamlet, dying, managed to kill his father's brother with his machete."

"You see, I was right!" exclaimed the elder.

"That was a very good story," added the old man, "and you told it with very few mistakes. There was just one more error, at the very end. The poison Hamlet's mother drank was obviously meant for the survivor of the fight, whichever it was. If Laertes had won, the great chief would have poisoned him, for no one would know that he arranged Hamlet's death. Then, too, he need not fear Laertes' witchcraft; it takes a strong heart to kill one's only sister by witchcraft.

"Sometime," concluded the old man, gathering his ragged toga about him, "you must tell us some more stories of your country. We, who are elders, will instruct you in their true meaning, so that when you return to your own land your elders will see that you have not been sitting in the bush, but among those who know things and who have taught you wisdom."

Thinking About the Text _____

1. Bohannan says that "one can easily misinterpret the universal by misunderstanding the particular." What does she mean by this? What significance does this have to the essay as a whole?

2. Before Bohannan shares *Hamlet* with the bushmen, she believes there exists only one interpretation of the text. Is she right? Does her universal interpretation change?

3. How does the African bushmen's culture affect the analysis of *Hamlet*? How do one's tradition and culture influence the interpretation of certain events?

Prologue from *The Invisible Man*

RALPH ELLISON

Ralph Ellison, an African American novelist, was born March 1, 1914, in Oklahoma City, Oklahoma. Ellison studied music from 1933 to 1936 at Tuskegee Institute, a college founded by Booker T. Washington. After moving to New York, he met Richard Wright who encouraged him to write. Ellison's writings focus on the strength of the human spirit and the need for racial pride. Ellison died April 16, 1994 of cancer.

I am an invisible man. No, I am not a spook like those who haunted Edgar Allan Poe; nor am I one of your Hollywood-movie ectoplasms. I am a man of substance, of flesh and bone, fiber and liquids—and I might even be said to possess a mind. I am invisible, understand, simply because people refuse to see me. Like the bodiless heads you see sometimes in circus sideshows, it is as though I have been surrounded by mirrors of hard, distorting glass. When they approach me they see only my surroundings, themselves, or figments of their imagination—indeed, everything and anything except me.

Nor is my invisibility exactly a matter of a biochemical accident to my epidermis. That invisibility to which I refer occurs because of a peculiar disposition of the eyes of those with whom I come in contact. A matter of the construction of their *inner* eyes, those eyes with which they look through their physical eyes upon reality. I am not complaining, nor am I protesting either. It is sometimes advantageous to be unseen, although it is most often rather wearing on the nerves. Then too, you're constantly being bumped against by those of poor vision. Or again, you often doubt if you really exist. You wonder whether you aren't simply a phantom in other people's minds. Say, a figure in a nightmare which the sleeper tries with all his strength to destroy. It's when you feel like this that, out of resentment, you begin to bump people back. And, let me confess, you feel that way most of the time. You ache with the need to convince yourself that you do exist in the real world, that you're a part of all the sound and anguish, and you strike out with your fists, you curse and you swear to make them recognize you. And, alas, it's seldom successful.

One night I accidentally bumped into a man, and perhaps because of the near darkness he saw me and called me an insulting name. I sprang at him, seized his coat lapels and demanded that he apologize. He was a tall blond man, and as my face came close to his he looked insolently out of his blue eyes and cursed me, his breath hot in my face as he struggled. I pulled his chin down sharp upon the crown of my head, butting him as I had seen the West Indians do, and I felt his flesh tear and the blood gush out, and I yelled, "Apologize! Apologize!" But he continued to curse and struggle, and I butted him again and again until he went down heavily, on his knees, profusely bleeding. I kicked him repeatedly, in a frenzy because he still uttered insults though his lips were frothy with blood. Oh yes, I kicked him! And in my outrage I got out my knife and prepared to slit his throat, right there beneath the lamplight in the deserted street, holding him in the collar with one hand, and opening the knife with my teeth—when it occurred to me that the man had not *seen* me, actually; that he, as far as he knew, was in the midst of a walking nightmare! And I stopped the blade, slicing the air as I pushed him away, letting him fall back to the street. I stared at him hard as the lights of a car stabbed through the darkness. He lay there, moaning on the asphalt; a man almost killed by a phantom. It unnerved me. I was both disgusted and ashamed. I was like a drunken man myself, wavering about on weakened legs. Then I was amused: Something in this man's thick head had sprung out and beaten him within an inch of his life. I began to laugh at this crazy discovery. Would he have awakened at the point of death? Would Death himself have freed him for wakeful living? But I didn't linger. I ran away into the dark, laughing so hard I feared I might rupture myself. The next day I saw his picture in the *Daily News*, beneath a caption stating that he had been "mugged." Poor fool, poor blind fool, I thought with sincere compassion, mugged by an invisible man!

Most of the time (although I do not choose as I once did to deny the violence of my days by ignoring it) I am not so overtly violent. I remember that I am invisible and walk softly so as not to awaken the sleeping ones. Sometimes it is best not to awaken them; there are few things in the world as dangerous as sleepwalkers. I learned in time though that it is possible to carry on a fight against them without their realizing it. For instance, I have been carrying on a fight with Monopolated Light & Power for some time now. I use their service and pay them nothing at all, and they don't know it. Oh, they suspect that power is being drained off, but they don't know where. All they know is that according to the master meter back there in their power station a hell of a lot of free current is disappearing somewhere into the jungle of Harlem. The joke, of course, is that I don't live in Harlem but in a border area. Several years ago (before I discovered the advantages of being invisible) I went through the routine process of buying service and paying their outrageous rates. But no more. I gave up all that, along with my apartment, and my old way of life: That way based upon the fallacious assumption that I, like other men, was visible. Now, aware of my invisibility, I live rent-free in a building rented strictly to whites, in a section of the basement that was shut off and forgotten during the nineteenth century, which I discovered when I was trying to escape in the night from Ras the

Destroyer. But that's getting too far ahead of the story, almost to the end, although the end is in the beginning and lies far ahead.

The point now is that I found a home—or a hole in the ground, as you will. Now don't jump to the conclusion that because I call my home a "hole" it is damp and cold like a grave; there are cold holes and warm holes. Mine is a warm hole. And remember, a bear retires to his hole for the winter and lives until spring; then he comes strolling out like the Easter chick breaking from its shell. I say all this to assure you that it is incorrect to assume that, because I'm invisible and live in a hole, I am dead. I am neither dead nor in a state of suspended animation. Call me Jack-the-Bear, for I am in a state of hibernation.

My hole is warm and full of light. Yes, *full* of light. I doubt if there is a brighter spot in all New York than this hole of mine, and I do not exclude Broadway. Or the Empire State Building on a photographer's dream night. But that is taking advantage of you. Those two spots are among the darkest of our whole civilization—pardon me, our whole *culture* (an important distinction, I've heard)—which might sound like a hoax, or a contradiction, but that (by contradiction, I mean) is how the world moves: Not like an arrow, but a boomerang. (Beware of those who speak of the *spiral* of history; they are preparing a boomerang. Keep a steel helmet handy.) I know; I have been boomeranged across my head so much that I now can see the darkness of lightness. And I love light. Perhaps you'll think it strange that an invisible man should need light, desire light, love light. But maybe it is exactly because I *am* invisible. Light confirms my reality, gives birth to my form. A beautiful girl once told me of a recurring nightmare in which she lay in the center of a large dark room and felt her face expand until it filled the whole room, becoming a formless mass while her eyes ran in bilious jelly up the chimney. And so it is with me. Without light I am not only invisible, but formless as well; and to be unaware of one's form is to live a death. I myself, after existing some twenty years, did not become alive until I discovered my invisibility.

That is why I fight my battle with Monopolated Light & Power. The deeper reason, I mean: It allows me to feel my vital aliveness. I also fight them for taking so much of my money before I learned to protect myself. In my hole in the basement there are exactly 1,369 lights. I've wired the entire ceiling, every inch of it. And not with fluorescent bulbs, but with the older, more-expensive-to-operate kind, the filament type. An act of sabotage, you know. I've already begun to wire the wall. A junk man I know, a man of vision, has supplied me with wire and sockets. Nothing, storm or flood, must get in the way of our need for light and ever more and brighter light. The truth is the light and light is the truth. When I finish all four walls, then I'll start on the floor. Just how that will go, I don't know. Yet when you have lived invisible as long as I have you develop a certain ingenuity. I'll solve the problem. And maybe I'll invent a gadget to place my coffee pot on the fire while I lie in bed, and even invent a gadget to warm my bed—like the fellow I saw in one of the picture magazines who made himself a gadget to warm his shoes! Though invisible, I am in the great American tradition of tinkers. That makes me kin to Ford, Edison and Franklin. Call me, since I have a theory and a concept, a "thinker-tinker." Yes, I'll warm my shoes; they need it, they're usually full of holes. I'll do that and more.

Now I have one radio-phonograph; I plan to have five. There is a certain acoustical deadness in my hole, and when I have music I want to *feel* its vibration, not only with my ear but with my whole body. I'd like to hear five recordings of Louis Armstrong playing and singing "What Did I Do to Be so Black and Blue"—all at the same time. Sometimes now I listen to Louis while I have my favorite dessert of vanilla ice cream and sloe gin. I pour the red liquid over the white mound, watching it glisten and the vapor rising as Louis bends that military instrument into a beam of lyrical sound. Perhaps I like Louis Armstrong because he's made poetry out of being invisible. I think it must be because he's unaware that he *is* invisible. And my own grasp of invisibility aids me to understand his music. Once when I asked for a cigarette, some jokers gave me a reefer, which I lighted when I got home and sat listening to my phonograph. It was a strange evening. Invisibility, let me explain, gives one a slightly different sense of time, you're never quite on the beat. Sometimes you're ahead and sometimes behind. Instead of the swift and imperceptible flowing of time, you are aware of its nodes, those points where time stands still or from which it leaps ahead. And you slip into the breaks and look around. That's what you hear vaguely in Louis' music.

Once I saw a prizefighter boxing a yokel. The fighter was swift and amazingly scientific. His body was one violent flow of rapid rhythmic action. He hit the yokel a hundred times while the yokel held up his arms in stunned surprise. But suddenly the yokel, rolling about in the gale of boxing gloves, struck one blow and knocked science, speed and footwork as cold as a well-digger's posterior. The smart money hit the canvas. The long shot got the nod. The yokel had simply stepped inside of his opponent's sense of time. So under the spell of the reefer I discovered a new analytical way of listening to music. The unheard sounds came through, and each melodic line existed of itself, stood out clearly from all the rest, said its piece, and waited patiently for the other voices to speak. That night I found myself hearing not only in time, but in space as well. I not only entered the music but descended, like Dante, into its depths. And *beneath the swiftness of the hot tempo there was a slower tempo and a cave and I entered it and looked around and heard an old woman singing a spiritual as full of Weltschmerz as flamenco, and beneath that lay a still lower level on which I saw a beautiful girl the color of ivory pleading in a voice like my mother's as she stood before a group of slaveowners who bid for her naked body, and below that I found a lower level and a more rapid tempo and I heard someone shout:*

"Brothers and sisters, my text this morning is the 'Blackness of Blackness.'"

And a congregation of voices answered: "That blackness is most black, brother, most black . . ."

"In the beginning . . ."

"At the very start," they cried.

". . . there was blackness . . ."

"Preach it . . ."

". . . and the sun . . ."

"The sun, Lawd . . ."

". . . was bloody red . . ."

"Red . . ."

"Now black is . . ." the preacher shouted.

"Bloody . . ."

"I said black is . . ."

"Preach it, brother . . ."

". . . an' black ain't . . ."

"Red, Lawd, red: He said it's red!"

"Amen, brother . . ."

"Black will git you . . ."

"Yes, it will . . ."

"Yes, it will . . ."

". . . an' black won't . . ."

"Naw, it won't!"

"It do . . ."

"It do, Lawd . . ."

". . . an' it don't."

"Halleluiah . . ."

". . . It'll put you, glory, glory, Oh my Lawd, in the WHALE'S BELLY."

"Preach it, dear brother . . ."

". . . an' make you tempt. . ."

"Good God a-mighty!"

"Old Aunt Nelly!"

"Black will make you . . ."

"Black . . ."

". . . or black will un-make you."

"Ain't it the truth, Lawd?"

And at that point a voice of trombone timbre screamed at me, "Git out of here, you fool! Is you ready to commit treason?"

And I tore myself away, hearing the old singer of spirituals moaning, "Go curse your God, boy, and die."

I stopped and questioned her, asked her what was wrong.

"I dearly loved my master, son," she said.

"You should have hated him," I said.

"He gave me several sons," she said, "and because I loved my sons I learned to love their father though I hated him too."

"I too have become acquainted with ambivalence," I said. "That's why I'm here."

"What's that?"

"Nothing, a word that doesn't explain it. Why do you moan?"

"I moan this way cause he's dead," she said.

"Then tell me, who is that laughing upstairs?"

"Them's my sons. They glad."

"Yes, I can understand that too," I said.

"I laughs too, but I moans too. He promised to set us free but he never could bring hisself to do it. Sill I loved him . . ."

"Loved him? You mean . . . ?"

"Oh yes, but I loved something else even more."

"What more?"

"Freedom."

"Freedom, " I said. "Maybe freedom lies in hating."

"Naw, son, it's in loving. I loved him and give him the poison and he withered away like a frost-bit apple. Them boys woulda tore him to pieces with they homemade knives."

"A mistake was made somewhere," I said, "I'm confused." And I wished to say other things, but the laughter upstairs became too loud and moan-like for me and I tried to break out of it, but I couldn't. Just as I was leaving I felt an urgent desire to ask her what freedom was and went back. She sat with her head in her bands, moaning softly; her leather-brown face was filled with sadness.

"Old woman, what is this freedom you love so well?" I asked around a corner of my mind.

She looked surprised, then thoughtful, then baffled. "I done forgot, son. It's all mixed up. First I think it's one thing, then I think it's another. It gits my head to spinning. I guess now it ain't nothing but knowing how to say what I got up in my head. But it's a hard job, son. Too much is done happen to me in too short a time. Hit's like I have a fever. Ever' time I starts to walk my head gits to swirling and I falls down. Or if it ain't that, it's the boys; they gits to laughing and wants to kill up the white folks. They's bitter, that's what they is . . ."

"But what about freedom?"

"Leave me 'lone, boy; my head aches!"

I left her, feeling dizzy myself. I didn't get far.

Suddenly one of the sons, a big fellow six feet tall, appeared out of nowhere and struck me with his fist.

"What's the matter, man?" I cried.

"You made Ma cry!"

"But how?" I said, dodging a blow.

"Askin' her them questions, that's how. Git outa here and stay, and next time you got questions like that, ask yourself!"

He held me in a grip like cold stone, his fingers fastening upon my windpipe until I thought I would suffocate before he finally allowed me to go. I stumbled about dazed, the music beating hysterically in my ears. It was dark. My head cleared and I wandered down a dark narrow passage, thinking I heard his footsteps hurrying behind me. I was sore, and into my being had come a profound craving for tranquillity, for peace and quiet, a state I felt I could never achieve. For one thing, the trumpet was blaring and the rhythm was too hectic. A tom-tom beating like heart-thuds began drowning out the trumpet, filling my ears. I longed for water and I heard it rushing through the cold mains my fingers touched as I felt my way, but I couldn't stop to search because of the footsteps behind me.

"Hey, Ras," I called. "Is it you, Destroyer? Rinehart?"

No answer; only the rhythmic footsteps behind me. Once I tried crossing the road, but a speeding machine struck me, scraping the skin from my leg as it roared past.

Then somehow I came out of it, ascending hastily from this underworld of sound to hear Louis Armstrong innocently asking,

What did I do
To be so black
And blue?

At first I was afraid; this familiar music had demanded action, the kind of which I was incapable, and yet had I lingered there beneath the surface I might have attempted to act. Nevertheless, I know now that few really listen to this music. I sat on the chair's edge in a soaking sweat, as though each of my 1,369 bulbs had every one become a klieg light in an individual setting for a third degree with Ras and Rinehart in charge. It was exhausting—as though I had held my breath continuously for an hour under the terrifying serenity that comes from days of intense hunger. And yet, it was a strangely satisfying experience for an invisible man to hear the silence of sound. I had discovered unrecognized compulsions of my being—even though I could not answer "yes" to their promptings. I haven't smoked a reefer since, however; not because they're illegal, but because to *see* around corners is enough (that is not unusual when you are invisible). But to hear around them is too much; it inhibits action. And despite Brother Jack and all that sad, lost period of the Brotherhood, I believe in nothing if not in action.

Please, a definition: A hibernation is a covert preparation for a more overt action.

Besides, the drug destroys one's sense of time completely. If that happened, I might forget to dodge some bright morning and some cluck would run me down with an orange and yellow street car, or a bilious bus! Or I might forget to leave my hole when the moment for action presents itself.

Meanwhile I enjoy my life with the compliments of Monopolated Light & Power. Since you never recognize me even when in closest contact with me, and since, no doubt, you'll hardly believe that I exist, it won't matter if you know that I tapped a power line leading into the building and ran it into my hole in the ground. Before that I lived in the darkness into which I was chased, but now I see. I've illuminated the blackness of my invisibility—and vice versa. And so I play the invisible music of my isolation. The last statement doesn't seem just right, does it? But it is; you hear this music simply because music is heard and seldom seen, except by musicians. Could this compulsion to put invisibility down in black and white be thus an urge to make music of invisibility? But I am an orator, a rabble rouser—Am? I *was*, and perhaps shall be again. Who knows? All sickness is not unto death, neither is invisibility.

I can hear you say, "What a horrible, irresponsible bastard!" And you're right. I leap to agree with you. I am one of the most irresponsible beings that ever lived. Irresponsibility is part of my invisibility; any way you face it, it is a denial. But to whom can I be responsible, and why should I be, when you refuse to see me? And wait until I reveal how truly irresponsible I am. Responsibility rests upon recognition, and recognition is a form of agreement. Take the man whom I almost killed: Who was responsible for that near murder—I? I don't think so, and I refuse it. I won't buy it. You can't give it to me. *He* bumped *me*, *he* insulted *me*. Shouldn't he, for his own personal safety, have recognized my hysteria, my "danger potential"? He, let us say, was lost in a dream world. But didn't *he* control that dream world—which, alas, is only too real!—and didn't *he* rule me out of it? And if he had yelled for a policeman, wouldn't *I* have been taken for the offending one? Yes, yes, yes! Let me agree with you, I was the irresponsible one; for I should have used my knife to protect the higher interests of society. Some day that kind of foolishness will cause us tragic trouble. All dreamers and sleepwalkers must pay the price, and even the invisible victim is responsible for the fate of all. But I shirked that responsibility; I became too snarled in the incompatible notions that buzzed within my brain. I was a coward . . .

But what did *I* do to be so blue? Bear with me.

Thinking About the Text _____

1. Who is Ellison's intended audience? What is he trying to convey to his audience? How successful are his strategies?

2. How does Ellison's use of light and invisibility contribute to the structure of his essay?

3. What rhetorical devices does Ellison employ in his essay? Are they effective or ineffective? Why or why not?

Section 4

Construction of Identity

Identities are constructed through media representations, through our own perceptions of who we are, and through our increasing awareness of how we fit in and where we fit in. The section starts off with the "Declaration of Sentiments and Resolutions" by Elizabeth Cady Stanton who argues for equal rights for women in all aspects of public and private life. Adrienne Rich in "Split at the Root: An Essay on Jewish Identity," continues the discussion of women's identity formation in a Jewish family, and Haunani-Kay Trask discusses her experiences as a Hawaiian living under the power of the United States. Warren Farrell, in "Men as Success Objects," argues that we need to reconsider our perspectives about the role of men in American society. In "Stranger in a Strange Land" and "Wanderers by Choice" Pico Iyer and Eva Hoffman look at how moving around in different parts of the States or moving to a different country impacts how we see ourselves. The two final selections by Joy Harjo and Aurora Levins Morales look at the construction of identity through poetry, addressing constructions of multicultural identities and the construction of "mestiza consciousness."

When you read this section, think about your own identity and how you construct your identity. Think too about how you look at the identity of those around you, whether you ask questions about who they are, or whether you make assumptions about them that you haven't yet explored.

- Think about three very different situations that you encountered. How did you adapt to these different situations? How would you describe yourself in each situation?

- Find an image in a magazine, newspaper, or on the web. How does the image reflect who you are? How does the image try to shape your identity?

- Write a poem or a narrative about something that is important to you. How does your writing reflect your identity? How do you construct your identity for your readers?

Declaration of Sentiments and Resolutions

Elizabeth Cady Stanton

Elizabeth Cady Stanton, one of the first activists for women's rights, was born in 1815 in Johnstown, New York and educated at an all-male school to which she was admitted under special arrangement. After several years of study at the Troy Female Seminary, she turned to law but was denied admission to the New York Bar because of her gender. After her marriage to abolitionist Henry B. Stanton, she was denied recognition as a delegate at London's World Anti-Slavery Convention in 1840 because only men were recognized. After facing such prejudice, Stanton dedicated the rest of her life to the abolition of laws that restricted the freedom and denied the rights of women. In 1848, Stanton helped organize the Seneca Falls Convention, which began the movement for women suffrage in the United States. In 1869, she was elected the first president of the National Woman Suffrage Association and held the post until 1890. Her writings include the three-volume *History of Women's Suffrage* (1896), *A Woman's Bible* (1895), and her autobiographical *Eighty Years and More* (1898). The following reading is a declaration which Stanton read at the Seneca Falls Convention.

When, in the course of human events, it becomes necessary for one portion of the family of man to assume among the people of the earth a position different from that which they have hitherto occupied, but one to which the laws of nature and of nature's God entitle them, a

Declaration of Sentiments and Resolutions, Seneca Falls, 1848.

decent respect to the opinions of mankind requires that they should declare the causes that impel them to such a course.

We hold these truths to be self-evident: that all men and women are created equal; that they are endowed by their Creator with certain inalienable rights; that among these are life, liberty, and the pursuit of happiness; that to secure these rights governments are instituted, deriving their just powers from the consent of the governed. Whenever any form of government becomes destructive of these ends, it is the right of those who suffer from it to refuse allegiance to it, and to insist upon the institution of a new government, laying its foundation on such principles, and organizing its powers in such form, as to them shall seem most likely to effect their safety and happiness. Prudence, indeed, will dictate that governments long established should not be changed for light and transient causes; and accordingly all experience hath shown that mankind are more disposed to suffer, while evils are sufferable, then to right themselves by abolishing the forms to which they were accustomed. But when a long train of abuses and usurpations, pursuing invariably the same object evinces a design to reduce them under absolute despotism, it is their duty to throw off such government, and to provide new guards for their future security. Such has been the patient sufferance of the women under this government, and such is now the necessity which constrains them to demand the equal station to which they are entitled.

The history of mankind is a history of repeated injuries and usurpations on the part of man toward woman, having in direct object the establishment of an absolute tyranny over her. To prove this, let facts be submitted to a candid world.

He has never permitted her to exercise her inalienable right to the elective franchise.

He has compelled her to submit to laws, in the formation of which she had no voice.

He has withheld from her rights which are given to the most ignorant and degraded men—both natives and foreigners.

Having deprived her of this first right of a citizen, the elective franchise, thereby leaving her without representation in the halls of legislation, he has oppressed her on all sides.

He has made her, if married, in the eye of the law, civilly dead.

He has taken from her all right in property, even to the wages she earns.

He has made her, morally, an irresponsible being, as she can commit many crimes with impunity, provided they be done in the presence of her husband. In the covenant of marriage she is compelled to promise obedience to her husband, he becoming, to all intents and purposes, her master—the law giving him power to deprive her of her liberty, and to administer chastisement.

He has so framed the laws of divorce, as to what shall be the proper causes, and in case of separation, to whom the guardianship of the children shall be given, as to be wholly regardless of the happiness of women—the law, in all cases, going upon a false supposition of the supremacy of man, and giving all power into his hands.

After depriving her of all rights as a married woman, if single, and the owner of property, he has taxed her to support a government which recognizes her only when her property can be made profitable to it.

He has monopolized nearly all the profitable employments, and from those she is permitted to follow, she receives but a scanty remuneration. He closes against her all the avenues to wealth and distinction which he considers most honorable to himself. As a teacher of theology, medicine, or law, she is not known.

He has denied her the facilities for obtaining a thorough education, all colleges being closed against her.

He allows her in Church, as well as State, but a subordinate position, claiming Apostolic authority for her exclusion from the ministry, and, with some exceptions, from any public participation in the affairs of the Church.

He has created a false public sentiment by giving to the world a different code of morals for men and women, by which moral delinquencies which exclude women from society, are not only tolerated, but deemed of little account in man.

He has usurped the prerogative of Jehovah himself, claiming it as his right to assign for her a sphere of action, when that belongs to her conscience and to her God.

He has endeavored, in every way that he could, to destroy her confidence in her own powers, to lessen her self-respect, and to make her willing to lead a dependent and abject life.

Now, in view of this entire disfranchisement of one-half the people of this country, their social and religious degradation—in view of the unjust laws above mentioned, and because women do feel themselves aggrieved, oppressed, and fraudulently deprived of their most sacred rights, we insist that they have immediate admission to all the rights and privileges which belong to them as citizens of the United States.

In entering upon the great work before us, we anticipate no small amount of misconception, misrepresentation, and ridicule; but we shall use every instrumentality within our power to effect our object. We shall employ agents, circulate tracts, petition the State and National legislatures, and endeavor to enlist the pulpit and the press in our behalf. We hope this Convention will be followed by a series of Conventions embracing every part of the country.

Resolutions

WHEREAS, The great precept of nature is conceded to be, that "man shall pursue his own true and substantial happiness." Blackstone in his Commentaries remarks, that this law of Nature being coeval with mankind, and dictated by God himself, is of course superior in obligation to any other. It is binding over all the globe, in all countries and at all times; no human laws are of any validity if contrary to this, and such of them as are valid, derive all their force, and all their validity, and all their authority, mediately and immediately, from this original; therefore,

Resolved, That such laws as conflict, in any way, with the true and substantial happiness of woman, are contrary to the great precept of nature and of no validity, for this is "superior in obligation to any other."

Resolved, That all laws which prevent woman from occupying such a station in society as her conscience shall dictate, or which place her in a position inferior to that of man, are contrary to the great precept of nature, and therefore of no force or authority.

Resolved, That woman is man's equal—was intended to be so by the Creator, and the highest good of the race demands that she should be recognized as such.

Resolved, That the women of this country ought to be enlightened in regard to the laws under which they live, that they may no longer publish their degradation by declaring themselves satisfied with their present position, nor their ignorance, by asserting that they have all the rights they want.

Resolved, That inasmuch as man, while claiming for himself intellectual superiority, does accord to woman moral superiority, it is preeminently his duty to encourage her to speak and teach, as she has an opportunity, in all religious assemblies.

Resolved, That the same amount of virtue, delicacy, and refinement of behavior that is required of woman in the social state, should also be required of man, and the same transgressions should be visited with equal severity on both man and woman.

Resolved, That the objection of indelicacy and impropriety, which is so often brought against woman when she addresses a public audience, comes with a very ill-grace from those who encourage, by their attendance, her appearance on the stage, in the concert, or in feats of the circus.

Resolved, That woman has too long rested satisfied in the circumscribed limits which corrupt customs and a perverted application of the Scriptures have marked out for her, and that it is time she should move in the enlarged sphere which her great Creator has assigned her.

Resolved, That it is the duty of the women of this country to secure to themselves their sacred right to the elective franchise.

Resolved, That the equality of human rights results necessarily from the fact of the identity of the race in capabilities and responsibilities.

Resolved, therefore, That, being invested by the Creator with the same capabilities, and the same consciousness of responsibility for their exercise, it is demonstrably the right and duty of woman, equally with man, to promote every righteous cause by every righteous means; and especially in regard to the great subjects of morals and religion, it is self-evidently her right to participate with her brother in teaching them, both in private and in public, by writing and by speaking, by any instrumentalities proper to be used, and in any assemblies proper to be held; and this being a self-evident truth growing out of the divinely implanted principles of human nature, any custom or authority adverse to it, whether modern or wearing the hoary sanction of antiquity, is to be regarded as a self-evident falsehood, and at war with mankind.

[At the last session Lucretia Mott offered and spoke to the following resolution:]

Resolved, That the speedy success of our cause depends upon the zealous and untiring efforts of both men and women, for the overthrow of the monopoly of the pulpit, and for the securing to woman an equal participation with men in the various trades, professions, and commerce.

Thinking About the Text _____

1. Why do you think Stanton chose the Declaration of Independence as the model for her Seneca Falls Declaration? Considering the context of the convention, how might this correlation between 'Declarations' aid Stanton's cause?

2. What is the effect of Stanton's assertion that man has had in his "direct object the establishment of absolute tyranny" over woman? What are some of the examples she gives to support her claim?

3. What purpose does Stanton's repetition of the word *Resolved* serve? Since the 1848 Seneca Falls Convention, how many of Stanton's Resolutions have actually been Resolved? Could Stanton's Declaration be applicable to other marginalized groups now? How?

Split at the Root:
An Essay on Jewish Identity

ADRIENNE RICH

Adrienne Rich was born in 1929 in Baltimore, Maryland. She received her bachelor's degree from Radcliffe College in 1951. Rich is considered to be one of America's premier poets and a devoted feminist. Her poetry, which has appeared in numerous collections over the past forty years, often addressed themes of social injustice, women's consciousness, and the need for an authentic human community. She has published a number of works, including *Diving into the Wreck* (1974) for which she received the National Book Award for Poetry, *The Dream of a Common Language* (1978), An *Atlas of the Difficult Life* (1991), and *What is Found There: Notebooks on Poetry and Politics* (1993).

For about fifteen minutes I have been sitting chin in hand in front of the typewriter, staring out at the snow. Trying to be honest with myself, trying to figure out why writing this seems to be so dangerous an act, filled with fear and shame, and why it seems so necessary. It comes to me that in order to write this I have to be willing to do two things: I have to claim my father, for I have my Jewishness from him and not from my gentile mother; and I have to break his silence, his taboos; in order to claim him I have in a sense to expose him.

And there is, of course, the third thing: I have to face the sources and the flickering presence of my own ambivalence as a Jew; the daily, mundane anti-Semitisms of my entire life.

These are stories I have never tried to tell before. Why now? Why, I asked myself some-time last year, does this question of Jewish identity float so impalpably, so ungraspably around me, a cloud I can't quite see the outlines of, which feels to me to be without definition?

And yet I've been on the track of this longer than I think.

In a long poem written in 1960, when I was thirty-one years old, I described myself as "Split at the root, neither Gentile nor Jew, / Yankee nor Rebel."[1] I was still trying to have it both ways: to be neither/nor, trying to live (with my Jewish husband and three children more Jewish in ancestry than I) in the predominantly gentile Yankee academic world of Cambridge, Massachusetts.

But this begins, for me, in Baltimore, where I was born in my father's workplace, a hospital in the Black ghetto, whose lobby contained an immense white marble statue of Christ.

My father was then a young teacher and researcher in the department of pathology at the Johns Hopkins Medical School, one of the very few Jews to attend or teach at that institution. He was from Birmingham, Alabama; his father, Samuel, was Ashkenazic,[2] an immigrant from Austria-Hungary, and his mother, Hattie Rice, a Sephardic[3] Jew from Vicksburg, Mississippi. My grandfather had had a shoe store in Birmingham, which did well enough to allow him to retire comfortably and to leave my grandmother income on his death. The only souvenirs of my grandfather, Samuel Rich, were his ivory flute, which lay on our living-room mantel and was not to be played with; his thin gold pocket watch, which my father wore; and his Hebrew prayer book, which I discovered among my father's books in the course of reading my way through his library. In this prayer book there was a newspaper clipping about my grandparents' wedding, which took place in a synagogue.

My father, Arnold, was sent in adolescence to a military school in the North Carolina mountains, a place for training white southern Christian gentlemen. I suspect that there were few, if any, other Jewish boys at Colonel Bingham's, or at "Mr. Jefferson's university" in Charlottesville, where he studied as an undergraduate. With whatever conscious forethought, Samuel and Hattie sent their son into the dominant southern WASP culture to become an "exception," to enter the professional class. Never, in describing these experiences, did he speak of having suffered—from loneliness, cultural alienation, or outsiderhood. Never did I hear him use the word *anti-Semitism*.

It was only in college, when I read a poem by Karl Shapiro beginning "To hate the Negro and avoid the Jew / is the curriculum," that it flashed on me that there was an untold side to my father's story of his student years. He looked recognizably Jewish, was short and slender in build with dark wiry hair and deep-set eyes, high forehead and curved nose.

My mother is a gentile. In Jewish law I cannot count myself a Jew. If it is true that "we think back through our mothers if we are women" (Virginia Woolf[4])—and I myself have affirmed this—then even according to lesbian theory, I cannot (or need not?) count myself a Jew.

The white southern Protestant woman, the gentile, has always been there for me to peel back into. That's a whole piece of history in itself, for my gentile grandmother and my mother were also frustrated artists and intellectuals, a lost writer and a lost composer between them. Readers and annotators of books, note takers, my mother a good pianist still, in her eighties. But there was also the obsession with ancestry, with "background," the southern talk of family, not as people you would necessarily know and depend on, but as heritage, the guarantee of "good breeding." There was the inveterate romantic heterosexual fantasy, the mother telling the daughter how to attract men (my mother often used the word "fascinate"); the assumption that relations between the sexes could only be romantic, that it was in the woman's interest to cultivate "mystery," conceal her actual feelings. Survival tactics of a kind, I think today, knowing what I know about the white woman's sexual role in the southern racist scenario. Heterosexuality as protection, but also drawing white women deeper into collusion with white men.

It would be easy to push away and deny the gentile in me—that white southern woman, that social christian. At different times in my life I have wanted to push away one or the other burden of inheritance, to say merely *I am a woman; I am a lesbian.* If I call myself a Jewish lesbian, do I thereby try to shed some of my southern gentile white woman's culpability? If I call myself only through my mother, is it because I pass more easily through a world where being a lesbian often seems like outsiderhood enough?

According to Nazi logic, my two Jewish grandparents would have made me a *Mischling, first-degree*—nonexempt from the Final Solution.[5]

The social world in which I grew up was christian virtually without needing to say so—christian imagery, music, language, symbols, assumptions everywhere. It was also a genteel, white, middle-class world in which "common" was a term of deep opprobrium. "Common" white people might speak of "niggers"; *we* were taught never to use that word—*we* said "Negroes" (even as we accepted segregation, the eating taboo, the assumption that Black people were simply of a separate species). Our language was more polite, distinguishing us from the "rednecks" or the lynch-mob mentality. But so charged with negative meaning was even the word "Negro" that as children we were taught never to use it in front of Black people. We were taught that any mention of skin color in the presence of colored people was treacherous, forbidden ground. In a parallel way, the word "Jew" was not used by polite gentiles. I sometimes heard my best friend's father, a Presbyterian minister, allude to "the Hebrew people" or "people of the Jewish faith." The world of acceptable folk was white, gentile (christian, really), and had "ideals" (which colored people, white "common" people, were not supposed to have). "Ideals" and "manners" included not hurting someone's feelings by calling her or him a Negro or a Jew—naming the hated identity. This is the mental framework of the 1930s and 1940s in which I was raised.

(Writing this, I feel dimly like the betrayer; of my father, who did not speak the word; of my mother, who must have trained me in the messages; of my caste and class; of my whiteness itself.)

Two memories: I am in a play reading at school of *The Merchant of Venice*. Whatever Jewish law says, I am quite sure I was *seen* as Jewish (with a reassuringly gentile mother) in that double vision that bigotry allows. I am the only Jewish girl in the class, and I am playing

Portia.[6] As always, I read my part aloud for my father the night before, and he tells me to convey, with my voice, more scorn and contempt with the word "Jew": "Therefore, Jew . . ." I have to say the word out, and say it loudly. I was encouraged to pretend to be a non-Jewish child acting a non-Jewish character who has to speak the word "Jew" emphatically. Such a child would not have had trouble with the part. But *I* must have had trouble with the part, if only because the word itself was really taboo. I can see that there was a kind of terrible, bitter bravado about my father's way of handling this. And who would not dissociate from Shylock[7] in order to identify with Portia? As a Jewish child who was also a female, I loved Portia—and, like every other Shakespearean heroine, she proved a treacherous role model.

A year or so later I am in another play, *The School for Scandal*, in which a notorious spendthrift is described as having "many excellent friends . . . among the Jews." In neither case was anything explained, either to me or to the class at large, about this scorn for Jews and the disgust surrounding Jews and money. Money, when Jews wanted it, had it, or lent it to others, seemed to take on a peculiar nastiness; Jews and money had some peculiar and unspeakable relation.

At this same school—in which we had Episcopalian hymns and prayers, and read aloud through the Bible morning after morning—I gained the impression that Jews were in the Bible and mentioned in English literature, that they had been persecuted centuries ago by the wicked Inquisition, but that they seemed not to exist in everyday life. These were the 1940s, and we were told a great deal about the Battle of Britain, the noble French Resistance fighters, the brave, starving Dutch—but I did not learn of the resistance of the Warsaw ghetto until I left home.

I was sent to the Episcopal church, baptized and confirmed, and attended it for about five years, though without belief. That religion seemed to have little to do with belief or commitment; it was liturgy that mattered, not spiritual passion. Neither of my parents ever entered that church, and my father would not enter *any* church for any reason—wedding or funeral. Nor did I enter a synagogue until I left Baltimore. When I came home from church, for a while, my father insisted on reading aloud to me from Thomas Paine's *The Age of Reason*—a diatribe against institutional religion. Thus, he explained, I would have a balanced view of these things, a choice. He—they—did not give me the choice to be a Jew. My mother explained to me when I was filling out forms for college that if any question was asked about "religion," I should put down "Episcopalian" rather than "none"—to seem to have no religion was, she implied, dangerous.

But it was white social christianity, rather than any particular christian sect, that the world was founded on. The very word *Christian* was used as a synonym for virtuous, just, peace-loving, generous, etc., etc.[8] The norm was christian: "religion: none" was indeed not acceptable. Anti-Semitism was so intrinsic as not to have a name. I don't recall exactly being taught that the Jews killed Jesus—"Christ killer" seems too strong a term for the bland Episcopal vocabulary—but certainly we got the impression that the Jews had been caught out in a terrible mistake, failing to recognize the true Messiah, and were thereby less advanced in moral and spiritual sensibility. The Jews had actually allowed *moneylenders in the Temple* (again, the unexplained obsession with Jews and money). They were of the past, archaic, primitive, as older (and darker) cultures are supposed to be primitive; christianity was lightness, fairness, peace on earth, and combined the feminine appeal of "The meek shall inherit the earth" with the masculine stride of "Onward, Christian Soldiers."

Sometime in 1946, while still in high school, I read in the newspaper that a theater in Baltimore was showing films of the Allied liberation of the Nazi concentration camps. Alone, I went downtown after school one afternoon and watched the stark, blurry, but unmistakable newsreels. When I try to go back and touch the pulse of that girl of sixteen, growing up in many ways so precocious and so ignorant, I am overwhelmed by a memory of despair, a sense of inevitability more enveloping than any I had ever known. Anne Frank's diary and many other personal narratives of the Holocaust were still unknown or unwritten. But it came to me that every one of those piles of corpses, mountains of shoes and clothing had contained, simply, individuals, who had believed, as I now believed of myself, that they were intended to live out a life of some kind of meaning, that the world possessed some kind of sense and order; yet *this* had happened to them. And I, who believed my life was intended to be so interesting and meaningful, was connected to those dead by something—not just mortality but a taboo name, a hated identity. Or was I—did I really have to be? Writing this now, I feel belated rage that I was so impoverished by the family and social worlds I lived in, that I had to try to figure out by myself what this did indeed mean for me. That I had never been taught about resistance, only about passing. That I had no language for anti-Semitism itself.

When I went home and told my parents where I had been, they were not pleased. I felt accused of being morbidly curious, not healthy, sniffing around death for the thrill of it. And since, at sixteen, I was often not sure of the sources of my feelings or of my motives for doing what I did, I probably accused myself as well. One thing was clear: there was nobody in my world with whom I could discuss those films. Probably at the same time, I was reading accounts of the camps in magazines and newspapers; what I remember were the films and having questions that I could not even phrase, such as *Are those men and women "them" or "us"?*

To be able to ask even the child's astonished question *Why do they hate us so?* means knowing how to say "we." The guilt of not knowing, the guilt of perhaps having betrayed my parents or even those victims, those survivors, through mere curiosity—these also froze in me for years the impulse to find out more about the Holocaust.

1947: I left Baltimore to go to college in Cambridge, Massachusetts, left (I thought) the backward, enervating South for the intellectual, vital North. New England also had for me some vibration of higher moral rectitude, of moral passion even, with its seventeenth-century Puritan self-scrutiny, its nineteenth-century literary "flowering," its abolitionist righteousness, Colonel Shaw and his Black Civil War regiment depicted in granite on Boston Common. At the same time, I found myself, at Radcliffe, among Jewish women. I used to sit for hours over coffee with what I thought of as the "real" Jewish students, who told me about middle-class Jewish culture in America. I described my background—for the first time to strangers—and they took me on, some with amusement at my illiteracy, some arguing that I could never marry into a strict Jewish family, some convinced I didn't "look Jewish," others that I did. I learned the names of holidays and foods, which surnames are Jewish and which are "changed names"; about girls who had had their noses "fixed," their hair straightened. For these young Jewish women, students in the late 1940s, it was acceptable, perhaps even necessary, to strive to look as gentile as possible; but they stuck proudly to being Jewish, expected to marry a Jew, have children, keep the holidays, carry on the culture.

I felt I was testing a forbidden current, that there was danger in these revelations. I bought a reproduction of a Chagall[9] portrait of a rabbi in striped prayer shawl and hung it on the wall of my room. I was admittedly young and trying to educate myself, but I was also doing something that is dangerous: I was flirting with identity.

One day that year I was in a small shop where I had bought a dress with a too-long skirt. The shop employed a seamstress who did alterations, and she came in to pin up the skirt on me. I am sure that she was a recent immigrant, a survivor. I remember a short, dark woman wearing heavy glasses, with an accent so foreign I could not understand her words. Something about her presence was very powerful and disturbing to me. After marking and pinning up the skirt, she sat back on her knees, looked up at me, and asked in a hurried whisper: "You Jewish?" Eighteen years of training in assimilation sprang into the reflex by which I shook my head, rejecting her, and muttered, "No."

What was I actually saying "no" to? She was poor, older, struggling with a foreign tongue, anxious; she had escaped the death that had been intended for her, but I had no imagination of her possible courage and foresight, her resistance—I did not see in her a heroine who had perhaps saved many lives, including her own. I saw the frightened immigrant, the seamstress hemming the skirts of college girls, the wandering Jew. But I was an American college girl having her skirt hemmed. And I was frightened myself, I think, because she had recognized me ("It takes one to know one," my friend Edie at Radcliffe had said) even if I refused to recognize myself or her, even if her recognition was sharpened by loneliness or the need to feel safe with me.

But why should she have felt safe with me? I myself was living with a false sense of safety.

There are betrayals in my life that I have known at the very moment were betrayals: this was one of them. There are other betrayals committed so repeatedly, so mundanely, that they leave no memory trace behind, only a growing residue of misery, of dull, accreted self-hatred. Often these take the form not of words but of silence. Silence before the joke at which everyone is laughing; the anti-woman joke, the racist joke, the anti-Semitic joke. Silence and then amnesia. Blocking it out when the oppressor's language starts coming from the lips of one we admire, whose courage and eloquence have touched us: *She didn't really mean that; he didn't really say that.* But the accretions build up out of sight, like scale inside a kettle.

1948: I come home from my freshman year at college, flaming with new insights, new information. I am the daughter who has gone out into the world, to the pinnacle of intellectual prestige, Harvard, fulfilling my father's hopes for me, but also exposed to dangerous influences. I have already been reproved for attending a rally for Henry Wallace[10] and the Progressive party. I challenge my father: "Why haven't you told me that I am Jewish? Why do you never talk about being a Jew?" He answers measuredly, "You know that I have never denied that I am a Jew. But it's not important to me. I am a scientist, a deist.[11] I have no use for organized religion. I choose to live in a world of many kinds of people. There are Jews I admire and others whom I despise. I am a person, not simply a Jew." The words are as I remember them, not perhaps exactly as spoken. But that was the message. And it contained enough truth—as all denial drugs itself on partial truth—so that it remained for the time being unanswerable, leaving me high and dry, split at the root, gasping for clarity, for air.

At that time Arnold Rich was living in suspension, waiting to be appointed to the professorship of pathology at Johns Hopkins. The appointment was delayed for years, no Jew ever having held a professional chair in that medical school. And he wanted it badly. It must have been a very bitter time for him, since he had believed so greatly in the redeeming power of excellence, of being the most brilliant, inspired man for the job. With enough excellence, you could presumably make it stop mattering that you were Jewish; you could become the *only* Jew in the gentile world, a Jew so "civilized," so far from "common," so attractively combining southern gentility with European cultural values that no one would ever confuse you with the raw, "pushy" Jews of New York, the "loud, hysterical" refugees from eastern Europe, the "overdressed" Jews of the urban South.

We—my sister, mother, and I—were constantly urged to speak quietly in public, to dress without ostentation, to repress all vividness or spontaneity, to assimilate with a world which might see us as too flamboyant. I suppose that my mother, pure gentile though she was, could be seen as acting "common" or "Jewish" if she laughed too loudly or spoke aggressively. My father's mother, who lived with us half the year, was a model of circumspect behavior, dressed in dark blue or lavender, retiring in company, ladylike to an extreme, wearing no jewelry except a good gold chain, a narrow brooch, or a string of pearls. A few times, within the family, I saw her anger flare, felt the passion she was repressing. But when Arnold took us out to a restaurant or on a trip, the Rich women were always tuned down to some WASP level my father believed, surely, would protect us all—maybe also make us unrecognizable to the "real Jews" who wanted to seize us, drag us back to the *shtetl*, the ghetto, in its many manifestations.

For, yes, that *was* a message—that some Jews would be after you, once they "knew," to rejoin them, to re-enter a world that was messy, noisy, unpredictable, maybe poor—"even though," as my mother once wrote me, criticizing my largely Jewish choice of friends in college, "some of them will be the most brilliant, fascinating people you'll ever meet." I wonder if that isn't one message of assimilation—of America—that the unlucky or the unachieving want to pull you backward, that to identify with them is to court downward mobility, lose the precious chance of passing, of token existence. There was always within this sense of Jewish identity a strong class discrimination. Jews might be "fascinating" as individuals but came with huge unruly families who "poured chicken soup over everyone's head" (in the phrase of a white southern male poet). Anti-Semitism could thus be justified by the bad behavior of certain Jews; and if you did not effectively deny family and community, there would always be a remote cousin claiming kinship with you who was the "wrong kind" of Jew.

I have always believed his attitude toward other Jews depended on who they were. . . . It was my impression that Jews of this background looked down on Eastern European Jews, including Polish Jews and Russian Jews, who generally were not as well educated. This from a letter written to me recently by a gentile who had worked in my father's department, whom I had asked about anti-Semitism there and in particular regarding my father. This informant also wrote me that it was hard to perceive anti-Semitism in Baltimore because the racism made so much more intense an impression: *I would almost have to think that blacks went to a different heaven than the whites, because the bodies were kept in a separate morgue, and some white persons did not even want blood transfusions from black donors.* My father's mind was predictably racist and misogynist;[12] yet as a medical student he noted in his journal that south- ern male chivalry stopped at the point of any white man in a streetcar giving his seat to an old, weary Black woman standing in the aisle. Was this a Jewish insight—an outsider's insight, even though the outsider was striving to be on the inside?

Because what isn't named is often more permeating than what is, I believe that my father's Jewishness profoundly shaped my own identity and our family existence. They were shaped both by external anti-Semitism and my father's self-hatred, and by his Jewish pride. What Arnold did, I think, was call his Jewish pride something else: achievement, aspiration, genius, idealism. Whatever was unacceptable got left back under the rubric of Jewishness or the "wrong kind" of Jews—uneducated, aggressive, loud. The message I got was that we were really superior: nobody else's father had collected so many books, had traveled so far, knew so many languages. Baltimore was a musical city, but for the most part, in the families of my school friends, culture was for women. My father was an amateur musician, read poetry, adored encyclopedic knowledge. He prowled and pounced over my school papers, insisting I use "grownup" sources; he criticized my poems for faulty technique and gave me books on rhyme and meter and form. His investment in my intellect and talent was egotistical, tyrannical, opinionated, and terribly wearing. He taught me, nevertheless, to believe in hard work, to mistrust easy inspiration, to write and rewrite; to feel that I *was* a person of the book, even though a woman; to take ideas seriously. He made me feel, at a very young age, the power of language and that I could share in it.

The Riches were proud, but we also had to very careful. Our behavior had to be more impeccable than other people's. Strangers were not to be trusted; nor even friends; family issues must never go beyond the family; the world was full of potential slanderers, betrayers, *people who could not understand.* Even within the family, I realize that I never in my whole life knew what my father was really feeling. Yet he spoke—monologued—with driving inten- sity. You could grow up in such a house mesmerized by the local electricity, the crucial mean- ings assumed by the merest things. This used to seem to me a sign that we were all living on some high emotional plane. It was a difficult force field for a favored daughter to disengage from.

Easy to call that intensity Jewish; and I have no doubt that passion is one of the qualities required for survival over generations of persecution. But what happens when passion is rent from its original base, when the white gentile world is softly saying "Be more like us and you can be almost one of us"? What happens when survival seems to mean closing off one emotional artery after another? His forebears in Europe had been forbidden to travel or expelled from one country after another, had special taxes levied on them if they left the city walls, had been forced to wear special clothes and badges, restricted to the poorest neighborhoods. He had wanted to be a "free spirit," to travel widely, among "all kinds of people." Yet in his prime of life he lived in an increasingly withdrawn world, in his house up on a hill in a neighborhood where Jews were not supposed to be able to buy property, depending almost exclusively on interactions with his wife and daughters to provide emotional connectedness. In his home, he created a private defense system so elaborate that even as he was dying, my mother felt unable to talk freely with his colleagues or others who might have helped her. Of course, she acquiesced in this.

The loneliness of the "only," the token, often doesn't feel like loneliness but like a kind of dead echo chamber. Certain things that ought to don't resonate. Somewhere Beverly Smith writes of women of color "inspiring the behavior" in each other. When there's nobody to "inspire the behavior," act out of the culture, there is an atrophy, a dwindling, which is partly invisible . . .

Sometimes I feel I have seen too long from too many disconnected angles: white, Jewish, anti-Semite, racist, anti-racist, once-married, lesbian, middle-class, feminist, exmatriate southerner, *split at the root*—that I will never bring them whole. I would have liked, in this essay, to bring together the meanings of anti-Semitism and racism as I have experienced them and as I believe they intersect in the world beyond my life. But I'm not able to do this yet. I feel the tension as I think, make notes: *If you really look at the one reality, the other will waver and disperse.* Trying in one week to read Angela Davis and Lucy Davidowicz,[13] trying to hold throughout to a feminist, a lesbian, perspective—what does this mean? Nothing has trained me for this. And sometimes I feel inadequate to make any statement as a Jew; I feel the history of denial within me like an injury, a scar. For assimilation has affected *my* perceptions; those early lapses in meaning, those blanks, are with me still. My ignorance can be dangerous to me and to others.

Yet we can't wait for the undamaged to make our connections for us; we can't wait to speak until we are perfectly clear and righteous. There is no purity and, in our lifetimes, no end to this process.

This essay, then, has no conclusions: it is another beginning for me. Not just way of saying, in 1982 Right Wing America, *I, too, will wear the yellow star.*[14] It's a moving into accountability, enlarging the range of accountability. I know that in the rest of my life, the next half century or so, every aspect of my identity will have to be engaged. The middle-class white girl taught to trade obedience for privilege. The Jewish lesbian raised to be a heterosexual gentile. The woman who first heard oppression named and analyzed in the Black Civil Rights struggle. The woman with three sons, the feminist who hates male violence. The woman limping with a cane, the woman who has stopped bleeding are also accountable. The poet who knows that beautiful language can lie, that the oppressor's language sometimes sounds beautiful. The woman trying, as part of her resistance, to clean up her act.

FOOTNOTES

1. Adrienne Rich, "Readings of History," in *Snapshots of a Daughter-in-Law* (New York: W. W. Norton, 1967), pp. 35–40. [Author's note]

2. *Ashkenazic*: Pertaining to descendants of the Jews who settled in middle and northern Europe after the Babylonian captivity (597–538 B.C.)

3. *Sephardic:* Pertaining to descendants of the Jews who settled in Spain and Portugal.

4. *Virginia Woolf:* English feminist, critic, and innovator in modern British fiction. (1882–1941), best known for her novels *Mrs. Dalloway* and *To the Lighthouse.*

5. *Final Solution:* Euphemistic name for the Nazi plan to execute Jews in "death camps" like Auschwitz and Dachau.

6. *Portia*: The heroine of Shakespeare's *The Merchant of Venice.*

7. *Shylock:* The Jewish moneylender and villain of *The Merchant of Venice.*

8. In a similar way the phrase "That's white of you" implied that you were behaving with the superior decency and morality expected of white but not of Black people. [Author's note]

9. *Chagall*: Marc Chagall, Russian painter (1887–1985), famous for surreal, dreamlike works inspired by his Jewish heritage.

10. *Henry Wallace:* American journalist (1888–1965), politician, and agriculturalist who was the Progressive party's candidate for the presidency in 1948.

11. *deist:* One who believes that human reason, not divine power, underlies the laws of the universe.

12. *misogynist*: A person who hates women.

13. Angela Y. Davis, *Woman, Race and Class* (New York: Random House, 1981); Lucy S. Davidowicz, *The War against the Jews 1933–1945* (1975; New York: Bantam, 1979). [Author's note]

14. *the yellow star:* The Star of David, used by Nazis during World War II to identify people who were Jewish.

Thinking About the Text _____

1. Why do you think Rich describes herself as "split at the root"? Does she, in her essay, ever make her roots "whole"? Why does she say that "flirting with identity" is dangerous?

2. How does Rich's father contribute to her Jewish identity? How does attending college affect Rich's perception of being a Jew? How do you think she feels about the term "Jew"?

3. As a poet, language is important to Rich. What do you think she means when she says "the poet who knows that beautiful language can lie" and "the oppressor's language sometimes sounds beautiful"?

From a Native Daughter

HAUNANI-KAY TRASK

Haunani-Kay Trask is a professor of Hawaiian studies at the University of Hawaii and Manoa. Many consider her work to be controversial; others refer to her as a scholar who is literally rewriting the history of Hawaii. Her books include *Eros and Power: The Promise of Feminist Theory* (1986) and *From a Native Daughter: Colonialism and Sovereignty in Hawaii* (1993).

E noi'i wale mai no ka haole, a,
'a' ole e pau na hana a Hawai'i 'imi loa
Let the haole *freely research us in detail*
But the doings of deep delving Hawai'i
will not be exhausted.

—*Kepelino, 19th century Hawaiian historian*

Aloha kākou. Let us greet each other in friendship and love. My given name is Haunaniokawēkiu o Haleakalā, native of *Hawai'i Nei.* My father's family is from the *'āina* (land) of Kaua'i, my mother's family from the *'āina* of Maui. I reside today among my native people in the community of *Waimānalo.*

I have lived all my life under the power of America. My native country, Hawai'i, is owned by the United States. I attended missionary schools, both Catholic and Protestant, in my youth, and I was sent away to the American mainland to receive a "higher" education at the University of Wisconsin. Now I teach the history and culture of my people at the University of Hawai'i.

When I was young the story of my people was told twice: once by my parents, then again by my school teachers. From my *'ohana* (family), I learned about the life of the old ones: how they fished and planted by the moon; shared all the fruits of their labors, especially their children; danced in great numbers for long hours; and honored the unity of their world in intricate genealogical chants. My mother said Hawaiians had sailed over thousands of miles to make their home in these sacred islands. And they had flourished until the coming of the *haole* (whites).

At school, I learned that the "pagan Hawaiians" did not read or write, were lustful cannibals, traded in slaves, and could not sing. Captain Cook had "discovered" Hawai'i and the ungrateful Hawaiians had killed him. In revenge, the Christian god had cursed the Hawaiians with disease and death.

I learned the first of these stories from speaking with my mother and father. I learned the second from books. By the time I left for college, the books had won out over my parents, especially since I spent four long years in a missionary boarding school for Hawaiian children.

When I went away I understood the world as a place and a feeling divided in two: one *haole* (white), and the other *kānaka* (native). When I returned ten years later with a Ph.D., the division was sharper, the lack of connection more painful. There was the world that we lived in—my ancestors, my family, and my people—and then there was the world historians described. This world, they had written, was the truth. A primitive group, Hawaiians had been ruled by bloodthirsty priests and despotic kings who owned all the land and kept our people in feudal subjugation. The chiefs were cruel, the people poor.

But this was not the story my mother told me. No one had owned the land before the *haole* came; everyone could fish and plant, except during sacred periods. And the chiefs were good and loved their people.

Was my mother confused? What did our *kūpuna* (elders) say? They replied: did these historians (all *haole*) know the language? Did they understand the chants? How long had they lived among our people? Whose stories had they heard?

None of the historians had ever learned our mother tongue. They had all been content to read what Europeans and Americans had written. But why did scholars, presumably well-trained and th   ', neglect our language? Not merely a passageway to knowledge, language is a form of knowing by itself; a people's way of thinking and feeling is revealed through its music.

I sensed the answer without needing to answer. From years of living in a divided world, I   w the historian's judgment: *There is no value in things Hawaiian; all value comes from things haole.*

Historians, I realized, were very like missionaries. They were a part of the colonizing horde. One group colonized the spirit, the other, the mind. Frantz Fanon[1] had been right, but not just about Africans. He had been right about the bondage of my own people: "By a kind of perverted logic, [colonialism] turns to the past of the oppressed people, and distorts, disfigures, and destroys it" (1968:210). The first step in the colonizing process, Fanon had written, was the deculturation of a people. What better way to take our culture than to remake our image? A rich historical past became small and ignorant in the hands of Westerners. And we suffered a damaged sense of people and culture because of this distortion.

Burdened by a linear, progressive conception of history and by an assumption that Euro-American culture flourishes at the upper end of that progression, Westerners have told the history of Hawai'i as an inevitable if occasionally bitter-sweet triumph of Western ways over "primitive" Hawaiian ways. A few authors—the most sympathetic—have recorded with deep-felt sorrow the passing of our people. But in the end, we are repeatedly told, such an eclipse was for the best.

Obviously it was best for Westerners, not for our dying multitudes. This is why the historian's mission has been to justify our passing by celebrating Western dominance. Fanon would have called this missionizing, intellectual colonization. And it is clearest in the historian's insistence that *pre-haole* Hawaiian land tenure was "feudal"—a term that is now applied, without question, in every monograph, in every schoolbook, and in every tour guide description of my people's history.

From the earliest days of Western contact my people told their guests that *no one* owned the land. The land—like the air and the sea—was for all to use and share as their birthright. Our chiefs were *stewards* of the land; they could not own or privately possess the land any more than they could sell it.

But the *haole* insisted on characterizing our chiefs as feudal landlords and our people as serfs. Thus, a European term which described a European practice founded on the European concept of private property—feudalism—was imposed upon a people halfway around the world from Europe and vastly different from her in every conceivable way. More than betraying an ignorance of Hawaiian culture and history, however, this misrepresentation was malevolent in design.

By inventing feudalism in ancient Hawai'i, Western scholars quick   transformed a spiritually-based, self-sufficient economic system of land use and occupanc   ito an oppres-sive, medieval European practice of divine right ownership, with the common   died like serfs to the land. By claiming that a Pacific people lived under a European sy   m—that the Hawaiians lived under feudalism—Westerners could then degrade a successful system of shared land use with a pejorative and inaccurate Western term. Land tenure changes instituted by Americans and in line with current Western notions of private property were then made to appear beneficial to the Hawaiians. But in practice, such changes benefited the *haole*, who alienated the people from the land, taking it for themselves.

The prelude to this land alienation was the great dying of the people. Barely half a century after contact with the West our people had declined in number by eighty percent. Disease and death were rampant. The sandalwood forests had been stripped bare for international commerce between England and China. The missionaries had insinuated themselves everywhere. And a debt-ridden Hawaiian king (there had been no king before Western contact) succumbed to enormous pressure from the Americans and followed their schemes for dividing up the land.

This is how private property land tenure entered Hawai'i. The common people, driven from their birthright, received less than one percent of the land. They starved while huge *haole*-owned sugar plantations thrived.

And what had the historians said? They had said that the Americans "liberated" the Hawaiians from an oppressive "feudal" system. By inventing a false feudal past, the historians justify—and become complicitous in—massive American theft.

Is there "evidence"—as historians call it—for traditional Hawaiian concepts of land use? The evidence is in the sayings of my people and in the words they wrote more than a century ago, much of which has been translated. However, historians have chosen to ignore any references here to shared land use. But there *is* incontrovertible evidence in the very structure of the Hawaiian language. If the historians had bothered to learn our language (as any American historian of France would learn French) they would have discovered that we show possession in two ways: through the use of an "a" possessive, which reveals acquired status, and through the use of an "o" possessive, which denotes inherent status. My body (*ko'u kino*) and my parents (*ko'u mākua*), for example, take the "o" form; most material objects, such as food (*ka'u mea'ai*) take the "a" form. But land, like one's body and one's parents, takes the "o" possessive (*ko'u 'āina*). Thus, in our way of speaking, land is inherent to the people; it is like our bodies and our parents. The people cannot exist without the land, and the land cannot exist without the people.

Every major historian of Hawaii has been mistaken about Hawaiian land tenure. The chiefs did not own the land: they *could* not own the land. My mother was right and the *haole* historians were wrong. If they had studied our language they would have known that no one owned the land. But was their failing merely ignorance, or simple ethnocentric bias?

No, I did not believe them to be so benign. As I read on, a pattern emerged in their writing. Our ways were inferior to those of the West, to those of the historians' own culture. We were "less developed," or "immature," or "authoritarian." In some tellings we were much worse. Thus, Gavan Daws (1968), the most famed modern historian of Hawai'i, had continued a tradition established earlier by missionaries Hiram Bingham (1848) and Sheldon Dibble (1909), by referring to the old ones as "thieves" and "savages" who regularly practiced infanticide and who, in contrast to "civilized" whites, preferred "lewd dancing" to work. Ralph Kuykendall (1938), long considered the most thorough if also the most boring of historians of Hawai'i, sustained another fiction—that my ancestors owned slaves, the outcast *Kauwā*. This opinion, as well as the description of Hawaiian land tenure as feudal, had been supported by respected sociologist Andrew Lind (1938).[2] Finally, nearly all historians had refused to accept our genealogical dating of over one hundred generations in Hawai'i. They had, instead, claimed that our earliest appearance in Hawai'i could only be traced to A.D. 700. Thus at least seven hundred years of our history were repudiated by "superior" Western scholarship. Only recently have archeological data confirmed what Hawaiians had said these many centuries (Tuggle 1979).

Suddenly the entire sweep of our written history was clear to me. I was reading the West's view of itself through the degradation of my own past. When historians wrote that the king owned the land and the common people were bound to it, they were saying that ownership was the only way human beings in their world could relate to the land, and in that relationship, some one person had to control both the land and the interaction between humans.

And when they said that our chiefs were despotic, they were telling of their own society, where hierarchy always results in domination. Thus any authority or elder is automatically suspected of tyranny.

And when they wrote that Hawaiians were lazy, they meant that work must be continuous and ever a burden.

And when they wrote that we were promiscuous, they meant that lovemaking in the Christian West is a sin.

And when they wrote that we were racist because we preferred our own ways to theirs, they meant that their culture needed to dominate other cultures.

And when they wrote that we were superstitious, believing in the *mana* of nature and people, they meant that the West has long since lost a deep spiritual and cultural relationship to the earth.

And when they wrote that Hawaiians were "primitive" in their grief over the passing of loved ones, they meant that the West grieves for the living who do not walk among their ancestors.

For so long, more than half my life, I had misunderstood this written record, thinking it described my own people. But my history was nowhere present. For we had not written. We had chanted and sailed and fished and built and prayed. And we had told stories through the great blood lines of memory: genealogy.

To know my history. I had to put away my books and return to the land. I had to plant taro in the earth before I could understand the inseparable bond between people and *'āina*. I had to feel again the spirits of nature and take gifts of plants and fish to the ancient altars. I had to begin to speak my language with our elders and leave long silences for wisdom to grow. But before anything else, I had to learn the language like a lover so that I could rock within her and lay at night in her dreaming arms.

There was nothing in my schooling that had told me of this, or hinted that somewhere there was a longer, older story of origins, of the flowing of songs out to a great but distant sea. Only my parents' voices, over and over, spoke to me of a Hawaiian world. While the books spoke from a different world, a Western world.

And yet, Hawaiians are not of the West. We are of *Hawai'i Nei,* this world where I live, this place, this culture, this *'āina.*

What can I say, then, to Western historians of my place and people? Let me answer with a story.

A while ago I was asked to share a panel on the American overthrow of our government in 1893. The other panelists were all *haole.* But one was a *haole* historian from the mainland who had just published a book on what he called the American anti-imperialists. He and I met briefly in preparation for the panel. I asked him if he knew the language. He said no. I asked him if he knew the record of opposition to our annexation to America. He said there was no real evidence for it, just comments here and there. I told him that he didn't understand and that at the panel I would share the evidence. When we met in public and spoke, I said this:

There is a song much loved by our people. It was sung when Hawaiians were forbidden from congregating in groups of more than three. Addressed to our imprisoned Queen, it was written in 1898, and tells of Hawaiian feelings for our land against annexation. Listen to our lament:

Kaulana na pua a'o Hawai'i	Famous are the children of Hawai'i
Kūpa'a mahope o ka 'āina	Who cling steadfastly to the land
Hiki mai ka 'elele o ka loko 'ino	Comes the evil-hearted with
Palapala 'ānunu me ka pākaha	A document greedy for plunder
Pane mai Hawai'i moku o Keawe	Hawai'i, island of Keawe, answers
Kokua na hono a'o Pi'ilani	The bays of Pi'ilani [of Maui, Moloka'i, and Lana'i] help
Kāko'o mai Kaua'i o Mano	Kaua'i of Mano assists
Pau pu me ke one o Kakuhihewa	Firmly together with the sands of Kakuhihewa
'A'ole a'e kau i ka pūlima	Do not put the signature
Maluna o ka pepa o ka 'enemi	On the paper of the enemy
Ho'ohui 'āina kū'ai hewa	Annexation is wicked sale
I ka pono sīvila a'o ke kānaka	Of the civil rights of the Hawaiian people
Mahope mākou o Lili'ulani	We support Lili'uokalani
A loa'a 'e ka pono o ka 'āina	Who has earned the right to the land
Ha'ina 'ia mai ana ka puana	The story is told
'O ka po'e i aloha i ka 'āina	Of the people who love the land

This song, I said, continues to be sung with great dignity at Hawaiian political gatherings. For our people still share the feelings of anger and protest that it conveys.

But our guest, the *haole* historian, answered that this song, although beautiful, was not evidence of either opposition or of imperialism from the Hawaiian perspective.

Many Hawaiians in the audience were shocked at his remarks, but, in hindsight, I think they were predictable. They are the standard response of the historian who does not know the language and has no respect for its memory.

Finally, I proceeded to relate a personal story, thinking that surely such a tale could not want for authenticity since I myself was relating it. My *tutu* (grandmother) had told my mother who had told me that at the time of annexation (1898) a great wailing went up throughout the islands, a wailing of weeks, a wailing of impenetrable grief, a wailing of death. But he remarked again, this too is not evidence.

And so, history goes on, written in long volumes by foreign people. Whole libraries begin to form, book upon book, shelf upon shelf.

At the same time, the stories go on, generation to generation, family to family.

Which history do Western historians desire to know? Is it to be a tale of writings by their own countrymen, individuals convinced of their "unique" capacity for analysis, looking at us with Western eyes, thinking about us within Western philosophical contexts, categorizing us by Western indices, judging us by Judeo-Christian morals, exhorting us to capitalist achievements, and finally, leaving us an authoritative-because-Western record of their complete misunderstanding?

All this has been done already. Not merely a few times, but many times. And still, every year, there appear new and eager faces to take up the same telling, as if the West must continue, implacably, with the din of its own disbelief.

But there is, as there has been always, another possibility. If it is truly our history Western historians desire to know, they must put down their books, and take up our practices. First, of course, the language. But later, the people, the *'āina*, the stories. Above all, in the end, the stories. Historians must listen, they must hear the generational connections, the reservoir of sounds and meanings.

They must come, as American Indians suggested long ago, to understand the land. Not in the Western way, but in the indigenous way, the way of living within and protecting the bond between people and *'āina*.

This bond is cultural, and it can be understood only culturally. But because the West has lost any cultural understanding of the bond between people and land, it is not possible to know this connection through Western culture. This means that the history of indigenous people cannot be written from within Western culture. Such a story is merely the West's story of itself.

Our story remains unwritten. It rests within the culture, which is inseparable from the land. To know this is to know our history. To write this is to write of the land and the people who are born from her.

FOOTNOTES

1. *Frantz Fanon:* French West Indian psychiatrist, author, and political leader. Fanon (1925–1961) is perhaps best known for his psychoanalytic study of Black life in a white-dominated world, *Black Skin, White Masks.* His *Wretched of the Earth* called for an anticolonial revolution by peasants; he anticipated that such a struggle would produce a new breed of modern people of color.

2. See also Fornander (1878–85). Lest one think these sources antiquated, it should be noted that there exist only a handful of modern scholarly works on the history of Hawai'i. The most respected are those by Kuykendall (1938) and Daws (1968), and a social history of the twentieth century by Lawrence Fuchs (1961). Of these, only Kuykendall and Daws claim any knowledge of pre-*haole* history, while concentrating on the nineteenth century. However, countless popular works have relied on these two studies which, in turn, are themselves based on primary sources written in English by extremely biased, anti-Hawaiian Westerners such as explorers, traders, missionaries

(e.g., Bingham [1848] and Dibble [1909]), and sugar planters. Indeed, a favorite technique of Daws's—whose *Shoal of Time* is the most acclaimed and recent general history—is the lengthy quotation without comment of the most racist remarks by missionaries and planters. Thus, at one point, half a page is consumed with a "white man's burden" quotation from an 1886 *Planter's Monthly* article ("It is better for the colored man of India and Australia that the white man rules, and it is better here that the white man should rule . . . ," etc., p. 213). Daws's only comment is "The conclusion was inescapable." To get a sense of such characteristic contempt for Hawaiians, one has but to read the first few pages, where Daws refers several times to the Hawaiians as "savages" and "thieves" and where he approvingly has Captain Cook thinking, "It was a sensible primitive who bowed before a superior civilization" (p. 2). See also—among examples too numerous to cite—his glib description of sacred *hula* as a "frivolous diversion," which, instead of work, the Hawaiians "would practice energetically in the hot sun for days on end . . . their bare brown flesh glistening with sweat" (pp. 65–66). Daws, who repeatedly displays an affection for descriptions of Hawaiian skin color, taught Hawaiian history for some years at the University of Hawai'i; he now holds the Chair of Pacific History at the Australian National University's Institute of Advanced Studies. [Author's note]

Cumulative Bibliography

Bingham, Hiram (1848). *A Residence of Twenty-one Years in the Sandwich Islands.* 2nd ed. New York: Converse.

Daws, Gavan (1968). *Shoal of Time: A History of the Hawaiian Islands.* Toronto and New York: Macmillan.

Dibble, Sheldon (1909). *History of the Sandwich Islands.* Honolulu: Thrum.

Fanon, Frantz (1968). *The Wretched of the Earth.* New York: Grove, Evergreen Edition.

Fornander, Abraham (1878–85). *An Account of the Polynesian Race: Its Origin and Migrations and the Ancient History of the Hawaiian People to the Times of Kamehameha I.* 3 vols. Vol. 1. London: Trübner.

Fuchs, Lawrence (1961). *Hawaii Pono: A Social History.* New York: Harcourt, Brace and World.

Kame'eleihiwa, Lilikala (1992). *Native Land and Foreign Desires.* Honolulu: Bishop Museum Press.

Kuykendall, Ralph S. (1938). *The Hawaiian Kingdom, 1778–1854.* Honolulu: Univ. of Hawai'i Press.

Land, Andrew (1938). *An Island Community: Ecological Succession in Hawaii*. New York: Greenwood.

Stannard, David (1989). *Before the Horror: The Population of Hawai'i on the Eve of Western Contact*. Honolulu: Social Science Research Institute, Univ. of Hawai'i.

Tuggle, H. David (1979). "Hawaii." In *The Prehistory of Polynesia*. Ed. Jesse D. Jennings. Pp. 167–99. Cambridge, Mass.: Harvard Univ. Press.

Thinking About the Text ——————————

1. Look closely at the essay and point out the different rhetorical appeals Trask uses. How does she establish ethos? Are the strategies she uses effective?

2. What is the main point of the piece, and how does she support the main point? What other ways of support can you think of?

3. What is the tone/voice of the essay, and which specific choices in the text help create it? How effective is her choice of tone/voice?

Men as Success Objects

WARREN FARRELL

Warren Farrell was born June 26, 1943, in New York, New York. Farrell attended Montclair State College where he received his B.A. in 1965. He received an M.A. at UCLA in 1966, and a Ph.D. in 1974 from New York University. He is an author, lecturer, and consultant on gender, male-female relationships, and men's issues.

For thousands of years, marriages were about economic security and survival. Let's call this Stage I in our culture's conception of marriage. Beginning in the 1950s, marriages became focused on personal fulfillment and we entered into the era of the Stage II relationship. In Stage II, love was redefined to include listening to each other, joint parenting, sexual fulfillment, and shared decision-making. As a result, many traditional marriages consummated in Stage I failed under the new Stage II expectations. Thus we had the great surge of divorces beginning in the '60s.

The increasing incidence of divorce altered the fundamental relationship between women, men, and the workplace. Before divorce became common, most women's income came from men, so discrimination in favor of a woman's husband benefited her. But, as the divorce rate mushroomed, the same discrimination often hurt her. Before divorce became a common expectation, we had two types of inequality—women's experience of unequal rights in the workplace and men's experience of unequal responsibility for succeeding in the workplace. To find a woman to love him, a man had to "make his mark" in the world. As women increasingly had to provide for themselves economically, we confined our examination of inequality between the sexes to inequality in the workplace. What was ignored was the effect of inequality in the homeplace. Also ignored was a man's feeling that no woman would love him if he volunteered to be a full-time househusband instead of a full-time provider. As a result, we falsely assumed that the experience of inequality was confined to women.

This article first appeared in the *Psychotherapy Networker* and is copied here with permission.

Because divorces led to a change in the pressures on women (should she *become* a doctor, marry a doctor, or have a career and marry a doctor?), that change became "news" and her new juggling act got attention in the media. Because the underlying pressures on men did not change (women still married men who earned more than they did), the pressure on men to succeed did not change, and, therefore, received no attention. With all the focus on discrimination against women, few understood the sexism directed against men.

The feminist perspective on relationships has become like fluoride in water—we drink it without being aware of its presence. The complaints about men, the idea the "men are jerks," have become so integrated into our unconscious that even advertisers have caught on. After analyzing 1,000 commercials in 1987, researcher Fred Hayward found that when an ad called for a negative portrayal in a male-female interaction, an astonishing 100 percent of the time the "bad guy" was the man.

This anti-male bias isn't confined to TV commercials. A sampling of the cards in the "Love and Friendship" section of a greeting card store revealed these gems:

"If they can send one man to the moon, why can't they send them all?"

"When you unzip a man's pants . . . his brains fall out."

"If we can make penicillin out of moldy cheese . . . maybe we can make men out of the low-lifes in this town."

A visit to the bookstore turns up titles like *No Good Men*. Imagine *No Good Women* or *No Good Jews*. And what do the following titles have in common? *Men Who Can't Love*; *Men Who Hate Women and the Women Who Love Them*; *Smart Women/Foolish Choices*; *Successful Women, Angry Men*; *Peter Pan Syndrome*.

Feminism-as-fluoride has left us acknowledging the working mother ("Superwoman") without even being aware of the working father. It is by now well recognized that, even among men who do more housework or more childcare than their wives, almost never does the man truly share the 24-hour-a-day psychological responsibility of ministering to everyone's needs, egos, and schedules.

But it is not so widely recognized that, despite the impact feminism has had on the contemporary family, almost every father still remains 24-hour-a-day psychological responsibility for the family's financial well-being. Even women who earn more than their husbands tell me that they know their husbands would support their decision to earn as much or as little as they wish. If a woman marries a successful man, then she knows she will have an option to work or not, but not an obligation. Almost all men see bringing home a healthy salary as an obligation, not an option.

A woman today has three options.

Option 1: *Full-time career.*

Option 2: *Full-time family.*

Option 3: *Some combination of career and family.*

A man sees himself as having three "slightly different" options:

Option 1: *Work full time.*

Option 2: *Work full time.*

Option 3: *Work full time.*

The U.S. Bureau of the Census explains that full-time working males work an average of eight hours more per week on their jobs than full-time working females.

Since many women now earn substantial incomes, doesn't this relieve the pressure on men to be a wallet? No. Why? Because successful women do exactly what less-successful women do—"marry up," that is, marry a man whose income is greater than her own. According to statistics, if a woman cannot marry up or marry someone with a high wage-earning potential, she does not marry at all. Therefore, a man often reflexively backs away from a woman he's attracted to when he discovers she's more successful than he is because he senses he's only setting himself up for rejection. Ultimately, she'll dump him for a more successful man. She may sleep with him, or live with him, but not marry him unless she spots "potential." Thus, of top female executives, 85 percent don't get married; the remaining 15 percent almost all marry up. Event successful women have not relaxed the pressure on men to succeed.

Ask a girl in junior high or high school about the boy whom she would "absolutely love" to ask her out to the prom and chances are almost 100 percent that she would tell you her fantasy boy is *both* good-looking *and* successful (a jock or student leader, or someone who "has potential"). Ask a boy whom he would absolutely love to ask out to the prom and chances are almost 100 percent his fantasy girl is good-looking. Only about 25 percent will also be interested in a girl's "strong career potential" (or her being a top female jock). His invisible curriculum, then, taught him that being good-looking is not enough to attract a good-looking girl—he must be successful *in addition* to being good-looking. This was his experience of inequality: "Good-looking boy does not equal good-looking girl." Why are boys willing to consider themselves unequal to girls' attention until they hit their heads against 21 other boys on a football field?

In part, the answer is because boys are addicted. In all cultures, boys are addicted to the images of beautiful women. And in American culture this is enormously magnified. Boys are exposed to the images of beautiful women about 10 million times per year via television, billboards, magazines, etc. In the process, the naturally beautiful girl becomes a *genetic celebrity*. Boys become addicted to the image of the quasi-anorexic female. To be the equal of this genetic celebrity, the adolescent boy must become an *earned celebrity* (by performing, paying on dates, etc.). Until he is an earned celebrity, he feels like a groupie trying to get a celebrity's attention.

Is there an invisible curriculum for girls and boys growing up? Yes. For girls, "If you want to have your choice among boys, you had better be beautiful." For boys, it's "You had better be handsome *and* successful." If a boy wants a romantic relationship with a girl he must not only be successful and perform, he must pay and pursue—risk sexual rejection. Girls think of the three Ps—performing, paying and pursuing—as male power. Boys see the three Ps as what they must do to earn their way to female love and sexuality. They see these not as power, but as compensations for powerlessness. This is the adolescent male's experience of inequality.

Thinking About the Text _____

1. Do you agree with Farrell's hypothesis that men are success objects? What strategies does he use to attempt to convince the reader of his hypothesis?

2. On the topic of gender and racial discrimination, some people would suggest that the white male is the only true minority. Would Farrell agree or disagree with this assumption? Why or why not?

3. In this essay, who is Farrell's intended audience? How is he trying to connect with this audience?

Stranger in a Strange Land

PICO IYER

In "Stranger in a Strange Land," Pico Iver looks at how moving around in different parts of the world impacts how we see ourselves and how we see others.

The biggest challenge today is how to make our peace with alienness. The villager in Cambodia (or Tibet or Ethiopia) suddenly runs into visitors from Stuttgart, or Vancouver, or Manchester; the person who has never left north London walks out of his door to find himself surrounded by signs he can't read and voices he can't follow. Never in human history have so many been confronted by so much they don't understand.

My answer to this global swirl is to live in a two-room apartment in rural Japan, in a mock-Californian suburb, none of whose buildings are older than I am. I live with a longtime love whose English is as limited as my Japanese, and her two children, who have even fewer words in common with me. You could say that much in the area is familiar—my apartment building is called the Memphis, and my girlfriend worked for years at a boutique called Gere. Gere is inside the Paradis department store, just across from a Kentucky Fried Chicken, a Mister Donut, and a McDonald's. A 10-minute bus ride takes me to the Bienvenuto Californian trattoria, the Hot Boy Club (with surfing shop next door), and a coffee shop above an artificial lake.

Japan is probably less apologetic about embracing artifice and plastic replicas than any country I know. Yet the children in the neighborhood call every older woman "Auntie," and the Aunties feed whoever's child happens to be around. At dawn, old women take showers in freezing cold water and shout ancestral prayers to the gods. The very cool clarity with which the neighborhood shuts me out, calling me a *gaijin*, or "outsider person," is partly what enables it to dispense courtesy and hospitality with such dependability, and to import so much from everywhere without becoming any the less Japanese. Surface is surface here, and depth is depth.

From *The Utne Reader*, July/August 2000. Reprinted by permission of the author.

Japan will never be entirely my home, of course, and Japan would never really want me to come any closer than I am right now. It assigns me a role. It asks me to go about my business, and to let it go about its own. It offers politeness and punctuality on cue, and it requests in exchange that I accept my fixed role in the cheerful pageant that is official life here. Coming from quicksand California, where newcomers are warmly welcomed to a vacuum and no one knows where he stands in relation to anyone else, I find comfort in this culture's lack of ambiguity.

One virtue of living in so strange a place is to be reminded daily of how strange *I* seem to *it*. When I am tempted to laugh at the notebook on my table that says, "This is the hoppest day of my life," or the message from the abbess of a local nunnery that prays (in translation) for "Peace on the earth and upon every parson," I recall that the real sense of local comedy, for the Japanese, is me: an unshaven, disheveled, seemingly unemployed Asian who speaks like a 3-year-old and seizes the senior citizen "silver" seats on the bus. "The most peaceful place on earth," as the writer Elias Canetti once said, "is among strangers."

And yet for all this mutual strangeness, I recognize in my neighborhood the outlines and emotions of the safe, protected England I knew when I was young, with its orderly, changeless world of corner shops and drizzly afternoons, with tea served promptly at 5 p.m. I recognize— more than the words, the codes and silences—the force of all the things unsaid. I recognize the imperial shelteredness, the island suspiciousness, the old-world cultivation of private hopes and habits that leave the status quo alone. On its surface, Japan is more alien than anywhere I know. Under the surface it speaks the language I was trained to hear.

I am reminded of how little I belong here each time I return. At the immigration desk the authorities scrutinize my passport with a discernible sense of alarm. I am a foreigner who neither lives nor works here, yet seems to spend most of his time here; an alien who is clearly of Asian ancestry, yet brandishes a British passport; a postmodern riddle who seems to fit into none of the approved categories.

I've been strip-searched for carrying over-the-counter allergy pills, for making a tele- phone call from the customs hall, for going to the men's room. Once I was taken aside because my overcoat was *abunomaru*, abnormal (I was flying to the Himalayas). I have shown them my *Time* business card, a book I wrote on Japan, interviews I have conducted in Japanese magazines. But these do not satisfy them. What concerns the Japanese, clearly, is that I am a modern citizen of nowhere and, more specifically, one who looks like exactly the kind of person who threatens to destroy their civic harmony. During the Gulf War, I was routinely treated as if I were Saddam Hussein's favorite brother; at other times I have been detained on the grounds of resembling an Iranian (thousands of whom live illegally in tent cities in Tokyo parks). The rest of the time I am suspected of being what I am—an ill-dressed, dark, and apparently shiftless Indian without a fixed address.

The mobile world and its porous borders present a challenge to a uniculture like Japan, which depends for its presumed survival upon its clear boundaries, its maintenance of a civil uniformity in which everyone knows everyone else—and how to work with them. And it is not always easy for me to explain that it is precisely this ability to draw strict lines—to sustain an unbending sense of within and without—that draws me to Japan. To invert Robert Frost, in the postmodern world home is the place where, when you have to go there, they don't have to take you in.

My daily life in Nara is a curious artifact, belonging to a kind of existence even I could not have imagined a decade ago, before technology made centrifugal lives possible. I go to bed every day by 9 p.m., in part so as to wake up at 5 a.m., when my New York employers (13 time zones away) are at their desks. My research facility is an English-language bookshop 90 minutes away by train, and my version of the Internet is a copy of the *World Almanac*. The person I see most often, outside my immediate household, is the Federal Express boy who collects and delivers packages from distant Osaka. In our shrunken world, I can complete articles or even books without having to exchange a word with editors, and can draw money in a local department store from a bank account on the other side of the planet.

For breakfast I enjoy some combination of asparagus cookies or "chlorella biscuits," chaperoned by what is here known as Royal Milk Tea. For lunch I go to a convenience store around the corner, where all the goods of England and America are on sale, yet nothing is quite as I would expect. Little old women are photocopying Chopin scores to the sound of piped-in Clash songs, and teenagers with safety pins all over their faces are consulting magazines with titles like *Classy*, *Waggle*, and *Bang*.

Usually, in the afternoons, I go to the post office next door. All the clerks look up as I enter, as at the arrival of their daily soap opera. My principal means of communicating with the world is fraught with hazards: The envelope I am using is too large—measured against a green post office ruler—or I have neglected to attach a PAR AVION sticker. Once I was re-buked for including too long a P.S. on the back of an envelope, and another time, during the holiday season, I was presented with an invoice for $30 when it was discovered that my New Year's greetings exceeded the five-word limit. Afterwards I walk around the local park, past the "bad boy" son of the electrician, polishing his Corvette until it is as red as his waist-length hair. And at one street corner, in this placid neighborhood, I pause before a set of vending machines where I can buy 49 kinds of cigarettes, 36 alcoholic drinks, and 92 nonalcoholic drinks.

Perhaps the way in which my neighborhood most solidly uplifts and steadies me, though, is its tonic blend of cheerfulness and realism, measured (as I see it) with the wisdom of a culture that has been around long enough to know how to mete out its emotions.

In practical terms, this serenity—some would say complacency—may be what gives an air of pink-sweater innocence to protected neighborhoods such as mine. Much of this can be regarded as hypocrisy, but it can also suggest a prudent drawing of boundaries in a world where they are in flux, and a sense of which illusions can be serviceably maintained and which cannot. Japanese society urges its members to conceive of a purpose and an identity higher than themselves. Even punky nose-ring boys and scruffy Indians are implicitly urged to tend to responsibilities beyond their mortal bodies. I find myself picking up stray pieces of trash as I walk down the street; getting up from my seat in the bank, I stop to brush it clean as I would never do "at home."

The homes we choose, in short, deserve a tolerance we might not extend to the homes we inherit. In a world where we have to work hard to gain a sense of home, we have to exert ourselves just as much to sustain a sense of Other. I choose, therefore, to live some distance from Kyoto's eastern hills, which move me like memories of a life I didn't know I had.

A large part of the liberation of living in suburban Japan comes, I think, from the enforced simplicities that accompany a very foreign life. Living far from anywhere, without a bicycle or private car, I conduct my days, nearly always, within the boundaries of my feet. Living without newspapers or magazines—and with a television whose spoken words are usually modern Greek to me—I can be free, a little, of the moment, and get such news as I need from the falling of the leaves, or the Emerson essays on my shelf. Living in a small room, moreover, prompts me to be sparing, and to live only with the books and tapes that speak to me in ways I can respect. And not knowing much of the local tongue frees me from gossip and chatter and eavesdropping, leaving me in a more exacting silence. I cannot hold very much to these austerities. (Nor can I really refuse technology, which allows me to communicate with bosses half a world away—and to get on a plane when I need a dentist.) Yet being in so alien an environment is the first step toward living more slowly and trying to clear some space, away from a world ever more revved up. In our global urban context, it is like living in the wilderness.

The person with whom I share these adventures is a little like the society itself, alluring both for the parts I recognize and for the parts I don't. Daily she recalls to me that the point of familiarity is to make one comfortable with mystery. All of us know, too well, that no place is more foreign than the face asleep by our side; yet in our modern world such old truths gain especial force, as more and more of us find ourselves sharing homes with our own private Japans, half strange and half strangely familiar.

Every couple has its private tongue. In my case, the setup is even stranger because I share no public tongue with Hiroko, my partner of 12 years. Because my Japanese has never been good enough to teach her English, nor her English good enough to teach me Japanese, we can communicate only in a kind of fluent pidgin with English words thrown into Japanese constructions. It sounds a little like the way the neighborhood looks to me.

This means, however, that we are free, for the most part, from subtexts, and from the shadows and hidden stings that words can carry. I can't make puns with her, spin ambiguities, or engage in very much verbal subterfuge, and she can't pore over my words to see what they mean or what they don't mean, what covert weapons they hide. Speaking across a language gap means speaking less to win than to communicate.

The global village has given us the chance to move among the foreign, and so to simplify and clarify ourselves. Even in the neighborhoods where we were born, often, we find ourselves speaking by gesticulation, or enunciating slowly to saleswomen and telephone operators. And living away from words means living away from the surfaces they carry. Neither my girlfriend nor I can read a word the other has written, and so we have to apprehend one another in some way deeper than the known.

I realize now that this is my home in incidental ways: I can tell when the trees in the park are going to change color, and when the vending machines will change their offerings from hot to iced. I know when my girlfriend will bring out the winter futons from the cupboard, and when her daughter will change her school uniform from white to blue. I read Thoreau on sunny Sunday mornings, as hymns float over from the nearby Baptist church, and think that in our mongrel, mixed-up planet, this may be as close to the calm and clarity of Walden as one can find.

One midsummer day last year, I took Hiroko to Kyoto on the final day of Obon, the traditional holiday in August when faithful Japanese return to their hometowns to pay respects to their departed ancestors—and when the departed ones themselves are believed to return to earth for three days. It is a time of solemn obsequies and traffic jams, as Kyoto comes alive with ghosts and lights.

Heading toward the eastern hills, the two of us walked along a broad avenue of trees, through a receiving line of lanterns. Old, old men walked past in kimonos, half-doubled over, to visit loved ones at their gravestones. Cicadas buzzed, and lanterns began to glow as the sky darkened. We followed the old men through a small entranceway and emerged in a world of shining lanterns as far as we could see, all across the slope above us, zigzagging toward the heavens. Below, at our feet, were the lights of the modern city, cacophonous, fluorescent, a distant hum; above us, stretching toward the heavens, was one shivering sea of golden lights. Then we walked back into town and dined on a summer platform along the Kamo River, while five great bonfires were lit up along the northern and eastern hills, spelling out a Chinese character.

That night I fell into a deep sleep and dreamed myself in a country house in England. Only a few other people were there: some flop-haired schoolboys, a woman who had been kind to me in my youth—and Hiroko. It was a lazy Sunday morning; we were reading the papers and making the occasional witticism. Once we went for a walk in green hills, encircled in mist; once I asked something about Egypt before the war. Somewhere Lou Reed played "Heroin." A few half-familiar figures drifted about—the unremarkable languor of a country weekend.

But something in this unexceptional scene felt absolutely right. I couldn't find the words, but as I slept I heard myself saying of the everyday English scene, "This is my home. This is where I belong. Usually I'm not very sociable, but this is me. This"—the large red-brick houses, the gray afternoons, the musty light and dullness, the sense of nothing special going on—"is who I am." Words I never thought to say in waking life. But here, suddenly, I could not only feel and see all the days of my childhood, but also taste them, and be inside them, in this distant science fiction land on the night when departed spirits find their way home.

Then I woke up—to the sounds of a bright Sunday morning in the northeast quarter of the ancient imperial capital of Japan, in the 10th year of the era known in English translation as Achieving Peace.

Thinking About the Text _____

1. What are some of the cultural differences that the author takes note of? How do these differences affect the way he interacts with Japan?

2. What is the structure of this piece (narrative, chronological, spatial, inductive, deductive, etc.)? How does the structure contribute to the success of Iver's piece? In other words, what tools does he use and how do they benefit his purpose?

3. In what ways is Iver's essay similar to Peay's? How could you synthesize the two essays?

Wanderers by Choice

Eva Hoffman

Born in Poland only two months after WWII, Eva Hoffman's parents were Holocaust survivors. Her parents moved to Canada when Hoffman was just a teenager, knowing little of the language and nothing of the culture. Hoffman has become a writer and academic; some of her most notable works are *Lost in Translation*, a biography, and *Exit into History: A Journey through the New Eastern Europe*.

Since Adam and Eve left the garden of Eden, is there anyone who does not, in some way, feel like an exile? We feel ejected from our first homes and landscapes, from our first romance, from our authentic self. An ideal sense of belonging, of attuning with others and ourselves, eludes us.

Historically, the symbolic meaning and experience of exile have changed. In medieval Europe, it was the worst punishment possible, because people's identities were defined by their role and place in society. This implied a highly charged concept of home—although home did not necessarily mean birthplace. For medieval clerics, it was the city that housed the papal seat. Jews nurtured a powerful idea of home that existed on two levels: the real communities they inhabited and "Israel," which became an imaginative center from which they derived their essential identity.

In recent years, great shifts in the political and social landscape have affected the very notion of exile. Cross-cultural movement has become the norm, which means that leaving one's native country is not as dramatic or traumatic as it used to be. The ease of travel and communication, combined with the looser borders, gives rise to endless crisscrossing streams of wanderers and guest workers, nomadic adventurers and international drifters. Many are driven by harsh circumstance, but the element of choice is there for most.

People who leave the former Soviet Union nowadays are likely to be economic migrants or Mafia tax dodgers rather than dissidents expelled by ruthless state power. One Bengali village has a tradition of long migrations: Many men leave for years or even decades, but always intend to return. They are not powerless victims of globalization; smart young men choose different countries for the economic advantages they offer. Almost all go back, a bit richer and more important in the eyes of their fellow villagers.

The *Herald Tribune* recently characterized the increasing number of American expatriates in Europe: "They are the Americans abroad, and their number is soaring in a time when travel is unblinkingly routine, communications easy and instant, and telecommuting a serious option. They are abroad in a world where they can watch the Super Bowl live from a Moscow sports bar or send an e-mail from an Internet cafe in Prague."

We all recognize these basic features of our new, fast-changing social landscape. Whether or not we have left, we know how easy it is to leave. We know that we live in a global village, although the village is virtual indeed—dependent not on locality but on the detachment of knowledge, action, information, and identity from a specific place. We have become less spacebound.

Exile used to be considered difficult. It involves dislocation, disorientation, self-division. But today we have come to value exactly those qualities of experience that exile demands— uncertainty, displacement, fragmented identity. Within this framework, exile becomes sexy and glamorous. Nomadism and diasporism have become fashionable terms in intellectual debate. Not only actual exile is at stake, but also how we situate ourselves in the world.

My emigration took place during the Cold War, though not in the worst Stalinist years. I happened to be a young, unwilling emigrant, yanked from my happy childhood. I felt the loss of my first homeland acutely, fueled by the sense that this departure was irrevocable. Poland was suddenly unreachable, and I felt as if I were being taken out of life itself.

Like so many emigrants, I was in effect without language. To lose an internal language is to slide into an inarticulate darkness where we become alien to ourselves; to lose the ability to describe the world is to render the world a bit less vivid. It takes time before a new language begins to inhabit us deeply, to enter the fabric of our psyches and express who we are.

As with language, so with culture: how much incoherence we risk if we fall out of its matrix. We know that cultures differ in customs, food, religions, social arrangements. What takes longer to understand is that each culture has subliminal values and beliefs. They inform our most intimate assumptions and perceptions, our sense of beauty, of acceptable distances between people, or notions of pleasure and pain. On that fundamental level, a culture gives form and focus to our mental and emotional lives. We are nothing more—or less—than an encoded memory of our heritage.

Real dislocation, the loss of all familiar external and internal parameters, is not glamorous or cool. It is an upheaval in the deep material of the self.

Exile, however, gives perspective, making every emigrant an anthropologist and relativist. To have a deep experience of two cultures is to know that no culture is absolute, to discover that the seemingly natural aspects of our identities and social reality can be arranged, shaped, or articulated in another way. Biculturalism has its pleasures—the relish of sharpened insight, the savviness of skepticism—and they can become addictive.

These virtues have serious defects. The addiction may be too seductive; as a psychological choice, being in exile may become not only too arduous but also too easy. The exile lives in a story in which one's past becomes radically different from the present. The lost homeland, sequestered in the imagination as a mythic, static realm, can be idealized or demonized, or become a space of projections and fantasies.

In our habitually diasporic and nomadic world, the playing field has changed. When all borders are crossable and all boundaries permeable, it is harder to imagine an idyllic realm or a permanent enemy. This situation is initially confusing, yet its merits are easily discernible. We move not only between places but also between cultures with grace and ease. We are less shocked by prevailing assumptions, less prone to absolute assertions. The literature of this new nomadism, represented by Salman Rushdie, is full of multiple cultural references colliding and colluding in robust, vital play. This is a vision of exile as comedy rather than despair.

But I wonder if, in our world of easy come, easy go, of sliding among places and meanings without alighting on any of them for very long, we don't lose an internal focus and certain strengths that come from gathering experiences and accumulating understanding, from placing ourselves squarely where we are and living in a shared framework. I wonder if, in trying to exist in barely perceivable spaces, or conceiving of experience as movement between discrete dots on a horizontal map, we don't risk what the novelist Milan Kundera calls "the unbearable lightness of being." It is the illness that comes upon unanchored people, those who travel perpetually to new moments and sensations and to whom no internal feeling is more important than another.

Among nomads, exile loses its charge because there is no place from which one can be expelled, no powerful notion of home. Indeed, now we are less likely to say that all fiction is homesickness than to say that all homesickness is fiction—that home never was what it was cracked up to be, the haven of safety and affection we imagine. Instead, we conceive of home mostly as a site of enclosure and closure, of narrow-mindedness and nationalism. There are two kinds of homes: the home of our childhood and origin, which is a given, and the home of our adulthood, which is achieved only through hard-earned, patient choice, the labor of understanding and gradual arrival.

In a parable about the founder of the Jewish Hasidic movement, thieves tell the Baal Shem Tov about a network of underground corridors that leads directly from Poland to Palestine and offer to take him there. With great difficulty, they walk through the tunnels more than halfway to their destination. Then, suddenly, the Baal Shem Tov sees before him "a flaming sword, turning this way and that," and decides to turn back.

On one level this parable shows the Baal Shem Tov's ambivalence about going to Palestine. On another, its unconscious, compressed message may be that we can't steal into paradise, or take a shortcut to the tree of life. Of course, the parable also suggests something about the fear of approaching our object of desire and finding ourselves in paradise—which may then turn out to be an ordinary garden, needing weeding, tilling, and watering.

To be sure, it takes long, strenuous work to find terrain of safety or significance or love. And it may often be easier to live in exile with a fantasy of paradise than to suffer the ambiguities and compromises of cultivating actual, earthly places. And yet, if we do not create home structures for ourselves, we risk exile that we do not even recognize as banishment. And, paradoxically, if we do not acknowledge the possibility and pain of expulsion, then we will not know that somewhere a tree of life—if we labor hard enough to approach it—can yield fruits of meaning after all.

Thinking About the Text _____

1. What is Hoffman's purpose in writing this essay? Who is her audience? What is the author's point of view? How does her perspective influence what she writes?

2. How does Hoffman's background affect her stance on the "global village"? What would be some other stances that the author could take?

3. Look at Hoffman's last paragraph again. How are her opinions similar to Peay's? How are they different? Who presents the most cohesive argument?

She Had Some Horses

JOY HARJO

Joy Harjo was born in 1951 in Oklahoma, a member of the Creek tribe. She strove to become a Muskogee painter, as other members of her family were, but found herself drawn toward poetry. She graduated in 1976 from the University of New Mexico with a BA in poetry. She then received her MFA in creative writing from the University of Iowa in 1978. Harjo now has several works of poetry published, including *The Woman Who Fell From the Sky* and *In Mad Love and War*.

She had some horses.
She had horses who were bodies of sand.
She had horses who were maps drawn of blood.
She had horses who were skins of ocean water.
She had horses who were the blue air of sky.
She had horses who were fur and teeth.
She had horses who were clay and would break.
She had horses who were splintered red cliff.

She had some horses.

She had horses with long, pointed breasts.
She had horses with full, brown thighs.
She had horses who laughed too much.
She had horses who threw rocks at glass houses.
She had horses who licked razor blades.

She had some horses.

She had horses who danced in their mothers' arms.
She had horses who thought they were the sun and their
bodies shone and burned like stars.
She had horses who waltzed nightly on the moon.
She had horses who were much too shy, and kept quiet
in stalls of their own making.

She had some horses.

She had horses who liked Creek Stomp Dance songs.
She had horses who cried in their beer.

Thinking About the Text _____

1. What specific stylistic strategies does Harjo use in her piece? How does her style contribute to the overall meaning of the piece?

2. To whom is Harjo writing this poem? What do you consider the most significant points she is making in the poem?

3. What are some of the metaphors that Harjo uses in this piece? What do the horses in her poem symbolize?

Child of the Americas

AURORA LEVINS MORALES

Aurora Levins Morales, the daughter of a Jewish father and a Puerto Rican mother, was born in the United States in 1954. At a young age, she moved with her family to Puerto Rico, but returned to the U.S. at thirteen years of age. As a teen, she was educated in American schools that taught her a culture and history other than her own. This lack of cultural diversity in her education motivated her, at a later age, to speak out against anti-Semitism and racism. Morales has taught at a number of universities where she has dedicated her life to educate others of the history of all peoples, not just one single nationality.

I am a child of the Americas,
a light-skinned mestiza of the Caribbean,
a child of many diaspora,[1] born into this continent at a crossroads.

I am a U.S. Puerto Rican Jew,
a product of the ghettos of New York I have never known.
An immigrant and the daughter and granddaughter of immigrants.
I speak English with passion: it's the tongue of my consciousness,
a flashing knife blade of crystal, my tool, my craft.

I am Caribeña,[2] island grown. Spanish is in my flesh,
ripples from my tongue, lodges in my hips:
the language of garlic and mangoes,
the singing in my poetry, the flying gestures of my hands.

From *Getting Home Alive* by Rosario Morales and Aurora Levins Morales, Firebrand Books, Milford, CT, with permission.

I am of Latinoamerica, rooted in the history of my continent:
I speak from that body.

I am not african. Africa is in me, but I cannot return.
I am not taína.[3] Taíno is in me, but there is no way back.
I am not european. Europe lives in me, but I have no home there.

I am new. History made me. My first language was spanglish.[4]
I was born at the crossroads
and I am whole.

FOOTNOTES

1. *diaspora*: Scattered colonies. The word originally referred to Jews scattered outside Palestine after the Babylonian exile; it is now used often to refer to African peoples scattered around the world.

2. *Caribeña*: Caribbean woman.

3. *taína*: Describing the Taíno, an aboriginal people of the Greater Antilles and Bahamas.

4. *spanglish*: Spanish and English combined.

Thinking About the Text _____

1. What does it mean to be American? How is your definition influenced by your background?

2. Morales says, "I am whole." Explain what she means by this.

3. Multiculturalism has sometimes been defined as melting pot or salad bowl theories. Does Morales's work confirm the truth of these theories? Or, does it suggest that a new one be formed?

INDEX

A

affirmative action, 117, 118
African-American culture, 82
African bushmen, Shakespeare and, 135–43
American culture, 12, 73–77
anglicisms, 52, 53
Anishinabeg culture, 14
anti-male bias, 186
anti-Semitism, 163–72
Anzaldúa, Gloria, 33, 49–59
Arendt, Hannah, 6
Armstrong, Louis, 148
artists, view of city, 5
assimilation, 96–97

B

Baca, Jimmy Santiago, 33, 41–46
Baker, Houston, 119
Baldwin, James, 82
Barber, James David, 120
baseball, 73–77
  crowds, 77
  origins of, 75
  poetry and, 74, 76
  sexuality of, 76–77
Bennett, William J., 29–30, 101
betrayal, of self, 168
biculturalism, 198–99
bilingual education, 90–97, 99–101
Bingham, Hiram, 178

body ritual, of the Nacirema, 130–33
Bohannan, Laura, 103, 135–43
Border Patrol, 123–27
broken English, 35–39
Butler, Renee, 5
bystander apathy, 17–19

C

Cao, Linh, 33, 61–70
Care of the Soul, The (Moore), 5
ceremony, 10
charm-box, 130–31
Chicano literature, 55
Chicano music, 55–56
Chicano Spanish, 51–54
Chicanos
  Americanization of, 50
  identity issues for, 49–59
"Child of the Americas" (Morales), 207–8
children
  effects of immigrant English on, 37–39
  immigrant, 66
  language acquisition by immigrant, 89–97
Christianity, 166–67
cities
  artists' view of, 5
  heart of, 5–6, 8
  history of, 5
  landscape of, 4–5

problems in, 6
public spaces in, 6–7
race problems in, 6
soul of, 3–7
class discrimination, 169–70
Codrescu, Andrei, 33, 73–77
colonialism, 176
communication
across language gap, 194
in immigrant families, 61–70
community
childhood, 1
construction of, 1–2
defined, 1
Native American, 13–15
town life, 3–7
consumerism, 12
Coor, Lattie, 115
corridos, 56
cultural destruction, 12
cultural diversity, in education,
105–11
cultural imagination, 4–5, 8
cultural traditions, parenting and,
10–13
culture
African-American, 82
American, 12, 73–77
Anishinabeg, 14
Chicano, 56–58
of domination, 107–8
Hawaiian, 175–83
Japanese, 191–95
knowledge of different, 198–99
loss of, 198
of the Nacirema, 129–33
Native American, 10–11
non-Western, 118–19
of sex, 21–22
Western, 81, 113
Cummins, Jim, 100

D

Daws, Gaven, 178
deculturalization, 12
desegregation, 106
Dewyer, John, 82
diaspora, 208
Dibble, Shelon, 178
differences, discernment of, 85–87
discrimination
class, 169–70
against men, 185–88
misuse of, 85–87
divorce, 185
Doctorow, E. L., 74–75
D'Souza, Dinesh, 103, 113–20
Duderstadt, James, 115

E

education
affirmative action in, 117, 118
bilingual, 90–97, 99–101
cultural diversity in, 105–11
multiculturalism in, 109–11
negative influence of multiculturalism in, 113–20
Ellison, Ralph, 103, 145–52
Elmer, Michael, 125–26
English
broken, 35–39
children of non-native speakers of,
37–39
non-native speakers of, 35–39
entertainment industry, culture of sex
and, 21–22
equality, female, 157–60
ethnic chauvinism, 79–80
ethnic identity, 54–58
exile, 197–200
extended families, 10

F

family
  conservative myth of, 108
  extended, 10
  feminism's impact on, 186
  immigrant
    isolation of, 90–92
    language use in, 61–70, 90–97
  language of, 90–97
  nuclear, 10
Fanon, Frantz, 176
Farley, Reynolds, 115
Farrell, Warren, 155, 185–88
female equality, 157–60
feudalism, 177–78
football, 76
foreign identity, 191–95
Freud, Sigmund, 74–75

G

Gates, Henry Louis, 33, 79–82
gay marriage, 25–26, 29–30
gender issues
  language and, 50
  Native American, 13–15
Genovese, Eugene, 120
Genovese, Kitty, 17
Gonzalez, Angelo, 33, 99–101
Goodman, Ellen, 21–22
group behavior, 17–19
Gutmann, Amy, 80

H

Hakuta, Kenji, 100
Halperin, Morton, 119
Hamlet, interpretation of, 135–43
Harjo, Joy, 155, 203–4
Hawaiian culture, 175–83
Hayward, Fred, 186
Hillman, James, 4–5, 7

history
  cities', 5
  distortion of, 176–81
  divided, 176–81
Hoffman, Eva, 155, 197–200
Hollywood, culture of sex and, 21–22
Holocaust, 167
holy-mouth-men, 131
homosexual marriage, 25–26
hooks, bell, 103, 105–11
household shrine, 130–31
Hulme, William Henry, 80
human body, 130
Hunger of Memory (Rodriguez), 64

I

I Am Joaquín (Gonzales), 55, 57
I, Rigoberta Menchú, 116
identity
  Chicano, 49–59
  construction of, 155
  exile and, 197–200
  as a foreigner, 191–95
  Jewish, 163–72
  linguistic, 55
  religious, 166
illegal immigration, Border Patrol and, 123–27
illiteracy, 41–43
immigrant children, 37–39, 66, 89–97
immigrant English, 35–39
immigrant families
  isolation of, 90–92
  language use in, 61–70, 90–97
immigrants, illegal, 123–27
Immigration and Naturalization Service (INS), 123–27
Indian. *See* Native American
Indigenous Women's Netwok (IWN), 14
individuals, in groups, 17–19
INS agents, 123–27

Invisible Man, The (Ellison), 145–52
isolation, 171
Iver, Pico, 155, 191–95

J

Jagger, Alison, 119
Japan, 191–95
Jewish identity, 163–72
Jews, in literature, 165–66
Johnson, John, 5–6
Jowett, Benjamin, 81

K

Kagan, Donald, 114–15
Kamenetz, Roger, 73–74
Kaufman, Gershen, 56
Kaye, Melanie, 55
Kennedy, Donald, 118
King, Martin Luther, Jr., 107–8, 111
King, Rodney, 17, 18
King, William, 116–17
Klepfisz, Irena, 51
Kundera, Milan, 199
Kuykendall, Ralph, 178

L

LaDuke, Winona, 9–16
land use, 177–78
landscape, 4–5
language
    of baseball, 76
    censorship of, 50
    Chicano Spanish, 51–54
    communication across gap in, 194
    construction of, 33–34
    family, 90–97
    forms of English, 35–39
    gender in, 50
    illiteracy and, 41–43
    in immigrant families, 61–70,
        90–97

loss of, 198
non-native speakers of English,
    35–39
power of, 33, 35, 43–46
public vs. private, 92–93
research on, 70
routinized interactions, 64
Spanish, 51–52
tolerance, 69–70
understanding through, 176, 178
latipso, 132
Lewis, Bernard, 117, 118–19
Lind, Andrew, 178
linguistic identity, 54–58
linguistic terrorism, 53–54
literature, portrayal of Jews in,
    165–66
loneliness, 171

M

male inequality, 185–86
Malinowski, Bronislaw, 133
Mansfield, Harvey, 118
marriage
    changing perceptions about,
        185–86
    same-sex, 25–26, 29–30
McLaren, Peter, 110
media, sex in the, 21–22
medicine men, 130–32
men, as success objects, 185–88
Mendoza, Lydia, 56
Mexican border, 123–27
Mexican identity, 56–58
Miller, Jeff, 73
Miller, Robert Keith, 33, 85–87
Miner, Horace M., 103, 129–33
minobimaatisiiwin, 14
Moore, Thomas, 5
Morales, Aurora Levins, 155, 207–8
Morrison, Toni, 110
mouth-rite, 131

Multi-Cultural Literacy, 116
multiculturalism
    in education, 109–11
    misunderstanding of, 79–82
    negative influence of, in education,
      113–20
music, Chicano, 55–56

N

Nacirema culture, 129–33
National Association of Scholars, 120
Native Americans
    community, 13–15
    culture of, 10–11
    tribal schools and, 12–13
nomadism, 197–200
non-Western culture, 118–19
nuclear family, 10

O

outsider, isolation of, 171

P

Pachuco, 52
parenting
    community, 10
    cultural traditions and, 10–13
    political activism and, 10–15
parents, limited-English speaking,
    35–39, 62–70
Parini, Jay, 119
Pattee, Fred Lewis, 80
Peay, Pythia, 3–7
pluralism, 82
pochismos, 52
Poe, Edgar Allen, 74
poetry
    baseball and, 74, 76
    transformative quality of, 46
political activism
    parenting and, 10–15

by women, 13–15
pregnancy, teen-age, 21–22
public policies, lack of discrimination
    in, 86–87

R

race problem, in cities, 6
racism, 105–11, 118
religious identity, 166
responsibility, diffusion of, 17–19
Rich, Adrienne, 155, 163–72
ritual, 10, 131–33
Rodriguez, Richard, 33, 64, 89–97
Rushdie, Salman, 199

S

Said, Edward, 81
same-sex marriage, 25–26, 29–30
schools
    desegregation of, 106
    tribal, 12–13
Sedgwick, Eve, 119
Seneca Falls Convention, 157
sex, culture of, 21–22
sexism, against men, 185–88
sexuality, of baseball, 76–77
Shakespeare, interpretation of,
    135–43
Shalala, Donna, 114
"She Had Some Horses" (Harjo),
    203–4
silence, 50
Silko, Leslie Marmon, 103, 123–27
Smith, Beverly, 171
Smith, Ray Gwyn, 50
soccer, 76
social loafing, 18
social reality
    construction of, 103–4
    racism and, 105–11
souls, of cities, 3–7

Spanish
  Chicano, 51–53, 53–54
  language, 51–52, 92
Stanton, Elizabeth Cady, 155, 157–60
Sullivan, Andrew, 25–26, 29–30
Supreme Court, on gay rights, 25
Sylvester, Kathleen, 21–22

T

taína, 208
Tan, Amy, 33, 35–39
Tavris, Carol, 17–19
teen-age pregnancies, 21–22
Tex-Mex
  language, 52
  music, 55–56
Thernstrom, Stephen, 115
Third World cultures, 118–19
Thomas, Gail, 4–5
Thomas, Lee, 33, 61–70
Thompson, Becky, 114
town life, 3–7
Trask, Haunani-Kay, 155, 175–83
tribal councils, 13–14
tribal school, 12–13

U

universities
  affirmative action in, 117, 118
  anti-Western bias in, 113–20
  changing curriculums at, 113–20
  cultural diversity in, 109–11
U.S.-Mexico border, 123–27

W

Washington, D.C., 3–7
Welty, Eudora, 3
Western culture
  academia's attack on, 113–20
  multiculturalism and, 79–82
Western history, 176–81
Where Do We Go From Here? (King),
  107–8
White Earth Land Recovery Project,
  9
White Earth reservation, 9–15
Williams, Ted, 75
Winson, Jay, 22
women
  equality for, 157–60
  political activism by, 13–15
  relationship between men and,
    185–88
Wong-Fillmore, Lilly, 66
writing, power of, 43–46